FLOYD W. REEVES

FLOYD W. REEVES

Innovative Educator and Distinguished Practitioner of the Art of Public Administration

Richard O. Niehoff

UNIVERSITY
PRESS OF
AMERICA

Lanham, New York, London

MICHIGAN STATE UNIVERSITY
East Lansing, Michigan

University Press of America®, Inc.
4720 Boston Way
Lanham, Maryland 20706

3 Henrietta Street
London WC2E 8LU England

Printed in the United States of America
British Cataloging in Publication Information Available

Co-published by arrangement with
Michigan State University

Library of Congress Cataloging-in-Publication Data

Niehoff, Richard O.
Floyd W. Reeves : innovative educator and distinguished
practitioner of the art of public administration
/ Richard O. Niehoff.
p. cm.
Includes bibliographical references (p.) and index.
1. Reeves, Floyd W. (Floyd Wisley), 1890-1979.
2. Educators—United States—Biography.
3. Government executives—United States—Biography.
I. Title.
LB885.R322N54 1991
370'.92—dc20 [B] 91-10191 CIP

ISBN 0–8191–7921–3 (alk. paper)

The paper used in this publication meets the minimum requirements of American National Standard for Information Sciences—Permanence of Paper for Printed Library Materials, ANSI Z39.48–1984.

To Hazel Beatrice Reeves

Dedicated wife, companion and supporter of Floyd Reeves for sixty-four years

Contents

PART II

MAJOR ACTIVITIES IN GOVERNMENT—PUBLIC ADMINISTRATION

Acknowledgments

My motivation for writing this volume is to record and to demonstrate in a small way my appreciation of the values and creative achievements of Floyd Reeves in education and public administration. I was warmly supported in this task, however, which began in 1982—interspersed with other activities appropriate to a so-called retiree and by many other persons and two sources of financial support. Without these tangible and intangible evidences of support, however, the writing of this book would not have been nearly as rewarding—perhaps not even brought to a satisfactory completion.

First on the list of acknowledgments should be Floyd Reeves himself, who during his later years, was a stimulating and enjoyable associate and friend. More specifically, for this task, he left an abundance of letters, memoranda, reports, books and other memorabilia in the Michigan State University Archives and Historical Collections with which I "lived" for several years. But the thought of trying to do justice to him, and his record of accomplishments, did not fully convince me that I should try until I had read President John A. Hannah's (President of Michigan State University for twenty-eight years) appraisal of his influence when he wrote in his *A Memoir*:

> If I were to identify a single individual to whom I think is due as much or more credit than any other single person for his contribution to making Michigan State move from the kind of institution it was in 1941 to the

---

*John A. Hannah - *Versatile Administrator and Distinguished Public Servant*, published by the University Press of America.

> kind of institution it was in 1969, I would put Floyd Reeves at the top of the list. (Page 48)

Dr. Hannah continued to encourage me in the task and was otherwise very supportive.

Hazel Reeves, to whom this volume is dedicated, and with whom I shared drafts of chapters from time to time, was an interested supporter as she was of her husband's many activities during his and her life time. She died in 1987.

My wife, Helen, was patient and steady in her support and willingly endured my "escapes" to the archives and library carrel, and at our home, when there were other activities which we could have done together.

Another constant supporter, helpful critic, and long-time associate and friend, Harry L. Case, was very helpful in his review and comments on the several chapters as they made their weary way through several revisions and rewrites. He also served as the copy editor in the final stages of the volume. His services were invaluable in improving the clarity and general quality of my efforts.

Without the patience, skill and experience of Jean Van Douser, a former secretary and long-time friend, in deciphering my bad handwriting when the manuscript was in various stages of creation, this volume would not have seen the light of day.

Dr. Ralph Smuckler, Professor of Political Science, Dean of the Office of International Studies and Programs and Assistant to the President of Michigan State University, and his colleagues provided encouragement and logistical support during the entire period of production of this volume.

Dr. David Anderson, an experienced biographer, Professor of American Thought and Language at Michigan State University, encouraged me somewhere near mid-point in the preparation of the first draft of the manuscript to believe that I had "a book." He also read a second-to-last version and made many helpful comments and suggestions.

Dr. Carl Gross, retired professor of Education and long-time colleague at Michigan State University, also read a draft of the manuscript and made several helpful and supportive comments. Dr. John Hannah, President, and Dr. John Cantlon, Vice President for Research and Graduate Studies and Dr. David Scott, Provost, also read an earlier chapter on Michigan State University and provided supporting comments. More recently, Dr. George Simpson, a later colleague in retirement, and former Chair of the Department of Anthropology and

Sociology at Oberlin College, read several chapters, raised a number of clarifying questions and made several comments which improved my efforts, as did Paul T. David, who was an associate of Reeves, and is quoted elsewhere in this volume.

And like all academic or non-academic enterprises there must be more than familial and collegial support. There must be funds for typing, travel, reproduction of copies, stamps and other out-of-pocket costs. These were generously provided, initially be the Spencer Foundation plus encouragement to undertake the work by its officers, H. Thomas James and Marian Faldet. A Trustee of the Foundation Ralph W. Tyler, encouraged by representation of a colleague, Paul W. Dressel, was instrumental in helping me to get financial assistance from the Spencer Foundation. The W. K. Kellogg Foundation generously provided funds for the final publication of this book.

The thoughtful responses to my letters from several friends and associates of Reeves are acknowledged in the text or footnotes.

The ever helpful assistance of Frederick L. Honhart, Director and his associates, Dorothy Fry and John D. Sanford, of the Michigan State University Archives and Historical Collections, who made the many hours in their basement quarters more pleasant than might have otherwise been the case, is much appreciated. In a similar, but in a less protracted way, the archivists at the Franklin Roosevelt, University of Chicago and Antioch College libraries were also pleasantly helpful.

But for all this help and encouragement, I stand, as do all authors, fully responsible for the end product.

Richard O. Niehoff
August 1990

FLOYD W. REEVES

Preface

This is a book primarily about the professional life of Floyd W. Reeves. It is not a conventional biography, although relevant general biographical data are woven into the account. Reeves had an outstanding career in education and public administration, and he was recognized for his major contributions by leaders in both fields. His initial and continuing career was essentially as an educator, but through a series of unusual opportunities, he was catapulted into positions and activities which were related to his work in education but which were more closely focused on federal governmental problems of the massive depression of the 30's and the war and post-war years. He incorporated an educational dimension in all of his work, however, and he may thus be remembered primarily as an innovative educator.

Although a teacher-scholar, author of many articles and several books, and editor of numerous publications, he was best known as a director of studies or chairman of major committees and commissions and as a wide ranging consultant to organizations which were primarily focused on action programs in education and on the organization, staffing and administration of governmental programs. He was an organizer, a director of studies, and a highly motivated activist. His major professional frustration was his failure to achieve his goal of writing a general theory of administration applicable to all types of human organizations.

His early upbringing in bleakly rural South Dakota, his fragmentary early formal schooling, and his early teaching experience in rural schools, in which he developed several innovative procedures in education, and his exposure to the discrimination of Indians and Negroes* and to the deprivations generally characteristic of life in rural areas provided his life-long determination to do all he could to alleviate such handicaps.

Several favorable circumstances in Reeves mid-career provided unusual opportunities for him to express his interests and abilities and provided broadened professional contacts, stimulating challenges, and personal and professional satisfaction. Foremost in this matrix of factors was his participation in Roosevelt's New Deal starting with the opportunity to serve as the first Director of the Personnel and Social and Economic Divisions of the Tennessee Valley Authority. From 1936 through the next fifteen years he was closely associated with a variety of activities with both Franklin and Eleanor Roosevelt, with Charles Merriam, Chairman of the Political Science Department and colleague at the University of Chicago, with Luther Gulick, Chairman of the Institute of Public Administration, and with several other leaders in government, labor, religion and business. Owen D. Young, former President of the General Electric Company, became one of his close associates. These professional and personal associations led to Reeves being named Chairman of the President's Advisory Committee on Education and to his active participation in the work of the President's Committees on Administrative Reform, Civil Service Improvement, and Selective Service; to his appointment as Director of Labor Supply in the Office of Production Management, and as a consultant and Director of Research for the Conference on Demobilization of Civilian and Military Personnel of the National Resources Planning Board. This latter responsibility led to the formulation of recommendations which formed the basis for legislation known generally as the G. I. Bill of Rights, and subsequent administrative action. At no time was he associated with either major political party.

In the field of education, his mentor and colleague, Charles Hubbard Judd, Chairman of the Department of Education at the University of Chicago, George Zook, President of the American Council on Education and several other educational leaders were instrumental in his receiving important appointments in Washington during the New Deal era. These appointments included the Directorship of the American Youth Commission, consultant/advisor to Aubrey Williams, Director of the National Youth Administration, to other agencies vitally interested in the problems of youth and youth organizations, and to com-

*The designation of "Negroes" was in common usage at that time.

mittees of the American Council on Education on discrimination in college and university admission policies and practices.

At an earlier time his association with Judd first as a graduate student and later, principally, as an early leader in making surveys of colleges and universities led to his appointment in 1929 as Professor of Education and Director of the comprehensive University of Chicago self-survey. During his first three years at the University of Chicago he directed many other surveys of colleges, universities and other educational institutions. Concurrently, he was very active as a leader of the work of the North Central Association of Colleges and Schools in establishing more flexible standards of accreditation which encouraged educational institutions to develop programs which were better tailored to their clientele and resources but still of creditable standards. Other noteworthy surveys included the New York "Regents Inquiry into the Character and Cost of Public Education," which was a forerunner to the more comprehensive study, directed by Reeves, of all higher education in New York State and which led to the establishment of the University of the State of New York. On the international front he served as head of a UNESCO consultative commission to the Philippines and as an advisor to the government of Pakistan.

An underlying factor which permitted and encouraged Reeves to engage in most of the activities mentioned above was the liberal policy of the University of Chicago for leaves of absence for faculty members to engage in projects of scholarly merit which were also socially useful and which provided feedback benefit to the research and instructional activities of the University.

Reeve's personal attributes, combined with the exceptional opportunities and linkages at a unique time, were key factors in his professional achievements. In both education and public administration he believed in ascertaining the basic facts of whatever project he undertook. The facts, combined with his judgment, and the judgment of his associates, provided the basis for formulating policy and program recommendations. His sympathies and interests were broad, thus making it possible for him to work effectively with a wide range of educational and civic leaders of varying backgrounds. He was motivated by a concern for fair play for those who were disadvantaged by reasons of race, color, religion, education, or economic status. He gave unstingingly of his time and energy to the work and causes in which he believed, even to the point of injury to his physical well being. Although he occupied a few administrative positions—notably Director of Personnel of the TVA and Acting Chairman of the Department of Education at the University of Chicago—he was essentially a staff officer, teacher, research director, consultant, and adviser. He knew that his interests and capabilities were primarily as a staff person, and he consistently turned down offers to accept high level administrative positions.

He had a certain "passion for anonymity" in the sometimes confidential and sensitive work which he did for the government. But when the results of his research and chairmanship of committees and commissions led to unanimous or near unanimous recommendations, he indefatiguably "took the stump" in speech making tours and conferences which involved criss-crossing the country to get acceptance and action on the recommendation.

He instilled confidence in his peers and administrative superiors, including FDR, who asked him to undertake several critical assignments. In turn, many of these led from one major undertaking to another.

Apart from his own energetic participation, Reeves had a penchant for identifying young men to whom he could delegate major responsibilities and coach them in achieving high levels of personal growth and competence. Outstanding among these persons was Gordon R. Clapp, who succeeded him as Director of Personnel in the Tennessee Valley Authority and went on to become General Manager and Chairman of the TVA Board. There were several others who became exceptionally competent in education and public administration, including Paul David, Maurice Seay, John Oliver, John Dale Russell, Cyril Houle, Harry L. Case and George F. Gant.

He ended his distinguished career at the University of Chicago to serve as Consultant to John A. Hannah, long-time President of Michigan State University, and as Professor of Education at Michigan State from 1953 until his retirement in 1962. He aided President Hannah, other officials and faculty members and the Board of Trustees, to develop Michigan State University from the Michigan State College of Agriculture and Applied Arts to a major land-grant, domestically and internationally distinguished University. He died on August 30, 1979 in East Lansing, Michigan. Descriptions of his work in educational projects follow in Part I of the volume; activities and projects in public administration are described in Part II. Preceding these sections are notes on his origins and major influences of his life and work. Appraisals of his colleagues and associates in all major activities are included in each chapter and reflective summary comments on "Reeves and the Art of Administration" are contained in the last chapter.

Origins and Influences

Floyd Reeves was born on November 6, 1890 in Castalia, South Dakota and lived to be 89 years of age. He spent most of his early years in the environment of his childhood and youth. During these years the United States was involved in the passing of the frontier; in great rural-urban migration; the rise of the great urban communities; and in other massive social and economic changes. We engaged in two world wars, and experienced several crippling depressions. During these years the roles of education and government in the affairs of the people were greatly expanded, and the United States became a responsible international political, industrial and economic leader. In his adult life Reeves was an active participant in various ways in this tumultuous period of U. S. History. He was a leader in education and public administration. His major activities in education were primarily directed to the creation of innovative policies and practices which enlarged opportunities for disadvantaged students and improved the organization and administration of education, principally at the college and university levels. As a student of government organization, policies and practices, he helped modernize governmental operations at the federal level, principally in the area of personnel and public administration. Although it is possible to make a reasonably sharp separation between the two "careers" of Reeves in education and public administration, this kind of demarcation of the professional life of Reeves would be essentially superficial at best. He did, indeed excel in both fields, and he was highly regarded by educators and public administrators, but in both careers he emphasized people, human and societal values.

The major purpose of this chapter, however, is to trace his origins and the early and later experiences which molded his development and influenced his values and gave direction to his many interesting and socially useful activities. He was physically small (5'7'') but a dynamic man of many talents, an excellent public speaker and a dedicated educator, public servant and citizen.

His forebearers came from England in 1824 and lived respectively in New York, Iowa and Illinois before finally settling in Castalia, South Dakota. Reeves father was a farmer, rancher and sometimes mill owner, and his mother was a school teacher before marriage. She taught him to read at home. His grandmother, who lived with the family, had an especially significant early influence on Reeves and also encouraged him to be an avid reader. She was an artist, musician, writer, and teacher. She operated a trading post for Indians and was an ardent prohibitionist, which sometimes interfered with her business relations with her Indian customers when they had too much to drink. There were three boys and two girls in the family—but little is revealed in the records or in personal conversations with the author as to the relationship to or influence of the siblings on Reeves.

Life was rugged in Reeves early years in rural South Dakota. In dry years there wasn't enough water to run his father's mill or enough fuel to fire the steam boiler to turn the mill. One of these years his father had to close down the mill and go to work in a gold mine near Deadwood to keep the family going. The deprivations resulting from these and other natural disasters did not appear to depress the family or to drastically change their life style. Instead the hardships appeared to fuel an ambition to overcome the difficulties and find innovative ways to survive if not prosper.

Some of Reeves early playmates were Indian boys and girls whom he came to respect. In his later years, he sought in a number of ways to diminish discrimination against them and young Negroes and to expand their educational opportunities.

Reeve's early formal education was pretty sketchy, with only two to three months of attendance each school year until he was twelve years old. Interrupted as it was with duties at home and on the farm tending cattle, he was largely self-taught. Fortunately, his grandmother provided him with books, such as Carpenter's *Geographical Reader* and Robinson's *Complete Arithmetic*, which he and his brothers avidly read and which introduced him to places beyond South Dakota and to the basic tools of mathematical computation. He also read Tennyson,

Shakespeare, Scott and Conan Doyle from his grandmother's library to while away the hours on the plains when tending the cattle.

His high school education was also interrupted with domestic duties, but he managed to attend the Academy at Dakota Wesleyan and Miller and Saint Lawrence High Schools in South Dakota for parts of the year and, as in elementary school, he continued to benefit from self-direction. His capacity for self-learning, aided by his grandmother, influenced him in his early teaching experience and later led him to espouse policies and organizational arrangements which credited students for what they knew and had learned informally without going through the formal classroom drills. He later applied these principles in his work at the University of Chicago as will be described in later chapters. His early love of books also contributed to his strong support for libraries generally, and especially for libraries that enriched rural life and encouraged life-long learning among adults.

Reeves was active in sports, especially in track, and in debating in which he continued to engage through college. He was salutatorian of his high school class, and in his commencement address stressed that "education should fit the individual rather than the individual fitting education"—a theme which he continued to expound in his later years as a teacher.

He enrolled in Huron College, in South Dakota, in 1912 and graduated three years later with a B. S. degree with majors in Public Speaking and English. Summers were spent earning enough money to see him through college. One summer he rode his bicycle around the state selling books, notably Bibles. Another summer he worked as a cashier at the State Fair dining hall. He also served as the local platform manager for the South Dakota Chautauqua and gave the oration that had won him a prize the year before. He accelerated his graduation from college by passing tests in subjects on which he had prepared himself by self-study. He won first prize in debating and continued his active participation in track. While at Huron College he came under the beneficial influence of Harry Morehouse Gage (later President of Coe College in Iowa) who saw Reeves's potential ability as a teacher and educational administrator.

After completing his undergraduate education and establishing the beginnings of a successful career as a teacher and educational administrator, he married Hazel Beatrice Flint in 1915 and became the father of two boys and one girl. Hazel Reeves became his constant companion and supporter through the many years of his varied careers—often "holding fort" for much of the time while he was away from home on missions and on many speaking, teaching and consultation engagements throughout the country and abroad.

He attended one summer term at the University of Wisconsin in 1916 where he took work with and was greatly influenced by Professor E. A. Ross, a distinguished professor of sociology, who expanded his horizons on a number of social and economic issues. In 1917 he received a fellowship in the graduate school at the University of Chicago where he earned an M. A. degree in 1921 and the Ph. D. degree, magna cum laude, in 1925.

Teaching

Reeves began his teaching career at seventeen years of age, before completing high school. The school at Hollister, South Dakota was a one-room school with an enrollment of thirteen students, several of whom had a reputation of having been, to say the least, reluctant students. To characterize the students as reluctant is a gross understatement as described by Opal David, a close friend, who wrote of Reeves first experiences as a teacher:[2]

> Boxing was never listed officially as a pre-requisite for teaching in the schools of South Dakota, but it was his mastery of this "subject" that clinched his first teaching job for Dr. Floyd W. Reeves . . . It was in a one-room school ten miles from his home, with a student body consisting primarily of the five large and unruly sons of the Chairman of the School Board. Three properly certificated teachers had resigned in as many weeks—the last one, an aunt of the boys, after one of them had knocked her out with a stove-poker and been sent to jail to cool off.
>
> The seventeen-year-old Reeves boy had no teacher's certificate but the school was offered to him anyway, with the understanding that he was to get forty dollars for every month he stayed. He asked for two weeks to get ready and spent the time learning to box. When he rode over to take charge of the school, his gloves hung from the saddle-horn, and this variation on the birch-rod proved a complete success. School "kept" for seven months . . .

At the Hollister School, Reeves emphasized independent study, in fact the school had no fixed curriculum for graduation.

After completing high school, he taught the first eight grades at the Swab School, in South Dakota, which enrolled thirty students. He continued to emphasize original recitations based on students' interests. Barbara Ann Nicholas, author of a Ph. D. dissertation on Reeves's early experiences as a teacher, summarized how these experiences influenced his later philosophy of education.

> Reeves's early educational background had a definite influence on his future philosophy of education. During the first two decades of the twentieth century Reeves's philosophy of education was being molded. It was at the age of seventeen in the one-room school where he taught that he felt the need to do away with the uniformity of the curriculum. He wanted the curriculum to be replaced with a child-centered education. He did not believe that the course of study had to be something "fixed," outside the child's experience, but rather that it could be somewhat free and flexible with his student's interests as the focal point. He attributed his own success, which he had achieved academically, professionally and personally to be due to the great freedom he had taken and had been given in his own education.
>
> He believed the job of the teacher was really to be a co-learner with the student—to learn about the students as the student learns about the teacher—to work together in doing things of interest to both. Furthermore, Reeves's early exposure to disadvantaged persons, initially Indians and later Blacks, as well as poor rural people generally, broadened his sympathies for underprivileged persons. His later years of dedicated, persistent and innovative activity to lessen discrimination and enlarge educational, economic and social opportunities for disadvantaged persons had their origins in these earlier experiences . . .[3]

Educational Administration

His first administrative job was as Superintendent of the Jefferson Schools in South Dakota, where he remained for two years from 1915–17 at a salary of $810 for the first year and $900 for the second. At the Jefferson Elementary School he also taught an evening course for adults at the Senior High School. The use of a public school for the teaching of adults was an innovation in South Dakota and in possibly most of the western and midwestern states at the time. After two years he moved on to the superintendency of the Gregory City, South Dakota, Schools, for three years where he taught courses in English and history. He believed, as a policy, that it should be standard practice for educational administrators to teach—a policy which he continued to espouse in his later years. His salary increased from $1400 to $2600 for a nine-month term. After the Superintendency at Gregory, he moved on to a bigger job as Superintendent of the Winner,

South Dakota, Schools for a substantial increase in salary from $3000 to $3800. At Winner he first met Ralph W. Tyler, who had been teaching science at the Pierre, South Dakota, High School. Tyler was to become the Chairman of the Department of Education and Dean of the Social Science Division at the University of Chicago during Reeves's tenure there. Tyler reported that Reeves's "vision and energy were then widely recognized in the state."

Reeves's first major experience as a college administrator was as Dean and Professor of Education at Transylvania College from 1923–25. Next he became Professor of Education and Director of the Bureau of School Service at the University of Kentucky. While at the University of Kentucky he began a career as a surveyor of school systems, colleges and universities, which became his major professional interest for about ten years thereafter. In 1942 he served for six months as acting chairman of the Department of Education at the University of Chicago. He had numerous opportunities to take on administrative positions—including college and university presidencies but preferred work as a teacher, and researcher or director of research.

Later Career

Although Reeves's basic values, motivation, and intellectual habits were well established in his youth and early professional experiences, the broader intellectual framework for his major mid-career and later achievements was essentially established in his work and association at the University of Chicago from 1929–1953. Thus his early proclivity to relate education to social, political, and economic trends, and his clear and often repeated distinction between *education* and *schooling* were enhanced by his affiliation with the University of Chicago Department of Education, which saw its research and teaching mission in this broader context.

His initial employment as a Professor of Education in 1929 coincided with the preparation of the massive review of *Recent Social Trends in the United States for 1890* (the year Reeves was born) *to 1933*. The survey was authorized by President Herbert Hoover and published in 1933, the year Franklin D. Roosevelt became President.[4] A number of professors at the University of Chicago were involved in the survey and shortly thereafter greatly influenced Reeves in his professional development. Furthermore, several of them became his close associates.

President Hoover's penchant for fostering surveys of various aspects of our national life, presumably to guide him in formulating national government policy in a possible second term which he failed to achieve, became useful guides for his successor, Franklin D. Roosevelt. Roosevelt demonstrated that he had a better grasp of the instrumentalities of government which could be utilized to do something about the problems which the surveys had documented and dramatized. Roosevelt's program and leadership were greatly influenced, of course, by the depression which engulfed the country in 1929 and later by preparations for and engagement in World War II.

Although it is impossible to document specific instances in which FDR was directly influenced by the major findings of the survey, it is quite clear that the survey influenced the President's creation of the National Resources Planning Board, the Tennessee Valley Authority and other actions to modernize governmental organization and operations in which Reeves was later engaged. The research involved in the preparation of the survey report and the follow-up activities collectively called the "New Deal" actively involved Charles E. Merriam, Vice Chairman of the President's Committee on Social Trends, who later (in 1938), appointed Reeves to be a member of the Department of Political Science, chaired by Merriam. Reeves was also a colleague of William Fielding Ogburn, who was the Director of Research for the survey. Charles Hubbard Judd, his mentor, colleague and Chairman of the Department of Education, wrote the chapter on education. The committee acknowledged the contribution of more than twenty-five other members of the faculty at the University of Chicago, among whom were colleagues of Reeves, including Robert Maynard Hutchings, Leonard White, Ralph W. Tyler, Marshall Dimock, Newton Edwards, Frank Freeman, Ernest W. Burgess and several others. Some twenty-five other persons not on the faculty of the University of Chicago who worked closely with Reeves on New Deal and other federal governmental activities included Luther Gulick, Louis Brownlow and Joseph Harris, associates with the National Resources Planning Board; Ismar Baruch and William Leiserson, associates in the Tennessee Valley Authority; and George Counts, a colleague at Michigan State University. These were the persons who engaged in animated discussions of social trends with Reeves in faculty meetings and informal lunches and dinners at the Quandrangle Club of the University of Chicago, the Cosmos Club in Washington, and in numerous committees and commissions with which these colleagues were associated. Important informal "seminars" with colleagues with whom he was associated in New Deal activities also occurred on the "Capitol Limited" train between Chicago and Washington, D. C. Marshall Dimock, distinguished professor of political science and public administration, who was then a young faculty member, wrote to the author of those heady days as follows:

> My immersion in the New Deal took two forms: the first was consulting, which began almost immediately, and lasted through the entire 1932–46 period. In addition I was involved in drafting the Social Security Act, working for the N.R.P.B. . . . and doing a major job in the Labor Department . . . The second part of my duties was to serve as an executive at both the Assistant Secretary and bureau chief level and this included posts in the Labor, Justice and War Shipping. One reason it was so much fun is that the University of Chicago during the New Deal period played a more prominent role than any other University . . . In the early days of the New Deal, it was not unusual for University of Chicago faculty to occupy, by prearrangement, one or more Pullman cars on the Baltimore and Ohio's "Capitol Limited" to Washington and return, later the same week, because so many of them divided their time between Washington and their teaching assignments. (Possibly not unlike Harvard academics in the Kennedy era!)

This was the intellectual environment in which Reeves worked. His values were compatible with the far reaching ideas and recommendations of this group of thinkers and leaders, and he expressed these values and convictions by his leadership and research in several major activities.

No attempt will be made to summarize the more than 1500 pages of the monumental survey report of social and economic trends or even the 66 pages which outline the major findings. Excerpts of the publication of particular relevance to Reeves are included in Appendix A.

Part I

Reeves As Educator

Chapter I

The University of Chicago: In Residence and on Leave

Introduction[1]

Floyd Reeves was appointed Professor of Education at the University of Chicago April 22, 1929 effective October 1, 1929, (at a salary of $6,500) and he continued his affiliation with the University until October 1, 1953. Reeves earlier had had a fellowship in the Department of Education at Chicago and had earned a Master of Arts Degree in 1921 and a Ph. D. degree, magna cum laude, in 1925. His dissertation on "The Political Unit of School Finance in Illinois," which involved research in economics and political science as well as in education, in a sense anticipated his later career activities of an interdisciplinary nature and his joint appointment with the Department of Political Science. Charles Hubbard Judd was Reeves's major professor and later close associate and supporter.

Reeves had at least one other vocational opportunity at the time of his appointment as attested by a letter which Judd sent to him on April 11, 1929 when he wrote:

> In the meantime let me express my own gratification that you selected this rather than the other opportunity offered to you. I will do everything I can to make your work successful and I am sure all of your colleagues in education will do the same. We are glad to have you join our group. I look forward optimistically to development of the work in higher education.[2]

Reeves came to the University from the University of Kentucky, where he had been Professor of Education and Director of the Bureau of School Service from 1925 to 1929. He had earlier been a professor and Dean of Education at Transylvania College, also in Kentucky, from 1923–25. He resigned from the University of Chicago in 1953 to accept an appointment as Consultant to President John A. Hannah and Professor of Education at Michigan State College, which became Michigan State University in 1955.

There were at least four major factors which were associated with the long and distinguished career of Reeves at the University of Chicago. First was the unique and warmly supportive relationship of Judd to Reeves. Their backgrounds were dissimilar but their views on education were similar. They were dissimilar in that Judd was a dignified foreign-born son of missionary parents in India and a somewhat austere professor of psychology, having taken his Ph. D. with Wilhelm Wundt in experimental psychology at Leipzig. His experience with the U. S. educational system was as an elementary, secondary and college student and as a professor of psychology at four U. S. universities. His familiarity with problems, issues, and developments in the American educational system in the early years of his career at Chicago was derived to a large extent from his chairmanship of the Editorial Review Board of two prestigious educational journals published by the University—*The School Review* and the *Elementary School Journal*. Reeves, on the other hand, was born in a sod-house in South Dakota of poor parents; was largely self-taught in his early years; and was a teacher, principal, school superintendent and college student in the rural state of South Dakota. In terms of personality, whereas Judd was dignified and not very approachable as indicated by the fact that graduate students kept an informal record of how many minutes were spent in conference with him, Reeves was very friendly and approachable and had a lively sense of humor. Judd was tall and impeccably dressed while Reeves was short of stature and somewhat indifferent to dress. Judd had great prestige in the University. President Robert M. Hutchins was reported to have said that he would not make a major move at the University without consulting with Judd, whereas Reeves was just starting his career at Chicago. Judd was seventeen years older than Reeves.

With these differences in background, what brought them into an effective professional relationship which extended over many years, on and off campus, is doubtless a tribute to the dedication that both men had to education. Their off-campus relationships were dramatized in part by the fact that Judd became immersed in a number of responsibilities in Washington, as did Reeves, both in the federal government and in educational activities under private auspices. The basis for their high degree of professional compatability is perhaps best expressed in comments made on occasion of Judd's death by Ralph W. Tyler, Chairman of the Social Science Division of the University. He commented that Judd's:

> wide interests, extraordinary powers and selfless devotion, the rante of his influence has been so great that it is impossible briefly to summarize his chief contributions. Among them there are three things which he advocated and consistently exemplified that illustrate the things for which he stood. The first was his belief that a sound foundation for educational policy and practice must be based upon facts and tested principles rather than upon speculation or collections of best practices . . . The second was his view that for the school to be effective, its aims and content must be derived both from a study of society and a study of the learner and that these aims and content must be translated into curriculum materials appropriate for the maturity level of the pupils . . . During the first world war he prepared some pamphlets for use as reading materials in the social studies, and under the auspices of the American Council on Education more were written. In the late 30's he developed additional materials of this sort for the National Youth Commission . . . The third illustrative contribution was his 'tough mindedness.' Because education involves the welfare of children, many educators become over sentimental and react in terms of emotion rather than on the basis of rational considerations . . . Mr. Judd's strict adherence to the canons of inductive and deductive logic, his willingness to face new facts that upset previous explanations, his unshaken attitude toward scientific method no matter how unpleasant the implications, represent 'tough mindedness' to an unusual degree.[3]

As will be described later, Reeves and Judd saw very much eye-to-eye on most or all of these convictions.

A second and critical factor in Reeves's career was the generous policy of the University of Chicago in granting leaves of absence for important activities off-campus. For example, Reeves was granted one leave of thirty months; two leaves of nine months each and one for three months for a total of over four years of his twenty-four years plus the normal quarter off each year for any activity in which he wished to engage. Furthermore, the University had a generous policy for consulting work—particularly if consulting contributed to the professinal stature of the individual and the University. This policy was expressed institutionally for a period under President Hutchins under so called 4 E contracts. Under these contracts professors were paid a fixed salary with certain patterns of consulting work taken into consideration in the formula. Compensation for other consulting work under these contracts, was then returned to the University. Reeves, for example, returned approximately $13,000 in 1947 and 1948 to the University for consulting services rendered to the State of New York, Michigan State College, National Advisory Board of Pepsi-Cola, Atomic Energy Commission, Kellogg Foundation, and the Tennessee Valley Authority.[4]

A third factor supporting Reeves's career at Chicago was related to the nature of the times and the social programs of President Franklin Delano Roosevelt. Roosevelt's *New Deal* had a large component of compassion for disadvantaged persons, especially youth, and for rebuilding the resources of the nation, including human resources through education. Reeves's values were highly compatible with Roosevelt and the New Deal. His first exposure to Roosevelt, while on his first leave from the University of Chicago, was as Director of the Personnel and Social and Economic Divisions of the Tennesee Valley Authority (TVA) from 1933–1936. During this period they had several opportunities to get acquainted and to build a relationship of trust and confidence. Harry Hopkins and Aubrey Williams were also involved in getting Reeves to direct or otherwise to participate in several national projects in education and public administration of significant interest to the President as described later in this study.

A fourth fact was Reeves's close association with Charles E. Merriam, Chairman of the Political Science Department of the University, who in 1938 joined with Judd in naming Reeves to a Professorship in Political Science in addition to his Professorship in Education. Merriam was one of three members of the Board of the National Resources Planning Board and of the President's Committee on Administrative Management in which Reeves was also involved.

What all of the above adds up to was that Reeves was the right person, with the appropriate talents and knowledge background; in the right institution; at the right time in history and with highly supportive colleagues to launch his exceptionally useful and creative career with the University of Chicago as a base.

1929–1933: The Period of Intensive Work at the University

The principal activity of this period was Reeves' direction of the comprehensive self-survey of the University.* The leadership of the

---

*See also "University of Chicago Survey in Chapter 2, Part I.

University had concluded that it was time to reexamine critically its development from its beginnings in 1892 and to establish directions for the future. Funds were provided for the survey by the General Education Board. This was a period in university administration when surveys were in vogue—but usually of a limited nature and usually made by outside consultants with emphasis on comparisons with the practices of other institutions and with heavy reliance on statistical data. The Chicago survey, however, was projected to be entirely internal and with greater emphasis on collective institutional judgment regarding policies and priorities. The timing coincided with the appointment of Robert Maynard Hutchins to the presidency of the University and the availability of Reeves to serve as the Director of the study. Reeves came to the task with extensive experience in university survey work and it took only a few weeks for President Hutchins, on Reeves's recommendation, to appoint a staff to work with him which included George A. Works, Frederick J. Kelly, John Dale Russell (a young associate of Reeves in survey work who was completing his Ph. D. with Reeves) and J. Mortimer Adler, a close associate of President Hutchins.

Judd acted as informal adviser to Reeves in formulating questions which needed to be addressed in the survey before being cleared with the President.[5]

Staff work continued on preparations for the survey—outlines of data needed, selection of staff and related matters. By April 1931, Reeves had received Hutchins's approval of a suggested organization of the University survey.[6] With outlines of key areas of University organization and operation defined and research staff selected, it took less than two years for the first of a series of twelve studies to be prepared, reviewed and published by the University of Chicago Press. The titles and authors of the complete set of publications follow:

Volume I: Trends in University Growth by Reeves, Ernest Miller and John Dale Russell.

Volume II: Organization and Administration by Reeves, F. J. Kelly and G. A. Works.

Volume III: The University Faculty by Reeves, Nelson B. Henry, F. J. Kelly, Arthur Klein and John Dale Russell.

Volume IV: Instructional Problems by Reeves, W. E. Peck and John Dale Russell.

Volume V:	Admission and Retention of Students by Reeves and John Dale Russell.
Volume VI:	The Alumni of the College by Reeves and John Dale Russell.
Volume VII:	The University Libraries by M. Llewellyn Raney.
Volume VIII:	The University Extension Service by Reeves, G. O. Thompson, A. J. Klein and John Dale Russell.
Volume IX:	The University Plant Facilities by Reeves, Kelly and John Dale Russell.
Volume X:	Some Student Problems by Reeves and John Dale Russell.
Volume XI:	Class Size and University Costs by Reeves, Nelson Henry and John Dale Russell.
Volume XII:	The Oriental Institute by James H. Breasted.

Each volume provided descriptive information on the subject and recommendations.

In addition to organizing and directing the entire survey, Reeves participated in the writing of all but two of the volumes, namely Libraries and the Oriental Institute.

The remarks made by President Hutchins in an address to the North Central Association of Colleges and Schools on March 19, 1931 provide evidence of the impact of the survey on the University:

> For a year and a half it (the University of Chicago) has through an internal survey been studying its own organization in the hope of eventually coming to understand itself. The process of becoming acquainted has been quite revealing. The gentlemen who are making the study are gazing upon us, all of us, with a cold and impartial eye. They are scrutinizing our teaching, our research, our administration, our expenditures, our income, our libraries, our laboratories—in short they are scrutinizing us from top to bottom. Since they are organized as a separate staff which has no affiliation with any department or school they cannot be accused of bias or prejudice. Since they have studied countless other institutions, they can hardly be accused of incompetence. Since they are considering every aspect of the University we shall have at the end a complete picture of the organization and operation of a large institution which should be of some use to institutions everywhere. As the survey has six more months to run its conclusions are as yet unformulated. Nevertheless its tentative findings have affected the whole scheme of budget making, have affected the plan of reorganization at every step, and in the construction of the

> new college curriculum have exerted a most imortant influence in showing the Committee what course our students were following.[7]

The University of Chicago survey became the model for university-self surveys.

Reeves continued his influence with Hutchins and the University of Chicago administration. Ten years later, when another reorganization was in process, Hutchins apparently consulted Reeves. Thus on July 1942 Reeves wrote to Hutchins:

> A few days ago Mr. Filbey gave me a copy of your confidential statement on "The organization of the University" with the request that I send you comments upon it. After careful consideration of the plan, I have reached the conclusion that its adoption would offer greater assurance of the development of the University along lines that will meet the future needs of the public than retention of the present plan of administration could offer. At all points, the proposed plan seems to me to be in full accord with sound principles of democratic administration.[8]

Apart from the work described above, Reeves served on an all-University Committee to Coordinate Degree Requirements and on two committees of the North Central Association of Colleges and Schools on Revision of Standard Reports for Institutions of Higher Education. He also participated in surveys of colleges and universities affiliated with the Methodist Episcopal Church and other surveys. He also taught two graduate courses in education and administration, and he was involved in the direction of several Ph. D. dissertations and master's theses.

He made major speeches on "Current Efforts to Improve the Liberal Arts College" to Iowa college presidents; on "The Needs for New Methods of Accrediting Institutions of Higher Learning to the National Association of Officers of Regional Standardizing Agencies"; and "Current Methods in the In-service Training of College Teachers" at a conference attended by representatives of forty-five colleges.

Besides the writing involved in the twelve survey volumes, he wrote a chapter on "Finance and Business Management in Institutions of Higher Education" published in the *Review of Educational Research* of the American Education Research Association, and other articles.

1933–1943: The Period of Extensive Involvement Principally in Off-campus Activities In Washington

The period of 1933–43 (as described in Part II) was undoubtedly the most active decade in the life of Floyd Reeves. It, indeed, must have stretched the liberal policy of leaves from the University to the limit. But they were all directly or indirectly related to New Deal efforts to cope with the problems of the depression, of governmental reorganization, planning, personnel policies and preparation for our entry into World War II. In these activities Reeves had the support of two major members of the Chicago faculty—Charles Hubbard Judd, and his new colleague Charles E. Merriam and President Hutchins, who was also involved in the American Youth Commission directed by Reeves.

Also related was the fact that the reporting system for members of the faculty provided a specific place for citing government services and activities which regularized their participation in such activities and made them an integral part of their work load. Some of the activities were part-time, some full-time and some were participated in during normal quarters off-campus. Several of them, however, required varying lengths of time on leave. The sequence of external activities began in July 1933 when Reeves was appointed Director of Personnel and of the Social and Economic Division of the Tennessee Valley Authority (TVA). (Chapter I Part II.)

Immediately after the above assignment, Reeves became involved in a significant educational project in New York State with Luther Gulick, Director of the Inquiry into the Character and Cost of Public Instruction in the State of New York, in which Reeves was given responsibility for directing the research on the adult education section of the inquiry. (Chapter II Part I.)

Concurrently with the Regents Inquiry, Roosevelt brought Reeves back into the federal scene, appointing him to chair the Advisory Committee on Education. This Committee, during the next eighteen months, produced the most complete analysis of the status, problems and needs of elementary and secondary education in the United States plus recommendations for greatly expanded federal support of such activities than had ever been made. (Chapter III Part I.)

The next major activity was his appointment in May 1939 as Director of the American Youth Commission (AYC) of the American Council on Education. (Chapter IV Part I.) The AYC was basically the privately funded research arm for a whole range of information about and problems of youth for the National Youth Administration (NYA). The NYA, the action agency, along with the Civilian Conservation Corps (CCC) of the government was headed by Aubrey Williams, who was a close associate and confidante of President Roosevelt. Reeves (and the ten volumes of research studies published by the AYC) was the linkage between the private coordinating body for American education and the well financed and far-flung federal government action programs for youth of the country—many of them disadvantaged by reasons of poverty, racial discrimination, unemployment, low morale and lack of appropriate educational opportunity. Besides the on-going interest of the President in youth programs, Eleanor Roosevelt was also interested and she formed a close working relationship with Reeves in the White House Conference and other youth activities. (Chapter IV Part I.)

The next major activity brought Reeves back into another federal problem in the personnel field. The problems of how to deal with the special problems of attorneys and administrators in the federal service led President Roosevelt to appoint a Committee on Civil Service Improvement under the chairmanship of Justice Stanley Reed. The special problems which the Committee addressed were, in a sense, left over and unresolved since publication of the report by the Committee on Administrative Management with which Reeves was previously involved. (Chapter II Part II.)

As preparations for war took on greater intensity, Reeves was again summoned to participate in the federal government as Executive Assistant to Sidney Hillman for Labor Supply in the War Production Board. He also served as a member of the President's Advisory Committee on Selective Service during the same period of approximately one year from June 1940. (Chapter IV Part II.)

Shortly thereafter Reeves became involved, also at the instigation of Charles Merriam, in the work of the National Resources Planning Board (NRPB). The NRPB was one of the agencies created as a result of the specific recommendation of the President's Committee on Administrative Management to improve the capacity of the Office of the President to grapple with the increasingly complex responsibilities of the federal government in economic and social problems. Of special importance was Reeves's chairmanship of a special committee (called a "conference" by President Roosevelt) of the NRPB on Post War Readjustment of Civilian and Military Personnel which provided the basis for legislation familiarly known as the G. I. Bill of Rights. (Chapter III Part II.)

Consultancies

Interspersed in the major activities noted above, Reeves engaged after he resigned from TVA, in consulting work with that agency on management problems; with Dexter Keezer of the Office of Price Administration on consumer relations; personnel and organization problems with the American Youth Commission (AYC) before he took over the directorship of the AYC; and with the Bureau of the Budget on problems of vocational rehabilitation, manpower and training. He also served as advisor to surveys on the Dental Curriculum of American universities and on programs of theological education in the USA and Canada.

He also served on the Boards of Trustees of Antioch and Huron Colleges and Roosevelt University.

His interest in post-war planning for educational institutions took him to meet and plan with educational officials and state legislators in Kansas, Missouri, Illinois and with Michigan State College.

National Committees

Reeves's work on major studies and surveys in education, planning, public administration and youth problems led naturally to persons who and organizations which wished to tap his knowledge, experience and judgment in these areas for varying periods of time. Among the national committees on which he served were: the National Committee on Standard Reports of Institutions of Higher Education; Advisory Committee on Youth Problems of the Office of Civilian Defense; Citizens Committee for the White House Conference on Youth—the latter two committees also included the active participation of Mrs. Roosevelt; National Committee of the International Student Service; American County Life Association; and a Planning Committee of the Civil Service Assembly of the United States and Canada.

Major Speaking Engagements

Reeves was clearly a highly popular and effective speaker—as numerous "fan letters" confirm. Most of the twenty or more speeches addressed to conferences and annual meetings of educational societies or organizations were based on research data and recommendations derived therefrom in the several areas of activities noted above.

Illustrative of speeches made to groups, not on the campus of the University of Chicago, were "Current Efforts to Improve the Liberal Arts College" before a group of presidents of Iowa colleges; "Post War Education" to the National Conference of the American Association of Collegiate Registrars; ''A Plan for Education after the War'' and ''Manpower Problems in Relation to Schools and Colleges'' to the meetings of the Educational Research Association; ''The Need for Social and Economic Planning'' to the League of Women Voters; ''Privileges and Duties of Citizens in a Democracy;'' the commencement address at Temple University in 1942; ''Organizing the Manpower of the Nation for Defense'' at the Annual Institute of Government at the University of Southern California; ''A Policy for Adult Education'' at the National Council on Education Conference; three speeches generally on ''Emergency Tasks Confronting Education'' at the 50th Anniversary Celebration of Stanford University; and the Inglis Lecture in 1942 at Harvard University on ''Education for Today and Tomorrow.''

While with TVA he made numerous speeches on the organization, personnel policies, and training programs of the Authority.

Meanwhile, Reeves did not neglect speaking engagements at the University, which included addressess to five annual conferences of administrative officers and public and private schools on such subjects as ''Regional and National Resources of Use to Localities in Solving School and Community Problems;'' ''Personnel Problems of Boards of Education Now and After the War;'' ''Leadership in the Formulation of Public School Policy;'' and ''Manpower and Defense Industries'' to the Institute of Military Studies.

Radio addresses were made on a local radio station's ''Prairie Farmer Discussion Club;'' and at the ''University of Chicago Round Table;'' national broadcasts with Ralph Tyler, Sam Nerlove and Robert Hutchins on ''When Johnny Comes Marching Home.'' He also testified at several Congressional hearings on proposed legislation addressed to funding for education growing out of the work and publications of the Advisory Committee on Education.

Major Publications

Reeves's published reports and articles, like his numerous speeches, were closely related to the research data, findings and recommendations of the organizations in which he was engaged. Practically all of the major publications were jointly authored. Ten of the twelve volumes of the University of Chicago Self-survey were jointly authored, though Reeves was listed as the senior author. The section on ''Personnel Administration in the Federal Service'' published in the comprehensive volume on "Administrative Management in the Government of the United States" was co-authored with Paul T. David. The volume on "Adult Education of the Regent's Inquiry into the Character and Cost of Public Education in the State of New York" included T. Fansler and C. O. Houle as joint authors. The twenty volumes and pamphlets on youth problems published by the American Youth Commission of the American Council on Education did not include Reeves's name on any volume except as Director of Research for the whole series. However, more than fifty articles in which Reeves was the sole author appeared in the *American Teacher*, *Survey Graphic*, *Journal of Educational Sociology*, *Educational Research*, *High School Journal*, *Illinois School Board Journal*, *Elementary School Journal*, *Harvard Educational Review*, *New Republic*, *Journal of Educational Research*, *Journal of Adult Education*, *Personnel Administration*, *School Life* and other journals.

University Committeees and courses taught

As time permitted, Reeves served on a number of all-University committees which were concerned with internal problems of the University.

Reeves taught very little except two courses in each of the summer quarters of 1933 and 1936 before he went to the TVA and after he returned. After returning to the campus he focused on adult education courses which were the initial courses in a program which was later enlarged and authorized for the Ph. D. degree. His extensive research and operational experiences in administration was recognized by the University in 1938 when his title was changed to Professor of Administration and a year later, he taught courses for graduate students in education, political science and business. In 1942 he developed a new course in "War and Post War Planning," which he gave in the Political Science Department. In 1943 he gave the same planning course in education and continued his "General Principles Course on Organization and Administration" in Political Science. After 1943 Reeves gave the course in General Principles to graduate students in education and political science and other students from the College of Business and other colleges of the University. The field of organization and administration became one of the areas of specialization for the Ph. D. degree in education.

He also had a relatively small quota of candidates for the masters and Ph. D. degrees. A small beginning was also made in the evolution of special programs in rural education which were developed in the years after 1943.

1944–1953: A Period of Continued Off-campus and Campus Activities

Off-campus Activities

Commission on Educational Reconstruction

Reeves continued a vigorous—although somewhat less hectic—series of off-campus activities and consultancies during this period. One of the principal activities was to serve as Chairman of the "Commission on Educational Reconstruction" as an active member of the American Foundation of Teachers (AFT). The principal purpose of this activity was to mobilize national educational organizations to support the basic recommendations of the Advisory Committee on Education. The recommendations of the Committee got into a log-jam of federal legislation which was stymied by the preoccupation of President Roosevelt with more urgent matters related to the war and to his loss of leadership of the Congress. One of the publications resulting from this effort—a small book with Lester Kirkendall as joint author, under title of "Goals for American Education," was printed in thousands of copies (20,000 were ordered by the Japanese Teachers Union) and widely quoted in *The New York Times* and other leading newspapers. The book, numerous speeches, conferences and aggressive committee work had positive results with Congress and throughout the nation. Reeves probably became as well known in all educational organizations nationally through his effort as he was through his extensive involvement in college and university surveys.

American Council on Education Committee on Discrimination

An activity which was likewise focused even more sharply on discriminatory practices in college admissions was his work as Chairman of the Committee on Discrimination in College Admissions organized under the auspices of the American Council on Education and funded in part by the Anti-Defamation League of B'nai 'Brith. Through a series of regional conferences of college and university presidents, deans, registrars and other educational officials and a large conference of students at Earlham College, plus the usual amount of speech making, correspondence and arm twisting, many of the discriminatory practices fell like the Walls of Jerico. (Chaper V Part I.)

UNESCO Mission and Other Activities

A first of three major experiences abroad (in addition to teaching college courses for the Education Branch of the Army in Florence, Italy) was Reeves's service on the UNESCO Consultative Mission to the Philippines. This project was the first of several somewhat experimental missions to countries in Asia to survey and document educational problems and needs which would form a basis for internal changes in policy and administration and for the encouragement of foreign technical assistance. Paul Hanna of Stanford University, a Canadian and a Costa Rican educator were members of the team headed by Reeves. (Chapter VI Part I.)

In addition to these major off-campus activities Reeves continued to serve as a consultant to the TVA—particularly on redefining TVA's program of regional studies and research and on TVA's involvement with the Oak Ridge Institute of Nuclear Studies in which a number of southern and other universities and the TVA participated. He also served as a consultant to the Council of State Governments on a study of the organization, control and financing of higher education in the then forty-eight states. Other short-term consulting services were provided to the Board for Southern Regional Education; Federal Civilian Defense Administration; the University of the State of New Mexico; President and faculty of the University of South Carolina; National Board for Granting Fellowships provided by the Pepsi-Cola Company; U. S. Atomic Energy Commission on organizational and personnel matters; and to President John A. Hannah of Michigan State College. (Chapter VII Part I.)

He also served on a number of national committees such as the Executive Committee of the Board of Directors of the American Country Life Association, Youth Committee of the American Council on Education and several other organizations.

He also taught at Claremont College in 1951 during his winter quarter off and continued his work as Vice President of the Howard University Board of Trustees and as a member of the Board of Trustees of Roosevelt University.

On-Campus Activities

Acting Chairman of the Department

Reeves was appointed Acting Chairman of the Department of Education by Chancellor Hutchins in December 1948 after Ralph Tyler was promoted to the deanship of the Social Science Division. He was to serve in an acting capacity until September 1949. During this period a committee of the department headed by Professor Newton Edwards, with Professor Guy T. Buswell and William S. Gray as members, made a search for a successor chairman. The faculty committee, after carefully considering the qualifications of all persons whose names were submitted to it by the faculty of the Department and by a number of outstanding educational leaders whom the committee consulted informally reported that: "The final choice of the committee unanimously arrived at, is Floyd W. Reeves." The committee expanded on its recommendation with these words:

> Mr. Reeves has achieved national recognition for distinguished work in the field of education and political science. He has exhibited an understanding of research in education and has contributed substantially to it as indicated in his extensive bibliography. He has (the) flexibility of mind required to initiate research in new areas. We believe that Mr. Reeves possesses in an unusual degree the qualities required to promote scientific inquiry in the field of education . . . Many of the activities which Mr. Reeves has directed have required a high order of administrative ability. His record clearly demonstrates that he ranks high in ability as an administrator . . . During the short period that Mr. Reeves has been acting chairman of the department, he has shown clarity in grasping the essential problems of the department and has demonstrated capacity to provide leadership in shaping the future policies of the department. The committee recommends Mr. Reeves to the Faculty of the Department of Education with full confidence that he would provide the kind of leadership the department needs.[9]

Following the recommendation of the committee, the faculty voted unanimously to recommend that Reeves be appointed chairman of the Department.

Reeves declined to accept the position on a permanent basis, as he did on several occasions before and after this show of confidence in his administrative ability. For example a letter to Judd from the

Executive Secretary of the Association of American Colleges in 1935 in which he asked for recommendations of some names he could pass along as possible presidents of colleges and universities, Judd responded: "Mr. Floyd W. Reeves, now on leave of absence from this institution, has made more surveys of colleges and universities, I suppose, than any other man in the country. He has refused a number of college presidencies and may not be disposed to assume the duties of such an office but he certainly has had the type of experience which qualifies him to administer any educational institution which he may be interested to join."[10] He was comfortable and happy to be a staff officer, advisor, consultant or director of research but did not wish to be involved directly in administration or management of any educational enterprise.

Speaking Engagements and Seminars

Reeves made somewhat fewer speeches and engaged in a smaller number of seminars and conferences during his last decade at the University. He did, however, continue to respond to several requests for speeches to educational and other organizations on their interests generated by the reports of the Advisory Commission on Education, school districting, rural education and other topics on which he had served as research director and spokesman. He also participated in a faculty seminar on "The Division of Labor Between the Federal Government and the States," limited to twenty persons organized by Leonard White, professor of Political Science in which members of the faculty invited from Economics, Sociology, Political Science and officials of state governments participated.

Teaching and Advising

Except for the period when Reeves was acting chairman and for the six months when he taught at Claremont College, he carried a normal teaching and advising load—plus doing a considerable amount of guest lecturing in other courses. The Chicago system of work allocation for the formula included "points" or "units" for teaching, research and writing and service for professors in the Departments of Education and Political Science and possibly other departments. In the Department of Education he taught the following courses and workshops during one or more quarters when he was in residence: "General

Principles of Organization and Administration,'' ''Education in Rural Communities,'' and ''Problems in Rural Education.'' He also taught the following courses in Political Science: ''General Principles of Organization and Administration,'' and a seminar with Professors Leonard White and Herman Pritchett.

He chaired or served on twenty-two doctoral and master degree candidate committees in 1948–49.

Reeves's teaching of courses in General Principles of Organization and Administration in the Department of Education and Political Science and for some students in the College of business, with basically the same material, underlined a thesis of Reeves, on which he continued to do research and writing, namely that the principles of administration had general applicability. A highly abbreviated outline of topics follows:

- The nature, characteristics, theory and practice of organization and administration.
- Nature and kinds of planning and forecasting; relationship between ends and means in planning; and the executive budget as an instrument of planning.
- The nature of organization; position and job classification; elements of formal organization structure; structural provisions for securing coordination and control and the use of committees and boards in formal organization structure; informal organization and related topics.
- Staffing, selection and assignment of personnel; delegating duties and authority; personnel development; employee-management relations and similar topics.
- Techniques for directing to secure coordination and control through means of the budget; memoranda of understanding, organization charts; and through informal methods; use of rewards and penalties; communication, both up and down the scales chain; and the interrelationship of all of the above factors.

In these courses and throughout his teaching career, Reeves was also highly involved in important research and educational advocacy projects which were addressed to then current needs and problems. The reactions of one of his students, Dr. D. B. Varner who later had a distinguished career in educational administration at Michigan State University and the University of Nebraska, wrote:

> My first experience with Floyd Reeves was as a student. I was in graduate school at the University of Chicago in 1946–48 and one of my classes was in the field of Public Administration under Floyd Reeves. He was an intriguing teacher. We had limited reference material and he had a tendency to substitute his own personal experiences for any of the literature in the field. He was a man of great experience and he lived them all intensely! He had an interesting characteristic in his class of teaching from this personal background. On two or three occasions, some of us kept a secret tally of the number of times he used the pronoun "I" in a 50-minute lecture. While I have forgotten the exact number, I can assure you that it was very, very high! This is not to suggest that he was an ineffective teacher—quite the contrary. He retained a high level of interest and I'm sure all of us gained substantially from his own wide basis of involvement with government and quasi-governmental agencies.[11]

Although Reeves lectured and wrote extensively on principles of organization and administration he failed to put all of his experience and knowledge together in the creation of a general theory on the subject.

Reeves did not, however, maintain an arms-length relationship with his students or with the young persons he engaged as his assistants in major undertakings. His record as a developer of able young people was one of his strongest personal characteristics.

Creation of an Institute for Rural Education[12]

Reeves's interest in neglected social and economic problems of the rural sector of our economy and particularly about education for youths and adults was deep. His rural upbringing, graduate study related to school districting, direction of studies for the American Youth Commission and the National Youth Administration, rural manpower and demobilization studies and other activities all came to focus in his creation of a rural education program at the University. The immediate antecedent of this program was Reeves's participation, in 1942, in a "Committee on Rural Education" of the National Education Association which was affiliated with the American Country Life Association. This Committee recommended that the American Council on Education take the initiative in arranging a conference of lay and professional persons, on post-war planning for rural education. Some of the topics which they identified as important to be examined were: the interrelationship of war and post-war problems; comprehensive integration of the rural school into the whole life of the community; and conditions necessary to develop a more effective rural education program. Reeves chaired the conference. The following are excerpts from his opening remarks:

> I don't need to tell this group the importance of this conference at this time. The report released two or three days ago from Washington indicates as I recall the figure, about thirteen million more people are going to be needed in our war industries and military forces in the year that lies ahead . . . now we know, if we think just a moment, what that is going to do to rural America, where such a large percentage of the youth who are called to military service and also called to war industries reside . . . It would be so easy, in the months that lie ahead, for our rural economy to be set back one or two generations . . . We cannot avoid the fact that the enrollment of our rural high schools will be cut drastically . . . We are going to hear some facts today about what is happening with reference to teacher supply . . . and we are going to face the situation that certain of these things are going to happen. They must happen. We can't prevent it. And then we must face . . . what can we, as a conference, do in the way of planning to make the impact on rural education less severe than it would be if we did not do that planning? . . . Now, that is what this conference means to me. We are faced by hard facts, but these facts are not of such a nature that by, carefully planning, we cannot devise means of meeting the situation better than we could meet it if we did not do that planning.[13]

The following actions resulting from the opening conference were taken by the University of Chicago:

- Acceptance in 1943 of an initial planning grant from the Farm Foundation to explore the possible creation of an "Institute of Rural Education" under the direction of Floyd Reeves.
- The appointment of an interdisciplinary committee (urged by Reeves) from the departments of Anthropology, Economics, Education, Geography, Political Science and from the Divinity and Business Schools and included the Provost of the University.
- After further exploratory work of the above committee the Farm Foundation made another grant, which was supplemented by University funds for a total of more than $40,000 to further the

University's involvement, in what some persons would regard as an unlikely field for the University of Chicago.

- After a still further year of discussion the exploratory committee published a report of its deliberations under title of "The Foundation for Research in Agriculture and Rural Life" which contained their appraisal for engaging in further activities:

Further activity which developed during the years 1943–46, in which Reeves served as Executive Director of the Committee, included:

- A conference on "Education and Rural Communication" which was attended by 130 faculty members, administrators of University, Land Grant colleges, State and Federal rural organizations, librarians, and others interested in and responsible for research and educational programs in rural education.
- Workshops in five midwestern states attended by state school supervisors of teachers in rural areas.
- Research by Reeves and a young associate, Laverne Burchfield, resulted in a book on *Education for Rural America.* [14]
- A summer workshop conducted in 1945 for editors of State Education journals.
- Field services to Superintendents of Public Instruction and postwar planning commissions in six midwestern states in analyzing relevant data regarding their rural sections and the problems of improving their programs for rural children was believed to produce excellent factual reports and suggestions.
- A report by the faculty on the thirty months of their experience in working on the program concluded that: "the project had made major contributions directly or indirectly to fundamental research, the interpretation of research findings of education and the other social sciences and in the translation of reserach findings into educational practices . . ."
- The last activity was a series of seminar sessions for 32 faculty members, including Floyd Reeves, which was led by Nobel Laureate, Theodore W. Schultz, Professor of Economics. The seminar sessions conducted over a period of more than a year, focused on such topics as: "The Political Setting for Policy Making in Agriculture;" "Agriculture Extension as the Crossroads;" "Quantitative Research in Agricultural Economics;" "Foundations for Research in Agriculture and Rural Social Life" and other topics. A book entitled *New Research Vistas for Agriculture and Rural Social Life*, was published on material presented in the seminar sessions.[15]

Reeves's Ambivalence about and His Frustrated Efforts to Develop a Comprehensive Theory of Organization and Administration

Some of the major expressions of his dilemma follow:[16]

• A letter to C. H. Judd from Reeves stated:

As far as my own work is concerned I find it difficult to distinguish between *research activities and service activities*. In connection with each of the four major investigations in which I have been engaged during the past three years, some of the work has been in the nature of research and some might be better classified as a service activity . . . This is true of the Survey of Institutions Related to the Methodist Episcopal Church, the Survey of the University of Chicago, the investigation of standards for the Committee on Revision of Standards for Institutions on Higher Education. For the National Committee on Standards Report I assisted in the preparation of three bulletins which represent largely committee judgments, and in the preparation of one bulletin which is a summary of the techniques employed and the findings of all of the important studies of unit costs which have been made in higher institutions. In addition to the four investigations mentioned above, last year I prepared a chapter on Finance and Business Managment in Institutions of Higher Education for the Review of Educational Research published by the American Educational Research Association.

• The minutes of eleven meetings of the Social Science Research Committee of the University or other exchanges of memoranda from January 1932 to 1952 reveal that Reeves was awarded grants and given time off from teaching duties to engage in research on underlying principles of organization and administration and supporting theory which would be applicable to education and other public and private organizations. His efforts to concentrate on this monumental task, as Tyler's letter indicates, were often, however disrupted or postponed as a result of involvement in important committees or commissions—principally national in scope. He continued, however, to relate these activities to his basic thesis and to write and teach theory and principles as they were maturing in his mind.

• The final episode in this chronology of frustration was a joint memorandum from C. Herman Pritchett of the Political Science Department and Maurice F. Seay of the Department of Education addressed to Ralph W. Tyler on May 16, 1952. The text of the memorandum follows:

Professor Reeves is engaged in writing a report of the important research which he has conducted over a period of years. Because of teaching duties and other instructional obligations Mr. Reeves has not been able to make the desired progress in preparing his publications. After studying this situation carefully we believe that it would be to the advantage of the Departments of Education and of Political Science to release Mr. Reeves during the Winter and Spring Quarters from teaching duties and to permit him to work on his publications during those quarters at the location which seems most desirable to him. We are also agreed that Mr. Reeves may carry out some special instructional or consultative assignments from other institutions during his absence from our campus provided these duties contribute to his major tasks of research and publication.

We are proposing this plan for the year 1952–53 and, unless some unforeseen circumstance develops, we anticipate making the same proposal for each year remaining before Dr. Reeves' retirement.

• Nearly fifty years later in a letter to the author from Ralph W. Tyler dated January 8, 1982, Reeves's ambivalence about research and service activities (or "operational research") again surfaced. Tyler had a long perspective on Reeves dating back to their association in South Dakota in 1921–22 and through his close association with him while Chairman of the Department of Education and as Dean of the Division of Social Science in the 30's and 40's.

In my opinion, Floyd established an aura of intense concern and energetic action on important educational and political issues that was viewed by his colleagues as the dominant basis of his relationships . . . I think he was viewed as a man who strongly pushed programs he thought important and could be depended upon to exercise initiative and put forth a great deal of energy on assignments that he viewed as socially significant. When his colleagues or administrative superiors could get him interested in an action program, he was like a 'fire horse' chomping at the bit to get out and do something. His causes were good ones, his judgment was unusually sound, his convictions were clear and stable. These characteristics were valuable assets to most social institutions including universities and governments, and he was frequently chosen to carry out an important and difficult assignment. But those outstanding positive qualities were sometimes in conflict with the traditional role of a university professor. He valued research but he found the patient search for knowledge somewhat incompatible with his zeal and urge for immediate action.

As far as I know, Reeves was never criticized by colleagues and

> administrators on these grounds. They valued his insights and the actions he advised or carried out. They accepted him fully for his exceptional talents. But I believe that he, Floyd Reeves, became increasingly uncomfortable with the contrast between what he, himself, believed to be the role of professor in a research university, and what he enjoyed most and spent most time doing. At one point, he asked me for time off to work on the development of a comprehensive theory of administration, which I gladly granted, but within a short time he asked, instead, for leave without pay to participate in the development of plans for a State University of New York. Interestingly enough, he kept increasing his emphasis on research in conversation and writing, while he reduced his own efforts on research to spend more energy on action programs . . . The administration of the University of Chicago and most of his colleagues were sorry to see him leave to accept an appointment as Consultant to President John A. Hannah of Michigan State College. We felt a profound loss, but I believed that he chose wisely in terms of his own sense of fulfillment—using his talents constructively without feeling that he was neglecting his primary task.[17]

Tyler's judgment of Reeves's values and preferences is supported by the record indicated above. It may only be added that Tyler's interpretation, with which I am in agreement, has to be thought of in terms of the kind of institution which the University of Chicago was and is—basically a research university. Reeves's principal supporters, Charles H. Judd and Charles E. Merriam were somewhat afflicted with the same ambivalence but perhaps less so as they too were frequently on missions comparable to those, and sometimes the same as those, in which Reeves participated. Furthermore, times had changed to a point when there was no more war to win or reconstruction to take place in which the University of Chicago had encouraged their faculty members to participate. Finally, although Reeves did not, in fact, produce a scholarly contribution to the theory of administration to which he aspired, he did produce an extra-ordinarily large—and for some items very significant and scholarly—number of articles and other writings which would be interpreted in some academic quarters as scholarly research. Furthermore, his writing of significant reports was basically depersonalized by the semi-anonymous role which he played as Director of Research or Studies or as Chairman of Committees or Commissions, the reports of which were credited—in most instances—to the Committees or Commissions, rather than to him. Nevertheless, it is true that Reeves did not achieve *his* goal of producing *the* basic, definitive, theoretical work on organization and administration.

Appraisal of His Career at the University of Chicago

Although Reeves, his colleagues, and interested publishers (e.g., Ordway Tead of Harper and Brothers) were disappointed that he did not write a scholarly work on the theory of administration which he aspired to do, his record of accomplishments at the University of Chicago and with the organization for which he served as Director of Research or Studies while affiliated with the University was outstanding. He directed the unique and highly useful self-survey of the University; he served as Acting Chairman of the Department of Education; was centrally involved in the creation of a Rural Development Project; was instrumental in establishing the first graduate programs in adult education and educational administration; was highly regarded as a professor in both education and political science; and was a stimulating colleague and teacher as indicated by previous citations. Furthermore, he added to the prestige of the University by service at the highest levels in the Roosevelt Administration, the North Central Association of Colleges and Schools, the American Council on Education and other organizations. Nevertheless, he was ready in his last years at Chicago, as Ralph Tyler had predicted, to respond to one more advisory and consulting challenge and assignment to an emerging and leading public land-grant university—under the leadership of another activist-administrator and public servant, John A. Hannah, President of Michigan State College.

Epilogue

Reeves continued to teach the principles courses in his last working days at Michigan State University apparently in much the same manner as he did at the University of Chicago. He also dictated several chapters for a volume which he never completed. Furthermore he continued, almost to his dying days, to sketch out (sometimes on cardboard from cereal or other boxes) "principles of organization and administration" in which he firmly believed. While a resident of the Burcham Hills Retirement Home, in East Lansing, Michigan, a fellow resident made a tape of his remarks in which he compared, in terms of principles, the organization and administration of the retirement home to large corporate and governmental organizations. But alas, maybe Robert Hutchins was right when he cast doubt on whether there was such a thing as a theory of or even principles of public administration and certainly whether they could be taught.[18] Notwithstanding Hutchins's skepticism, Reeves had something important in mind, even though he didn't write the definitive theory, as attested to by at least some of his students and young colleagues who distinguished themselves and their former teacher with their organizational and administrative competence. Reeves deeply influenced a number of young leaders in educational and public administration who demonstrated the validity and applicability of the concepts and principles of administration which he espoused. These included George Gant and John Oliver, both General Managers of TVA; Paul David, Professor of Politial Science at the University of Virginia; and John E. Ivey, former Executive Vice President of New York University, and several others who were not as closely associated with Reeves, but who were students of his or otherwise greatly influenced by his ideas and motivation. One such was Harry L. Case, former Director of Personnel at the TVA, United Nations and Ford Foundation official and Professor at Michigan State University.

First among those former persons was Gordon R. Clapp who was a Ph. D. candidate at the University of Chicago under Reeves before joining the TVA as Reeves assistant. Clapp's career in TVA was meteoric, rising as he did from assistant to Reeves through successive promotions and Presidential appointments to Chairman of the Board over a period of twenty-two years. He later served as Deputy City Manager of the City of New York and President of the Development and Resources Corporation

Clapp was invited back to the University of Chicago to give the Walgreen Lecture in 1954; it was published under the title *The TVA: An Approach to the Development of a Region*[19] Clapp, inscribed a copy of the volume to Reeves as "Your Life Long Student."

Chapter II

Surveys of Colleges, Universities and Other Educational Institutions and Work with the North Central Association of Colleges and Schools, 1927–36

Surveys

Surveys of colleges, universities (and to a lesser degree of public school systems) were a highly popular mode of examining the organization, instructional programs, method of financing, personnel, and strengths and weaknesses in the performance of educational institutions from about 1908 through the early 40's. Floyd Reeves was a recognized leader and innovator in this field.

The number and range of surveys of educational institutions were analyzed in 1933 by the then president of the Carnegie Foundation for the Advancement of teaching, Dr. Walter Crosby Eells, professor of education at Stanford University, who made a comprehensive examination of the field.[1] Over 500 surveys were identified in the first tabulation, of which 230 were printed. He submitted copies of these surveys to 41 of the most experienced surveyors of institutions of higher education to select the 30 outstanding surveys. Reeves was director of three of those rated as outstanding.

The Foreword to the Eells report by Howard J. Savage, staff member of the Carnegie Foundation, written in 1936, provides perspective on the survey movement at its most active stage. As to the methods of making surveys, Savage points out that the Eells' study:

> makes clear that those who over the past thirty years have studied American higher education have contributed much to the statistical methods of treating data. Many of the processes they have thus applied have come from other fields of inquiry. Some have been devised afresh to fill needs as they have appeared. On the whole, it would seem that the surveyors of our higher education have not been by any means exempt from the passion for statistics that have come to possess the American mind. The industrious collection of facts alone does not constitute science or the scientific method. Interpretations, with understanding and intelligence, must follow, by whatever method good judgment indicates. Here as elsewhere statistics are no adequate substitute for common sense.[2]

In his introduction to the first volume of the University of Chicago survey Reeves wrote: "Any discussion of the organization and administration of the University of Chicago will have to be largely in terms of judgment rather than scientific established conclusions. These judgments, however, have been arrived at after a study of principles as seem to apply and after a review of the experience which many universities have had with the several practices involved."

Savage appraised the surveys as varying "materially in worth and in the values of the recommendations they contain, if one is to judge by the proportion of the recommendations which public and educational opinion has been strong enough to effectuate. The best of these reports have had a profound and lasting effect upon the national welfare; the less practical have had small result." He continued with these observations: "However diverse and individual our colleges and universities—and ought to be—each of them has access to a common body of administrative wisdom, which can be applied to new but similar conditions. Useful as educational surveys may be, their effect in many cases has been principally to corroborate conclusions arrived at long before through sound reasoning and understanding of human nature."

He continued with this prophetic note, "The survey, as we know it even at its best, may not turn out ultimately to be the most fruitful avenue of approach to every problem of our higher education. It is conceivable that, in some cases the extensive amassing of data . . . may give place to less formalized and less obtrusive advisory services without any written report at all."[3] Reeves would have also concurred in this view. Reeves consistently used data primarily as a means of illuminating problems but relied heavily on involvement of the persons responsible for the work of the institution in appraising the meaning of the data and, through non-threatening discussion and counseling to find more effective solutions to the problems.

Summary of Reeves's Involvement in Surveys as Reported by Eells

Eells noted ninety-six surveys of all types of educational institutions in which Reeves was involved. Sixty-four were directed by Reeves. In most instances he had one or more collaborators. Most of them were colleagues from Kentucky educational institutions and from the University of Chicago. John Dale Russell, a former student of Reeves who was one of his proteges, was his principal collaborator. The surveys varied in scope from a few mimeographed pages to the twelve volume record of the University of Chicago self-survey. The institutions surveyed ranged from very small colleges to large universities.

Between 1924 and 1935 all of the educational institutions in West Virginia; all of the state universities in Indiana; and the curricula and programs of theological and dental schools were reviewed and 25 educational institutions affiliated with the Baptist and Discipiles of Christ Churches were surveyed. A major survey of 35 colleges and universities affiliated with the Methodist Episcopal Church included Northwestern University and 34 smaller institutions. The results of this project were published by the University of Chicago Press under the title of *The Liberal Arts College*. Reeves and Russell also collaborated in writing a widely used textbook, also published by the University of Chicago Press under the title of *College Organization and Administration*.

Quality of Surveys Directed by Reeves

As indicated above, three of the larger surveys directed by Reeves were evaluated as among the best. Five other surveys directed by Reeves also received high votes of approval. Many of the surveys were evaluated as being of considerable value to the institutions which were surveyed. For example E. C. Elliott, President of Purdue University, speaking for the universities of the state of Indiana reported:

> The beneficial effects of the survey were immediate. Many of the long-standing doubts as to the place of higher institutions in the social economy of the state were removed. Beginning with the legislative session of 1927 a more favorable and constructive attitude prevailed and this attitude has continued to the present time.[4]

President Robert M. Hutchins of the University of Chicago also expressed his approval as follows:

> The survey of the University of Chicago has important results in three particulars. In the first place it is a reference work and as such is constantly used by the administration, the faculty and the trustees . . . In the second place certain volumes (twelve in all) have been important in presenting various aspects of the University to prospective donors . . . In the third place the survey has had important effects on the organization of the University . . . The recommendations of the survey, since they assisted us to a simpler organization, also assisted us to meet the depression.[5]

Reeves's Approach and Method of Work in Making Surveys

First as to the "general method of presenting reports" Eells wrote:

> A variety of methods have been used for presenting the completed survey report to the sponsoring body. At one extreme may be placed the 'poker face' type described by one of the men who has had much experience in higher educational surveys as follows: 'I used to think that the proper way to conduct a survey was to go into an institution, collect all the information possible, present a poker face throughout the entire period, give no one the slightest inkling of the nature of my conclusions, present a final report at the meeting of the Board of Trustees later in the evening and take the midnight train out of town!' Fortunately, this notion of survey work has tended to give place to a more rational cooperation throughout the survey. In the surveys undertaken under the direction of Dr. Floyd W. Reeves, for example, quite a different philosophy has prevailed; recommendations have frequently been made and put into effect during the progress of the work. Note, for example, the procedure in the Methodist Survey. 'The president of the college (presumably each of the 36 presidents of the colleges surveyed) was asked to read this report in this preliminary form in order to catch any errors of fact and to criticize in general the attitude taken by the survey staff toward the problems of his institution. This reading of the preliminary report also served to give those connected with the college a preview of the findings;

> in many cases a large number of the recommendations made in the report were thus actually put into effect before the official delivery of the survey. The Director took the position of the adviser and counselor to these committee groups and not that of a surveyor hunting for faults to be kept dark until they could be written out in the form of a report.[6]

This point of view characterized Reeves's approach to consultation as he became increasingly involved in that level of work.

Reeves also served as a member of the standing committee of the Association of American Colleges which had as its function "to keep the members of the Association advised of significant college surveys, developments in survey technique and the actual or suggested solutions to pertinent problems of administration."

Also D. Henderson, former President of Antioch College, Professor of Higher Education at The University of Michigan and Associate Director of Studies in 1946 for the "State of New York Temporary Commission on the Need for a State University," directed by Reeves, evaluated Reeves's work as follows:

> There is no question that Floyd Reeves was an expert, perhaps *the* expert on institutional surveys. He always knew what he wanted to accomplish. He organized well for the field work and the collection of data. He approached every activity with great enthusiasm, and I think this quality of leadership is responsible for getting acceptance of his ideas and methods. His firm convictions—'There is no question but' made it difficult to disagree with him, because he had such a command of what he wanted to do . . . He was creative in the survey work. He was innovative and creative in redesigning the methods used by the North Central Association.[7]

Norman Burns, formerly Professor of Education at the University of Chicago, commented on Reeves's work as a surveyor of colleges and universities and the relationship of surveys to the practical impact on the accrediting process as follows:

> More than anyone I have ever known Floyd Reeves was always ready to question established practices and entertain new ideas. In the area of evaluation and accrediting of colleges and universities, the area in which I worked closely with him, Floyd was one of the first to recognize the faculty degrees, class size, student-faculty ratios, library holdings, income and expenditures per student and the like. He frankly recognized and accepted the importance in the evaluative process of judgment of

> institutional quality by knowledgeable persons. Floyd was instrumental, first as Executive Secretary of the North Central Association's Commission of Institutions of Higher Education, then as advisor to me when I succeeded him in that position, in effecting significant changes in the accrediting processes and activities of the Commission.[8]

Dr. Burns responded affirmatively to the author's question about a comment which he had heard Reeves make on several occasions about his favorable appraisal of Antioch and Oberlin Colleges—two very different institutions.

The mode of operation, principles and values which Reeves espoused, and some of the most important findings and recommendations made in two of the comprehensive surveys conducted by Reeves and staff associates who were recruited by him are described in the following.

Survey of Colleges Related to the Methodist Episcopal Church—1930–32

The conduct of this extensive survey by Reeves and Russell catapulted him into the top group of surveyors of educational institutions and probably led to his selection as Director of the University of Chicago self-survey which represented his most complex undertaking in this field.

The general conference of the Methodist Church had several objectives in authorizing and funding the surveys which would put them in a better position to: (1) know the quality of the service rendered by each of the institutions; (2) suggest improvements in their performance; (3) increase confidence in their work and provide the basis for more generous support, and (4) provide a better basis for making annual appropriations to the institutions which sought support from the conference.

The final report was published by the University of Chicago Press. Illustrative observations and recommendations of particular interest to Reeves and which reveal some of the values and principles of administration which he held follow: (1) He strongly urged a reduction of the size of boards (characteristically large) to seven or eight which would increase the sense of responsibility of each member; (2) Ecclestical control would be assured by requiring that only a majority of the trustees be elected for that purpose. This recommendation opened the door to other influences which are relevant to serve varied clientele in multi-purpose institutions; (3) Age of board members should include some trustees who were relatively young, a majority middle aged and only a few older persons. This would increase receptivity to new ideas and focus institutional objectives on the needs of youth; (4) Women should be elected to membership on the Boards to increase representation of the needs and interests of women in all institutions which were then admitting women students; (5) Boards were recommended to focus on policies leaving the application of those policies to the executive officers chosen by the Boards; (6) After detailing the principal duties of the presidents, academic deans, registrars and business officers, Reeves's proclivity for some flexibility and recognition of personality factors in administration is illustrated by the following:[9]

> A college should not be criticized adversely because it departs from the general pattern in its assignment of administrative duties. Responsibilities should be assigned to the person who can perform them best, regardless of the manner in which this policy may disarrange the usual assignment of administrative functions. Thus administration in a college becomes more a matter of adaptation to personnel than a matter of adherence to formal principles.*

Reeves's view of the function of committees in the administration of educational institutions is illustrated by the following:

> Observations made in this group of colleges lead very definitely to the conclusion that administrative matters are usually better handled when specifically assigned to responsible executive officers than when handled through committees of the faculty. As one college president expressed it, the most effective committee is a committee of one . . . These criticisms of faculty committees for administrative purposes do not imply that all faculty committees are subject to the same objection. There is a clear place for committees of the faculty to deal with matters of policy formation. For the most part committees of this sort will be temporary, rather than standing committees, and will be discharged upon the completion of the task assigned.**

University of Chicago Survey

Reeves was brought back to the University in 1929, after having been awarded his doctorate in 1925, to organize and direct a three-year comprehensive internal survey to review its past and to chart its future.

---

*Page 88.
**Pages 106 and 107.

Reeves secured a number of important suggestions from Judd and others to formulate a plan for the survey before selecting a research staff. Approximately 50 University of Chicago faculty and administrative staff plus six from other educational institutions and one banker participated in the research and formulation of recommendations. Twelve areas were defined for study and later published as separate volumes by the University of Chicago Press.[10]

In addition to organizing and directing the whole survey, Reeves was listed as the prime surveyor in ten of the volumes along with John Dale Russell. Some prior study was made of the organization and administration of other large private universities broadly comparable to the University of Chicago. As a matter of procedure all of the recommendations were concurred in by the three or four principal investigators for each area after full consultation with the responsible academic and administrative persons.

Even a highly abbreviated summary of all of the recommendations made would be excessive in light of the primary purpose of this work. It is relevant, however, to provide a brief resumé of the area in which Reeves was personally expert—namely the "Organization and Administration of the University" even though one of the staff, Frederick J. Kelly, was credited, by Reeves, as being largely responsible for writing the report. The areas studied were: (1) University Control: The Board of Trustees; (2) The Management of Investments; (3) Operating the University: The Office of the President; (4) Instruction and Research; (5) Non-curricular interests of Students; (6) Business Management; (7) Accounting and Budget Control; and (8) Public Relations.

Reeves noted in the Foreword that "all members of the survey staff have participated in gathering the original data for the report and in criticizing the manuscript throughout its successive stages of preparation. The findings and recommendations represent the combined judgments of the four members of the survey staff." Reeves also listed in the Foreword three factors which made the preparation of the report a difficult task as follows: the difficulty of ascertaining exactly the present administrative practices in the University because of the absence of common understanding among administrative officers; the rapid changes in the organization and administration of the University; and recognition of the fact "that there are few scientifically validated standards for determining good practice in University organization and administration."

Reeves adopted the procedure, previously mentioned in the survey of Methodist institutions, of submitting the tentative report to numerous administrative officers, colleagues and members of the Board of Trustees for detection of errors of fact and interpretation. Corrections were incorporated in the final text. Reeves praised the cooperation which he and his colleagues received in these words: "The spirit of cooperation is in itself perhaps one of the most important commentaries upon the administration and organization of the University." Many recommendations were adopted as the results of the survey became known and evaluated. Some of the more important observations and recommendations follow:

Role of the President

> The President represents the interests of the faculty on one hand and the Board (of Trustees) on the other. His effectiveness depends equally upon the confidence placed in him and the good will toward him which are present in each group. His selection, which technically is a responsibility of the Board, should be made with the hearty cooperation of the faculty . . . (page 6)

Relationship of the Board to Administrative Officers

> To maintain this delicate balance between the responsibility of the Board, which delegates its authority, and the judicious exercise of that delegated authority by an administrative officer is the severest test of the mutual confidence and sound judgment of both the Board and the administrative officer. Where the balance is best maintained, the Board recognizes that, with only extraordinary exceptions, recommendations and actions of administrative officers are to be approved and confirmed even in those occasional cases where the Board finds itself in disagreement with the proposed action. But in such cases, the Board uses the occasion to make clear that such actions appear not to be in accord with approved policies. In return for such supporting attitude of the Board, the administrative officer must exercise scrupulous care not to place the Board in such a position often . . . (page 8)

Guidelines for Relationships of the Board to Instructional Matters

> In the type of organization which prevails in American universities, the final responsibility for question pertaining to education as well as to other matters must lie with the board of trustees. Because of the special training of the president and members of the faculties in matters of education, the board may meet its responsibility best by delegating authority in educational matters to them. Such delegation of authority imposes upon the

president, faculty members, and trustees the obligation to counsel freely together with respect to all important educational questions.

The foregoing statements suggest the desirability at the University of Chicago of organizing groups including both faculty members and trustees, where the free interchange of fact and opinion may not be impeded by the feeling of authority on either side . . . (page 23)

Special Responsibilities of the President's Office

Among the responsibilities that cannot be shifted from the President's office by any process of distributing functions is the preparation of the budget of expenditures. The budget of a University is a clear reflection of its educational policies. The budget was strongly recommended as being non-confidential . . .

Next to budget making, no other duty is so clearly a function of the President's office as the final approval of major appointments which are to be recommended to the Board. (page 47)

Relationships between Academic Offices and Administrative Offices with reference to Instruction and research were recommended as follows:

Faculties should control the policies—curriculums, instructional procedures, research programs, and the like—which govern instruction and research. The time and interest of faculty members should be conserved for the work of instruction and research and should not be dissipated in administrative and executive functions that might better be left to individuals chosen for the purpose. (page 60)

Clarification in the Language of the Statues which Governed the 19 Ruling Bodies of the University was recommended as follows:

As long as there is lacking a common understanding of the meaning of 'administrative,' it would be well to omit the word from the statutes which define the functions of the University Ruling Bodies. The functions of these bodies are essentially legislative. Executive functions with few exceptions should be placed by statute in the hands of executive officers. (page 75)

Responsibilities of Deans Set Forth in the Statutes was expressed in the following:

Each Dean supervises in general the administration of his school, division or college under the direction of the President; recommends to the

President faculty appointments; recommends annually a consolidated budget for all departments and activities under his supervision; and approves appointments to the staff of advisers of students, as recommended to the President by the Dean of Students, for work in his school, division, or college. (page 78)

Other recommendations were made regarding the functions of the business manager and comptroller.

With reference to Public Relations—the survey group recommended the establishment of a Division of Public Relations to be headed by the Secretary of the University including administrative jurisdiction over the alumni organization insofar as the activities of the alumni organization represents the University officially.

On the occasion of a dinner given to Mr. Judd, on April 15, 1948 tribute was paid by President Hutchins to Mr. Judd (the University of Chicago did not designate anyone as Doctor) and to Reeves and those who were involved with him in the reorganization of the University Hutchins said:

The first telegram I received congratulating me on my election as president came from the School of Education. I did not know till after how much effort this must have cost Mr. Judd. He finally revealed to me that when I was elected he had got in touch with one of his most intimate friends at Yale, who told him that he must prepare for the worst. His friend told him that I had gone to a private preparatory school and an endowed university, that I had no knowledge of or interest in public education, and that there was no hope that I could possibly understand any of the issues which concerned Mr. Judd and the School of Education.

Of course Mr. Judd's friend in New Haven was right. What he did not reckon on was that Mr. Judd was a great teacher. He could teach even a university president. And he was not easily dismayed by the difficulty of a task. I was willing to learn, because he made an enormous impression on me. He began to teach me about the organization of education, the relation of public and private education, and the relation of the Federal government to education. When he got tired, he got George Works and Floyd Reeves to help him. He and these two assistants not only did all they could with their pupil; they also played a great part in the reorganization of the University that went on in 1930 and 1931; the creation of the College and the Divisions, the establishment of the Board of Examinations and the Dean of Student's office, and the ultimate formation of the four-year college.[11]

The Regents Inquiry into the Character and Cost of Public Education in the State of New York

Reeves was persuaded to participate in the New York State University Regents Inquiry by Luther Gulick, who had served as one of the members of President Roosevelt's Advisory Committee on Education, chaired by Reeves and as a colleague on the President's Committee on Administrative Management. (Chapter II Part II.) Gulick had developed respect for Reeves's competence in both education and public administration, which Reeves had successfully combined or interrelated throughout most of his career. The assignment to direct the section of the Regents Inquiry on adult education harked back to Reeves's experience in 1915 when he taught a group of adults in the Huron, South Dakota, High School and his earlier and later work at the University of Chicago in adult education as an aspect of a comprehensive policy and program of education. As was characteristic of Reeves's work method—partly by design and partly by necessity, because of his involvement in several activities concurrently, he engaged two of his former students Cyril O. Houle and Thomas Fansler, to serve with him in the research and as co-authors of the published report of the study.[12]

The frame of reference of the inquiry was well expressed in the Foreword to the published report of the study by Luther Gulick as follows:

> The work of the Inquiry has been divided into three major undertakings: first, the examination of the educational enterprise of the State and the analysis of its outcome, methods, and costs; second, the critical appraisal of the work now under way; and third, the formulation of policies and programs for dealing with the immediate problems and issues, and long-range objectives of the educational system of the State. The purpose of the Inquiry has not been to gather great masses of statistics, to devise numerous questionnaires, or to present meticulous factual descriptions of every phase of education within the State. Rather, the Regents' Committee and the staff of the Inquiry have been interested in isolating major issues and in hammering away at the problems which presented themselves in order to find a reasonable comprehensive solution which would commend itself to the forward-minded people of the State of New York.[13]

More specifically, the special problems of the large variety of adult education problems in New York State was cogently expressed by Edward C. Elliott, President of Purdue University in these words:

> Throughout the preparation of this analysis of the adult education problem in the State of New York, the twofold nature of adult education has been kept in mind: first, indirect adult education—an incidental, by-product of the ever-present disposition of a certain few to influence, to convert, or to salvage the uncertain many. This may be classified as altruism, as mutual aid, or as sheer propaganda; and, second, direct adult education—an intentional organization and direction of effort for the increase of individual opportunity. The State of New York now has a vast amount of indirect and direct adult education carried on with little or no government organization, oversight, or support.
>
> The lack of organization results in enormous wastage—wastage of time, money, and even of human lives. It is no exaggeration to suggest that the total moneys spent by the citizens of New York on adult education that is inefficient and disorganized, and perhaps even harmful, more than equals the total bill for public schools.[14]

In accordance with the framework indicated above, Reeves and his colleagues examined the scope of the varied programs under public and private auspices which were recognized as part of "an adult education movement" in 1924; the dynamic social forces such as urbanization, increased leisure, influence of radio and other communications media; the emancipation of women and other social forces which created a challenge to adult educators to adapt their programs to meet new needs and opportunities; and the increased public support for many of these activities several of which were initially organized and funded by private organizations. Reeves and his associates defined adult education as any purposeful effort toward self-development carried on by an individual without direct legal compulsion and without such effort becoming his major field of activity. It may be concerned with any or all three aspects of his life, his work life, his personal life, or his life as a citizen. Although this study takes into consideration the broadest implications of adult education, in general its concentration must be on the narrower aspects . . ." The clientele for adult education activities, however, was hardly restrictive as indicated in the following.

The research revealed that very large numbers of men and women voluntarily engaged in a variety of educational activities to: (1) make up for lost opportunities because of dropping out of school at early ages; (2) learn the new language and customs of their adopted country by the large number of immigrants who had come to New York City and the State of New York and to prepare for naturalization; (3) "fill in gaps" of their previous formal educational experiences; (4) improve home life, family relations and health; (5) increase opportunities for cultural and "appreciational" development which was largely limited to adults living in urban areas; (6) increase "civic effectiveness" by a smaller number who recognized the limitations of their earlier courses in civics; (7) engage in vocational rehabilitation for those seeking to retain their jobs because of technological changes or prepare for new jobs, and (8) for a variety of other purposes.

Organizations fostering programs of adult education included the public schools, public libraries, agricultural extension, labor unions and private corporations apprenticeship and other in-service training programs, university extension and several others.

Evaluation and Recommendations

On the basis of an evaluation of the several aspects of the adult education program illustrated by the above and other evaluative judgments, Reeves and his collaborators pointed out the needs for: better definitions and sharper objectives to guide the several types of programs; better guidance programs for general and vocational education to help adults choose the most appropriate programs for their needs and interests; the development of more appropriate teaching methods for adults to take account of their greater maturity, individual differences and motivations—in short the need for more appropriate "adult pedagogy;" and more adequate financial support and better coordination of the programs. On these latter points the language of the report was very clear. On financial support for adult education in the context of a total educational program the report pointed out that:

> The distribution of the population according to age groupings indicates that there are approximately three times as many adults as there are children of school age; also, that the span of adult life is approximately three times as long as that of school life during childhood. By concentrating planning and expenditures for public education on only the first one-fourth of life, society puts itself in the position of declaring that education must be preparation and not participation.[15]

On the entire need for better coordination, the language of the report is also emphatically critical as follows:

> For the most part, agencies at both the state and local levels pursue their ways, serenely unconscious of other closely related programs in existence. When consciousness of these programs exists, it frequently

results in bitter jealousy, and coordination is the exception rather than the rule.[16]

While it is not possible in a report of several authors and other contributors specifically to identify proposals authored by Floyd Reeves personally, enough is known of his values, principles and convictions to quote or paraphrase selected points in the proposed program as being those which he probably initiated and strongly suggested.

General Policy Considerations

As to general policy considerations underlying future plans for adult education he and his colleagues saw adult education as an integral part of a comprehensive program of public education to be funded with the object of equalization of opportunity in both "quantitive and qualitative" terms. The need for a variety of agencies and programs to accommodate the many different types of needs and interests of adults was recommended. The work of these varied agencies, however, must be coordinated to achieve a complete and balanced program. The values and usefulness of privately supported activities in the context of a public-private mix of programs was seen as best utilized "not through regulations and competition on the part of public agencies, but through coordination at local and state levels of administration."

The report consistently espoused the importance of a proper organization structure to give effect to the achievement of program objectives, expressed as follows:

> Whatever determination may be reached as to the structural organization of the State Education Department, it is urged that the field of adult education be placed on a parity with the fields of elementary, secondary and higher education . . . Furthermore, "while it is recognized that inspired leadership can overcome limitations of department organization, the elevation of adult education to equality with other levels through structural reorganization will of itself lend inspiration and dignity to whatever leadership may in time become available.[17]

Recognizing the multiplicity of problems facing adult education, including the absence of clear standards of performance; creative methods of instruction adapted to the needs and interests of adults; more attention to research and experimentation; use of advisory councils; demonstration centers, improved counseling service and similar devices to make adult education activities more effective were urged.

While $1,275,000 was recommended to be spent to implement the various proposals during a five-year period, continuous evaluation as to results of the expenditures was recommended:

> During the five-year period continuous evaluative procedures be carried on. Certainly before any recommendations are accepted to increase the suggested amounts or to extend the experimental period, studies should be undertaken for the purpose of determining what ways the whole program of state support for education may best be revised to include adult activities upon a basis proportionate with the needs and aspirations of the whole people.[18]

The findings of this somewhat limited study of educational problems and needs in the state of New York greatly influenced a comprehensive study of the need for a state university which is described in the following section.

State of New York Temporary Commission on the Need for a State University

Background and Summary[19]

Called away from a vacation in South Dakota in September 1946 by Owen D. Young, Floyd Reeves, then back at the University of Chicago, embarked upon a seventeen-month part-time task of helping the State of New York determine whether or not it should establish a State University. The establishment of a State University had been proposed by Governor Thomas E. Dewey to the State Legislature in February of that year. The Legislature shortly thereafter approved the appointment of a Temporary Commission to examine the question. On July 14, the Governor had named a group of distinguished citizens as members of the Commission, headed by Owen D. Young. Dr. Oliver Carmichael, President of the Carnegie Foundation for the Advancement of Teaching and formerly President of Vanderbilt University, was named Vice Chairman. Other members of the Commission included Sarah Gibson Blanding, President of Vassar College; Edmund Ezra Day, President of Cornell University; Alvin S. Johnson, President of the New School for Social Research, and other qualified educators, business and civil leaders plus eleven members appointed by the Senate and the Assembly. Francis T. Spaulding, Commissioner of Education for the State and eight other key educators, public officials and prominent citizens served in an ex-officio capacity. The Commission was bi-partisan in composition.

The first meeting of the Commission was held on August 23, 1946 and the last on January 12, 1948. The final draft report, approved unanimously by the Commission, was submitted to Governor Dewey on February 16, 1948. The Governor proposed legislation to implement the far-reaching recommendations of the Commission, which made a positive answer to the question of the need for a state university plus numerous other recommendations which would drastically transform institutional arrangements and educational procedures to meet the needs for improved post-secondary education in the State. Most of the recommendations of the Commission, supported by the Governor, were acted on favorably by the legislature.

Some of the Major Problems Pointed Out by Governor Dewey in His Annual Message to the Legislature, February 4 1946[20]

In the annual message, the Governor reminded the legislature that the high level of financial support for higher educational institutions provided by private gifts had substantially declined because of the decrease in personal fortunes, which combined with the greatly increased demand for higher education, had put added pressure on the government for public support of higher education. The need for additional facilities to accommodate the needs of returning veterans and non-veteran high school gradutes were also on his mind. Also high on the list of major problems which the Governor thought should be examined by the Commission related to discrimination in admission. On this point he expressed himself forcefully:

> Racism (is) alien to our way and to our spirit. At this time, or at any time, we should not give up the fight or yield to segregation as an ill conceived compromise in the peace of outright discrimination. We are in a fight in which we are winning and we choose neither to appease nor to compromise.

With reference to the research procedures to be followed by the Commission he spoke equally clearly:

> I am sure that (the Commission) will examine all the issues, ascertain all the divergent views and give hearing to all interested persons to the end that we will have a sound evaluation of our system of higher education and its need without commitment in advance to any particular solution.

Governor Dewey saw several possible solutions to the massive educational problems and varied choices, interlaced with political problems and entrenched positions with which the Commission would need to deal. Some of these were: for the state to take over some private institutions and expand and maintain them; retain private institutions but create new public institutions; greatly expand the number of scholarships to relieve the problems of economically disadvantaged but qualified youth; and improve the use of existing facilities. The most comprehensive solution would be for the state to create a state university which would be an organization of schools and colleges strategically placed on campuses throughout the state. The creation of a state university should, furthermore, be built to "serve the needs of those who may have been discriminated against in some existing institutions."

Specifics on the Size and Complexity of the Problems to be Examined by the Commission

There were 92 educational institutions chartered and established by the state in 1941. Seventy-seven of these were private and fifteen public institutions. Four of the publicly controlled institutions were municipal colleges in New York City, nine were state normal schools and two were state teachers colleges. Of the seventy-seven private institutions, twelve were liberal arts colleges not affiliated with universities, thirty-eight were professional schools not affiliated with universities, nineteen were junior colleges and eight were other types of institutions. In addition, there were six agricultural and technical institutions and several hundred private institutions which did not grant degrees.

Since 1941 a number of major additions or changes had been made including: the New York Maritime Academy was established as a four-year degree granting institution; five institutes of applied arts and science were established; changes in the charters of twenty-three other degree institutions were made to expand their programs or for other reasons; three emergency institutions were created to accommodate returning veterans; one college was converted into a university; and nine institutions expanded their off-campus or extension centers in two different locations to accommodate increased pressure for their facilities.

In brief, higher education in New York State was indeed a jumble of uncoordinated institutions.

The Employment of Floyd W. Reeves

Owen D. Young made a recommendation on October 1, 1946 to the Commission that Floyd Reeves be employed as Director of Studies to help it sort out the problems and options. Reeves was no stranger to Young, as they had served together in several major federal organizations. Furthermore, Reeves was well known to Young for his extensive experiences in making numerous college and university surveys, for his major efforts to reduce discrimination in college admissions, and in other activities relevant to the New York assignment. The approval of his appointment, however, was most carefully evaluated as indicated by Oliver Carmichael.[21]

> The first order of business for the joint subcommittees was the selection of the director of studies. The list of nominees had been reduced to one man, Floyd W. Reeves, who, by invitation, was present at the meeting. It was suggested that if he were acceptable to the subcommittee, he would immediately begin work with the committee on program research, thus speeding up the process of program development. Prior to approving Dr. Reeves' nomination, the subcommittee entertained a lengthy discussion of his background, qualifications, and experience.

During a lengthy discussion of Reeves's personality and individual qualities the personal feelings of certain Commission members toward him emerged. Dr. Francis T. Spaulding's comments were particularly relevant, in view of his having worked with Dr. Reeves on several projects. He described Reeves as a ". . . rather demanding person, and if the Commission wants the study to go in a way different from what Reeves wants it to go, the Commission will have to push, but it is much more satisfactory to deal with a person of that sort than one who has no will of his own. I think he would be a good choice for the job."

Mr. Mahoney, another member of the Commission, wondered, in light of Dr. Spaulding's comments whether Dr. Reeves would "dominate the Commission and do things his way and not the way of the

Commission. That leaves me in a little doubt as to where we will end up."

In response to Mr. Mahoney, Dr. Spaulding then clarified his comments:

> If I left that impression, what I intended to convey is that he is a man with distinct convictions of his own, which is to his credit, and if just left to his own devices, he will plan this study and carry it through . . . All I was trying to convey was that with a man of that sort, it is important that the Commission work along with him to make sure that in his plan the Commission's own plans are adequately reflected. When I spoke of conviction I did not mean convictions that were closed or pre-arranged conclusions, because he is not guilty of either, but he is a man of so much drive that the Commission ought to be aware that it is getting a self-starter who will not wait for the Commission if he feels the job will not be done.

Dr. Edmund Ezra Day added his appraisal:

> I know what the Commissioner is talking about and to be quite candid, Reeves will take some handling on this job becaue he has great drive of his own, and if the Commission doesn't develop its own thinking, he will move in and endeavor to supply it. I don't know if that is altogether obejctionable because I think it puts a challenge to the Commission to develop its own ideas as to what the Commission should report to the state in regard to this complex subject . . . I don't think he will dominate this Commission, but he will keep it under steady pressure to push its own thinking through to pretty definite conclusions, which I think is quite all right.

Mr. Mahoney summarized his appraisal:

> I think we ought to accept the challenge of Reeves to put us on our mettle and see what we can do with this Commission.

After the proper motion, Dr. Reeves was nominated to serve as the Director of Studies.

The appointment of Reeves was confirmed by the full committee the next day at a salary of $6,500 plus expenses for a period of six months, which was later extended. Reeves was also authorized to appoint Algo Henderson,[22] Assistant Commissioner of Education for the State of New York and former President of Antioch College as the Deputy Director of Studies and to select subject to final approval of the

Commission, various other consultants, attorneys and other staff members. The Commission was given an initial budget allocation of $100,000, which was augmented by $125,000 concurrently with the extension of the date for submitting its final report on February 16, 1948.

Organization of the Research Studies

Prior to Reeves's appointment, the Commission had made some preliminary plans for organizing the relevant studies under the able leadership of Oliver Carmichael. The areas of study needs carved out initially included: a survey of post-secondary education at all levels; appraisal of existing facilities; comparison of needs and existing facilities; economic barriers; barriers of race, creed or color; availability of scholarships; and needs for extension and adult education and related areas.

This preparatory thinking was presented by Carmichael at its first meeting. Carmichael's tentative suggestions were concurred in by Reeves. He thus had a firm basis for organizing the research staff, which included some highly qualified experts, into three major clusters of topics as follows:

- Economic, academic, geographic and minority barriers to college and university enrollment.
- Educational facilities and needs including population and enrollment projections for general and undergraduate education; graduate education; medical, dental and nursing education; teacher education and the programs of "State Contract Colleges," state institutions and New York City municipal colleges.
- Finance, organization and control including costs, available revenues and all possible contributions to both public and private institutions.

Reeves assembled, with the help of his deputy Algo Henderson, a full-time and part-time research staff of seventeen major experts and others in the three areas of research noted above.[22] The staff included Paul Studenski, Professor of Economics at New York University, for fiscal matters; Robert D. Leigh, former President of Bennington College and Director of the Commission on the Freedom of the Press, to do research on minority group barriers to enrollment in higher education; Edward Franklin Frazier, Professor and Head of the Department of Sociology at Howard University, to document the extent of discrimination against Negroes; Elbridge Sibley of the Social Science Research Council for a study of economic barriers; Professor Louis Wirth, Professor of Sociology and Associate Dean of the Social Science Division of the University of Chicago and President of the American Sociological Society and the American Council on Race Relations, to study and provide counsel on problems of discrimination. Ten other researchers, of comparable qualifications, were recommended by Reeves to do research and make recommendations on various problems.

David S. Berkowitz, sometime Professor of History at Harvard and Emerson Colleges and Executive Officer of the Association of Private Colleges and Universities, served as liaison officer to the Commission and Warnick J. Kernan and Arthur H. Schwartz served as attorneys.

Thus Reeves's knowledge of top flight scholars whom he had come to know through his extensive knowledge of university and public policy oriented personnel qualified him to assure the Commission of a highly capable research and consulting staff.

Preliminary Report

A preliminary report on the work of the research staff was submitted to the Commission on January 8, 1947. The report included tentative policy options in addition to those which Governor Dewey had projected to be considered by the Commission—singly or in some combination; expand present facilities; establish new state supported colleges at present or new locations; convert selected private colleges into public institutions; add programs of general education and other programs to existing state teachers colleges; expand non-degree programs; and authorize cities and intermediate school districts to establish free or low-cost institutions; provide state support for educational buildings or student housing; provide free transportation within 20–25 miles of a college center; subsidize room and board expenses for students away from local public institutions; establish a decentralized state university system in most major cities; and provide a liberal program of scholarships and fellowships.

The draft findings of the research program which included staff studies on "Barriers to College Attendance," "Educational Facilities and Needs," "Finance, Organization and Control" were presented and discussed. A bibliography of selected studies by others bearing on the problems faced by the Commission was also presented.

The reactions of citizen groups which were consulted including the National Conference of Christians and Jews, the Mayor's Committee on Unity and the Public Education Association were reported.

The Commission heard and discussed the reports of the research staff and suggested other topics which should be undertaken but made no recommendations at this time. An extension of time to February 16, 1948 was approved.

Major Public Hearing

The critical importance of the reaction of citizen groups to the issues and choices faced by the Commission led to the organization of a large scale open meeting on October 20, 1947. Forty-one speakers represented a wide variety of groups such as: the B'nai B'rith Anti Defamation League, American Jewish Congress, New York City Committee for Equality in Education, Chamber of Commerce, Urban League, American Labor Committee, Liberal Party, Federation of Teachers Unions, Columbia University Medical School, Association of Colleges and Universities and many others. Rabi Stephen Wise and Governor Herbert Lehman were two of the key speakers.

Some of the major issues brought out by the speakers were: the extent and effects of discriminatory practices in admission and the need for corrective legislation regarding quota systems and other barriers to open admissions; the lack of financial support for higher education; the failure of private institutions to meet the needs; the need for better administration of existing laws and policies; and the unmet needs of veterans; and many other barriers to access to higher education in the state. Obviously these representatives felt that they had a major stake in the outcomes of the Commission's proposed recommendations. *The New York Times* and other papers with large circulations in the state gave extensive coverage to these open hearings, and other information provided by the Commission and the research staff. A highly important result of the hearings and the publicity regarding the work of the commission was near universal endorsement of the idea of creating a University of the State of New York.

This endorsement was not, however, shared by all members of the Commission who had been examining and discussing the research reports made by Reeves and his associates. But by September 1947, a year after the first meeting of the Commission, a draft report was ready for the Commission and staff to discuss in depth. This meeting was planned to take the whole range of viewpoints into account. Chairman Owen D. Young, fully cognizant of the divergence of viewpoints, and experienced at dealing with dissension, concluded that the Commission should discuss the draft report for three days in the more relaxed environment of a conference site on Lake George.

> He knew well that the members of his varied and often antagonistic group could come nearer to understanding each other, and could speak more frankly, sitting on the wide piazzas of the hotel, glass in hand, than in the overheated atmosphere of Albany.
>
> Young urged that each member must lay all the cards on the table and negotiations must be conducted face to face without instructions from constituency or special interest. He conducted all discussions on an 'off the record' basis and requested that they be considered as confidential.' Young also demanded ultimate unanimity on the recommendations of the report, knowing well that, on publication, any dissent would attract more attention than the much greater areas of agreement.
>
> Inevitably dissension arose, not so much as to whether New York should have a state university or not, for everyone on the Commission agreed that it should; the questions were rather what kind, where and—above all—how much would it cost?[23]

Supplementing Young's strategy in resolving problems of wide diversity of opinion were the methods of work attributed to Reeves as he directed the staff reports on which the Commission relied. Carmichael describes the exchange of ideas of staff and Commission:

> Dr. Reeves recognized that although considerable guidance is provided by strong chairmen and committee heads, it is incumbent upon the professional staff member to plan the projects and to obtain criticisms and suggestions from the Commission leaders; and secondly, that one of the basic jobs of staff is to attempt to find the point of compromise among the divergent viewpoints of the Commission members in order to steer the project ahead.
>
> Dr. Reeves used several techniques for accomplishing these purposes. He instructed his staff to follow the basic procedure of entering the discussions in the Commission meetings only for the purpose of answering questions on a particular report. He advised against arguing and debating points with the Commission members. To increase the effectiveness of the staff, he suggested that each member familiarize one or more of the Commission members with a given report in order that the latter could carry the brunt of the discussion in the formal Commission meeting.

> With few exceptions these instructions were carried out, and seldom was there any debate between Commission and staff.
>
> By careful questioning, the Director of Studies was able to engender heated discussions on vital issues and thereby gain ideas about the thinking of the Commission. For example, Dr. Reeves asked: Should New York adopt a policy of extending free public education two years beyond the high school? If so, should the state operate the program of the 13th and 14th years, or should the program be operated locally with the financial support provided jointly by the state and local government units? In answering, not only did the Commission members discuss financial responsibility and costs, but debated at length on educational issues.[24]

After the discussion of cost and state responsibility for educational facilities, Reeves, by questions, directed the discussion to the type of education which should be offered: liberal arts, technical terminal programs, or a combination of both. These questions remained as key issues throughout the Commission's existence. By this technique, Carmichael noted that the Director of Studies never became embroiled in the debates and yet was able to force the issues for decision.

In May and June 1947, Governor Dewey on more than one occasion expressed concern over the work of the Temporary Commission. Although Dewey had been kept informed of the progress of the staff, in early June 1947 a joint conference was arranged between the Governor, Reeves, Burton, Schwartz and Carmichael. The Governor, Carmichael reported, "spent most of the time asking questions, usually aimed at the Director of Studies."

Final Report of the Commission[25]

The final report, including the recommendations for action of the Commission, was submitted to Governor Dewey on March 5, 1948. After each recommendation explanatory comments were included. Four major reports which incorporated research data to support the recommendations were also submitted along with the recommendations. The fact that the text of the report and appendices was boiled down to fifty-six pages was in itself a remarkable achievement and, no doubt, facilitated the understanding of the issues and recommendations and its prompt acceptance by the Legislature. Governor Dewey's transmittal to the Legislature was highly laudatory of the Commission's work:

> The report is the product of two years' unceasing report by the Temporary Commission and is the most comprehensive report of its kind in the

> educational history of the state . . . The Commission recommends a program of greatly expanded operations by the state itself. It also recommends a system of state support for community or municipal colleges. Further, the Commission recommends that the state, in addition to state institutions, extend state assistance to certain professional schools that may prove to be in need of assistance to maintain the quality and quantity of their important work. There is no precedent in any state for the type of joint state-local-private effort contemplated . . . The program is unique and of major importance to the future of the people of our state. It warrants our most favorable consideration.

With reference to an earlier expression of the Governor's views regarding racial and religious discrimination which the Commission fully documented, he urged enactment of appropriate legislation to eliminate such practices. It is important, he said, "that not only economic barriers to higher education be removed, but that also barriers based upon distinction of race, color, creed or national origin be removed."

The Governor estimated that the recommendations of the Commission would increase the state's annual expenditure for higher education to some 50 million dollars plus capital expenditures in excess of 125 million dollars over the period of two years during which the program would develop.

The Governor summarized his transmittal of the report:

- The plan embraced by the Commission's report and the legislation that will implement it constitutes a new charter for the youth of the state of New York . . . The barriers imposed by economic needs and those imposed by restrictions on members of minority groups will be overcome.

In addition to the aspects of the report which the Governor commented upon, the Commission made several specific detailed recommendations, including:

- The immediate establishment of a state university as a corporate entity which should place prime emphasis upon the development of widely distributed and greatly expanded facilities throughout the state . . .
- The establishment of full four-year college programs in certain sections of the state not adequately served by any college or university; establishment of two medical centers by the state including schools of medicine, dentistry, nursing and public health

and the establishment of an additional state-supported school of veterinary medicine.

- Broadening of the programs of the state teachers college and provision of state aid for teacher education in the four municipal colleges of New York City.
- Establishment, with state aid, of locally administered public community colleges.
- An expanded scholarship program.
- The development of a comprehensive system of counseling service which Reeves persistently had recommended in other situations.
- Finally, the Board of Regents was charged with responsibility for insuring admission to colleges and universities without regard to race, color, creed or national origin, with power to enforce its orders.

The last recommendation was expanded in four additional detailed recommendations by the Commission ending with the directive that "If upon all the evidence the Board of Regents should find that an institution has engaged in discrimination, it shall direct the issuance of such order as is just and proper, including in an appropriate case a cease and desist order, and upon failure of the institution to comply with such order it shall seek an order of the Supreme Court of the State of New York for its enforcement."

The Commission's work, based largely on the reports and recommendations made by Reeves and his staff was overwhelmingly supported by the Governor, the legislature and the people of New York.[26]

With reference to Reeves' work as Director of Studies Dr. Algo D. Henderson his Deputy, appraised his contribution:

> Floyd designed the study, and although because of his teaching at Chicago he could give only part-time to the work, he carried the principal responsibility for supervision. The final report, though based on many special reports, was clearly his work. He was able continuously to inject ideas, many of which were adopted. In defining the nature and scope of the needs in New York, partly through empirical data we assembled, and partly by his personal persuasion, Floyd had more impact on the eventual legislation and the results that ensued than any other individual.[27]

It is perhaps relevant to note that Thomas Hamilton, the second Chancellor of the University of the State of New York, was a former student of Reeves at the University of Chicago and colleague at Michigan State University.

Some time later, Hamilton was succeeded by Clifton R. Wharton, Jr. who had served as President of Michigan State University for seven years and is now (1990) President and C.E.O. of the TIAA/CREF Insurance and retirement annuity program for college and university academics and persons employed by other educationally related organizations.

The North Central Association of Colleges and Schools, 1927–1936 (NCA)[28]

The North Central Association came into being in 1895 largely on the initiative of James B. Angell and William Rainey Harper, Presidents of the University of Michigan and Chicago respectively, W. H. Butts of the Michigan Military Academy and a few others. Thirty-six educators met at the invitation of the instigators at Northwestern University in Evanston, Illinois to consider organizing . . . "if deemed expedient, an association of colleges and secondary schools in the North Central States, representatives of universities, colleges, scientific schools, normal schools, high schools and academics." Organize they did for the broad general objective, reflected in their first constitution, for establishing "closer relations between the colleges and the secondary schools of the North Central States"—an objective which has guided the work of the Association for its entire history. All decisions regarding management of higher and secondary institutions were to be strictly advisory.

The early meetings were largely devoted to scholarly seminars on educational problems and developments, but by 1900 the Association recognized that the evaluative procedures which the University of Michigan had employed, since 1871, for accrediting high schools and for admission to the University could be more broadly adopted. A decision to apply evaluative procedures to high schools led to the approval of 156 schools by 1904. Concurrently, committees were established on methods of improving the teaching of English and mathematics, which were later adapted to commercial subjects, mechanical arts and other subjects as the curricula of high schools were expanded to accommodate students who did not expect to go on to colleges and universities.

By 1907 the idea of evaluating colleges began to be accepted and standards formulated—aided and abetted in part, by the practical necessity of colleges becoming eligible to participate in retirement benefits for accredited institutions, being offered by the Carnegie Foundation. By 1913 the first list of accredited colleges was published and the Association clearly moved away from a debating society to a power in education. On the high school side, standards for high schools were formulated for graduation with the popularization of the "Carnegie Unit"—15 of which being required for graduation.

By 1918 the Association grouped higher education instutitions into separate bodies as: (1) colleges and universities; (2) junior colleges, and (3) teacher-training institutions with different evaluative criteria for each division. Louis Geiger reported that despite the numerous changes and efforts to improve evaluative criteria—"the standards seemed inadequate for measuring the effectiveness of educational institutions. Criticisms were voiced about certain published standards and methods of enforcement; formal, arbitrary and *exparte* criteria for judging an institution's quality; failure to strike a balance between the weaknesses and strengths in an institution's program; lack of recognition of unique and specialized aims of an institution; and over-emphasis on quantitative rather than qualitative factors."

The continuous drive for flexibility and improvement in standards was eloquently and humorously articulated in a speech on March 19, 1930 by Ray Lyman Wilbur, former President of Stanford University, who was then acting as Secretary of the Interior. The speech was to the Joint Meeting of the four Commissions of the Association under the title of "Flexible Standards." Although the whole speech is worth quoting, the possibly over-serious focus by the Commission on the details of accrediting criteria and procedures needed a bit of comic relief, which the following story provides. Drawing upon his long association with the medical profession, he said:

> It happens that as a member of the Council on Medical Education . . . I have had for some years an opportunity to watch the effect of a more or less rigid curriculum in medical education. We had to have, in order to cure medical education of some of its ills, a fairly strong curricular set up. We made one and then we began to develop it and improve it. After a while I think we got into the condition somewhat like that (which) is illustrated by the story of a man who had sent his wife to the hospital for an operation. He was not familiar with hospitals and their ways, but when he went the next day and inquired about her, the nurse said she was improving. He next went again that evening and was met by an intern who assured him that she was still improving, and the next morning the superintendent also said she was improving. But later the next afternoon the doctor who had operated on her met him and said that he was sorry to say that his wife had died. Vell then vat did she die of, improvements?[29]

Reeves participated in creating a factual and judgmental basis for recommending numerous improvements—and the "patient" thrived!

Concurrently, while debate on the standards for accrediting took place and revisions made to reflect various institutional aims and programs and to foster experimentation, two major societal developments were taking place. The greatly expanded participation by the federal government in education, related in part to preparation for our entry into World War II, and the rehabilitation of returning veterans after the war—with which developments Floyd Reeves was prominently associated. (Chapter III Part III).

On the matter of colleges and universities adjusting to the influx of returning veterans the Association's Commission on Colleges and Universities, for example, reminded member institutions "that it was their responsibility to accept all students they could house and teach" even though concessions on faculty qualifications were strictly on an emergency basis.

Specific Activities of Reeves in the N.C.A.
1927: The Cost of Education in Liberal Arts Colleges

The research was undertaken at the behest of the "Commission on institutions of Higher Education" of the Association and published in the *North Central Quarterly* for December 1927.[30]

Seventeen colleges were involved in the research, which included an examination of: salary costs in the junior college and senior college divisions of the liberal arts colleges; current expenditures for each of the divisions; relationship between various sources of income and current education expenditures; and relationships between total current educational expenses and total instructional salaries; ten tables of data were prepared for each of the above five areas. Although the findings and conclusions were in no way startling, they did illuminate variability between institutions and between junior and senior college divisions. For example, the instructional salary expenditure per student for nine institutions was $109 for junior college divisions and $190 for senior college divisions; instructional salaries ranged from 51% to 68% of total costs for thirteen of the institutions; for all seventeen of the institutions, 64% of the income for current educational expenditures came from students; 25% from endowment and 11% from other sources; and there was little relationship between salaries of full-time instructors and income from endowment.

In this study, Reeves enhanced his reputation for providing a factual basis for policy formation and for utilizing cost-analysis data as one of the factors in making administrative judgments.

1928: Financial Standards for Accrediting Colleges

The Commission acted favorably on the study of the 17 colleges previously reported and authorized him to extend the research to 15 additional colleges, some of which were outside of the North Central area. Again tables of comparable data were presented on the topics mentioned above and searching questions raised as to the adequacy of expenditures per student to achieve a satisfactory quality level of education. The research, after extensive review, eventuated in creating "Financial Standards for Accrediting Colleges"—a landmark in the process of clarifying standards.

1928: Standards for Accrediting Colleges

The Commission, appreciative of Reeves's research reported above, further expanded the scope of the study to include the original seventeen institutions and twelve more including Oberlin College—which many years earlier had been one of the first colleges to be surveyed. Reeves was still Director of the Bureau of School Service of the University of Kentucky and was joined by John Dale Russell, who became principal collaborator over several years to follow. In addition to data secured in previous studies, personal visits were also made to all 29 institutions lasting from one-half day to one to three weeks each. Considerable refinements in research techniques were devised and in-depth judgments applied in this more intensive study of factors already noted.

Some of the major, although tentative, conclusions reached by the Committee on the basis of data and judgments presented by Reeves and Russell were:

> The present standards of the Association for Accrediment of Colleges are not resulting in a satisfactory state of excellence in every accredited college. One needs only to cite the enormous range of all the factors studied in proof of this point. With many institutions having annual salaries of faculty members below $2,000, and average annual expenditures per student for strictly educational purposes below $200, it should

be apparent without additional statistical proof that the present standards for accreditment are not guaranteeing a satisfactory college.

Since the evidence in the present standards is not guaranteeing a satisfactory college, and in view of the fact that no evidence is found to warrant the discarding of the present standards, the only course is to seek new bases upon which additional standards may be founded.

It is obvious that such measures as the North Central Association have employed heretofore, as well as those which are suggested in this report are quantitative in character. They deal only with externals of excellence. Sooner or later the Association must find ways of evaluating the quality of work and of measuring the outcome of the instruction offered by the college. Experimentation with comprehensive examinations and with every other device which seems likely to throw light upon the character of the results obtained by the colleges should be encouraged by this Association.[31]

The Commission finally recommended that: provision should be made for continuation of the study including personal inspection of fifty or more colleges by at least three trained observers; and that "institutional members of the Association should be urged to set up their accounting systems so as to disclose the annual expenditures per student for strictly educational purposes."

Thus it became clear to the Commission that the critical statistical measure of excellence was the per capita student expenditure for purely educational purposes—an index figure which Reeves spoke of long after this survey had been made as the one single most meaningful measure of excellence. The conclusion of the Committee to extend the study and to broaden the factors considered was clearly a tribute to Reeves's capacity to illuminate critical issues in the appraisal of educational effectiveness with facts and judgments thereon.

1929–36: The Evaluation of Higher Institutions

By 1929 it became apparent that an even more comprehensive examination of the problem of evaluating higher institutions was needed to arrive at more objective, holistic and acceptable standards. Accordingly, a special Committee on Revision of Standards, within the Commission on Higher Institutions, was appointed. The Committee was headed by Lotus D. Coffman, President of the University of Minnesota and included Chancellor Capen of the University of Buffalo; Professor W. W. Charters of Ohio State University and Charles Hubbard Judd of the University of Chicago, all of whom were well acquainted with Reeves's previous work for the Association. A special planning subcommittee which took responsibility for developing a strategy for the study, for advising during its execution and for preparing reports was chaired by George F. Zook and included Dean M. E. Haggerty of the College of Education of the University of Minnesota and Floyd W. Reeves. John Dale Russell succeeded Reeves when Reeves accepted the position of Director of Personnel at the Tennessee Valley Authority in 1933. Thus, there was assured continuity in the endeavor. The study was funded by a grant of $135,000 from the General Education Board and included fifty-seven colleges and universities in all parts of the North Central area. Seven monographs were published by the University of Chicago Press; Reeves and Russell wrote the monographs on Administration and Finance.[32]

Framework and Rationale for the Study of Administration and Finance

Reeves provided the following rationale for this study:

> The standards of the North Central Association have never made reference to the characteristics of administrative organization that are desirable in a college or university. This is a topic which has generally been avoided in the standards of all accrediting agencies dealing with institutions of higher education, those of the American Medical Association being the only standards that refer specifically to institutional administration . . . The Committee in charge of the present study early decided to explore the possibility of using measures of administrative effectiveness as a part of the accrediting procedures. The experiences of investigators in previous studies had revealed cases in which an unusually effective administration had been able to mold a satisfactory educational program out of relatively meager resources. On the other hand, instances are not unknown in which an institution with well qualified faculty and satisfactory financial support is rendering only a mediocre educational service because of ineffective administration.

The research report was organized into ten chapters as follows: method of the study; general administration and control; academic administration; business administration; financial administration; administration of student personnel services; administration of special educational activities; personnel for administrative services; records and reports; and total pattern of administrative organization.

Method of Analysis Used in the Study

The basic analytical tool or procedure used in the study was a carefully designed rating scale or score card for the several specific elements for each aspect of administration. Written definition of terms and other guidelines were designed in advance for the use of each investigator to secure the highest possible level of objectivity. Each major topic of the study was subdivided into elements of administration and assigned a score in terms of the importance of the element.

Each of the major aspects of administration had similar breakdowns of components: e.g., "Administration of Student Personnel Functions" had fifteen components: These score cards were taken to each of the fifty-seven institutions by Reeves and a research colleague. In the process of testing each of the items for feasibility of application some were modified, and some dropped. Individual and groups of items, one hundred seventy-seven in total, were related to an "entire subdivision of the whole administrative process and to the educational excellence of the institution as indicated by an independent criterion of excellence." Reeves's appraisal of the score card technique follows: "The score card technique was especially valuable in providing a composite rating for each instutition on a number of items related to a single phase of administrative practice . . . the score card technique thus permits a comparative evaluation of administrative practices and enables the investigator to assign to a college a percentile score that expresses its general standing in the group with reference to any particular phase of administrative service."

Because of the serious attention which was given by the Association to finding an objective basis for a major revision of standards, it was highly relevant, and certainly in accordance with Reeves's general work style, that standards for accreditation should be evolved through a process of research of the facts about institutional practices and discussion of the application of the facts and judgments before the new standards were adopted. Accordingly, Reeves made several progress reports to the Association through the Commission on Institutions of Higher Education.

The first such report was given by him on "The Study of College Administration Plant Facilities and Finance" and published in the September 1932 issue of the *Quarterly*. In this report Reeves explained the approach which he and his colleagues planned for the research, some of the problems which they anticipated addressing, and the "score card" device described earlier. He had already arrived at the conviction, based in part no doubt on his earlier experiences of surveying colleges and universities that "the problem facing this Association is something more than that of developing a new set of standards. Equally as important is the problem of developing a new method for the administration of institutional inspections if inspections are to be continued."

The second report was published in the *Quarterly* in September 1933 under the title of "A New Type of Standard and its Explication Relative to Administration" which Reeves had presented at the 38th meeting of the Association in March 1933. In this report Reeves stated that "The study of standards has progressed far enough to lead to a tentative conclusion that institutional excellence is closely related to the quality of the administration. It appears that poor administration constitutes a direct weakness in a number of institutions now accredited. There is evidence, also, to show that some institutions fail to meet certain of the present standards primarily because of inadequate control and direction of their resources." Continuing the report, he said: "The correlation between a rating of the fifty-seven institutions on the basis of general excellence and a rating of the same institutions on the basis of a judgment of the general effectiveness of the personnel for administration is both positive and high. While these ratings are still tentative and subject to modification in the light of a further analysis of the data assembled, it appears probable that further study will not result in any marked change in the relationship discovered." The standard which he then tentatively recommended was: "The institution should have a competent administrative staff of a size adequate to perform the necessary administrative functions. The emphasis will be placed upon the performance of administrative function rather than upon administrative personnel or organization." Reeves noted, in the same report, that the Committee had agreed that the standards, as above, would be stated in general terms, with interpretations—to accompany the standards, written in the form of a discussion of principles and a presentation of examples. He then proceeded to raise questions about the meaning of "good administration" and to provide examples of different practices from three different types of higher institutions on such topics as organization, membership and functions of governing boards, functions of administrative officers, variable practices with reference to efforts of administrative officers to stimulate the staff to bring about improvement in scholarship and instruction, participation of students in governance of the institutions, administrative records, and other topics in which administration was a significant factor. With reference to the relative importance of administrative organization as compared with personnel, Reeves indicated a conviction which he applied elsewhere, that ". . . the personnel factor is more important than the type of organization set up for administration. By this statement I do not mean that organization is not an important factor—but of the two factors, personnel for administration on one hand and machinery set for administration on the other, the personnel is more important than the machinery."

At the same meeting L. D. Coffman, Chairman of the Committee, in reporting more broadly on the work of the Committee, which relied heavily on the work of the research staff headed by Reeves, had the following to say about the evolving standards:

- A standard should not be regarded as final but as referring to something that is alive and developing.
- The North Central Association should be less a judge and more a creator.
- The North Central Association standards should be statements of policy, not the framework or skeleton outline of a scheme.
- The standards of the North Central Association should be such that a school will know whether it is improving and measuring up to reasonable conditions.

The general debates about standards during this session were essentially supporting of the above principles.

By the July 1937 meeting of the Association a statement of policy relative to the accrediting of institutions of higher education was adopted and reported in the July issue of the *Quarterly* (pages 67–70). Several of the key standards of special importance to Reeves for which he and his colleagues had provided the factual basis and arguments, became the recommendation of the Commission and finally the standards of the Association. They follow:

Basis of Accrediting

> An institution will be judged for accreditment upon the basis of the total pattern it presents as an institution of higher education. While institutions will be judged in terms of each of the characteristics noted in this statement of policy, it is recognized that wide variations will appear in the degree of excellence attained.

Individuality of Institutions

> In its accrediting procedures the Association intends, within the general pattern of higher education, to observe such principles as will preserve

whatever desirable individual qualities member institutions may have. While it is necessary to emphasize certain characteristics as are recognized as basic, such as the competence of the faculty, the representative character of the curriculum, effective administration, standards of student accomplishment and financial adequacy, it is regarded as of prime importance also to protect such institutional variations as appear to be educationally sound . . .

Administration

The administrative organization should be suitable for accomplishing the objectives of the institution. Adequate provision should be made for the performance of all administrative functions by personnel competent in their respective lines of activity. In evaluating the administration of an institution, the emphasis will be placed upon the manner in which the functions are performed rather than upon the organization or the personnel, although the suitability of the organization and the competence of the personnel cannot be ignored.

Like other research projects which Reeves had directed, implementation followed closely on the heels of the research. There were not extended time gaps between finding the facts and judgments to support action and the adoption of the necessary measures to give effect to the recommended action.

Before Reeves gave his papers and books to the MSU Archives and Historical Collections he wrote on the margins of one of the studies: "False Use of a Tool (of analysis) Destroys Its Value." It is clear throughout Reeves's work in surveying and accrediting educational institutions that he regarded all statistical or quantitative techniques as imperfect even though useful to stimulate further analysis and judgment. The processes of evaluation were in his view basically modes of stimulating reflection and securing insights into administration translated into principles which must be adjusted as new insights are acquired. It is a continuous process!

In the Foreword to each of the volumes of the study published in 1936, President Coffman wrote:

In the opinion of the Committee on Revision of Standards this is the most comprehensive and constructive study of this particular problem which has ever been made and it represents an advance, in fact, a new day with history of the North Central Association in consideration of colleges that apply for its approval.

Chapter III

The President's Advisory Committee on Education[1]

Background and Summary

The Advisory Committee on Education was appointed by President Franklin Delano Roosevelt on September 19, 1936.[2] Floyd W. Reeves was appointed Chairman of the Committee by the President on September 26, 1936. He initially served on a part-time basis while on leave from the University of Chicago but later devoted varying amounts of time up to and including full-time to the task, depending on his work at the University, the status of research for the Committee, and the increased pace of Committee deliberation geared to reporting requirements set by the President. The initial task of the Committee focused on "existing programs of federal aid for vocational education, the relation of such training to general education and to prevailing economic and social conditions, and the extent of the need for an expanded program; and to develop recommendations that would be available to the Congress and the Executive."

Although this assignment was broad enough to keep an able group of advisors and researchers busily occupied for some time, it became increasingly clear to the Committee—its Chairman, Floyd Reeves, and to the President that the task could not be fully carried out without giving consideration to the broader questions of the need for and possible components of an expanded program of federal aid to the major aspects of a comprehensive educational system. The mood of the Congress to introduce numerous, but piece-meal measures, to deal with various problems—primarily vocational education—without adequate factual bases for their legislative acts was also a factor in the President's decision to take the initiative in appointing the committee and later to expand its assignment.

Concurrently, the President had taken measures to improve planning for governmental programs of expenditures through the creation of the National Resource Planning Board. He perceived the need for a functional joining of the assignment given to the Advisory Committee on Education to the need for better general planning—for both executive and legislative actions.

Reeves and the Committee fully concurred in this broadened assignment, which the President made on April 19, 1937, seven months after the appointment of the original Committee. Five additional members were appointed to the Committee on the recommendation of Reeves. The carefully selected Committee of twenty-three members came from a variety of backgrounds including business, industry and government—with only a few professional educators. The Committee was greatly aided in the preparation of reports and other ways by Paul David, who served as Secretary and Assistant Director of Studies, and by a large staff of researchers and consultants. Furthermore, the Committee authorized the Chairman and staff to convene conferences, hold meetings and otherwise aggressively seek the advice, counsel and experience of educators and educational organizations, local, state and national governmental officials, persons from business and labor, religious leaders and citizens interested in education.

The Committee, after an extension of time, delivered its report to the President on February 18, 1938, which he transmitted to Congress on February 28, 1938. The report was approved by all members of the Committee except one, whose minority report was made an official part of the report to the President. His basic objection was to the size of the proposed grants for the several purposes—$120,000,000 over a three-year period instead of $855,500,000 over a six-year period proposed by the Committee.

The total cost of the study was approximately $300,000, most of the services, having been given by members of the Committee and others in and out of government without compensation except travel and other expenses for attendance at Committee meetings. Salaries and honoraria were, however, provided for the staff and consultants.

Highlights of the Recommendations of the Committee

The recommendations of the Committee were grounded in objective, factual studies which were later published in nineteen staff studies, ranging from fifty-five to three hundred twenty-five pages in length, plus numerous memoranda, conference reports and other data. Apart from the general policy question of the propriety and desirability of an expanded program of federal aid to education, the Committee was faced with several complex questions which included: (1) equalizing, or improving the gap of educational opportunity between rich and poor states, Negro and white pupils, and rural and urban communities; (2) federal-state-local-community control of schools and the avoidance of federal controls which were feared as a result of increased federal expenditures and questions related to what proposed expenditures could be allocated to private schools as defined by state school authorities, and (3) the creation of formulae for the allocation and definition of responsibility for distributions of funds at the federal, state and local levels on an objective non-political basis.

Also faced were questions related to the advisability of providing federal funds for older established programs of vocational education and new programs. These newer programs included counseling, library services for rural adults, improvement of teacher preparation, construction of school buildings, educational research and other programs to improve the quality, efficiency and general performance of school officials, the U.S. Office of Education and the Land-Grant Colleges and Universities. The final product of Committee study was bold and broadly gauged to be helpful to industry, labor and rural people and broadly humanitarian in scope. Possibly one of its unique features was the attention paid to programs for the improvement of the educational system for young adults and for their readjustment which had been initiated by the programs of the Civilian Conservation Corps (CCC) and the National Youth Administration (NYA).

Without pretending to do more than highlight the 243 pages of the full report of the Committee,[3] or even the more comfortably sized 31 pages of an official abbreviated report, the following will provide essential information on the scope and magnitude of the Committee's recommendations. All the recommendations of the Committee were justified by data derived from special studies, and from information and judgment secured through conferences and other modes of communication.

General Federal Aid for Elementary and Secondary Education

The overall general purpose of providing additional federal funds "would be primarily for improving the schools that are *least* satisfactory"—many of the schools in the south, especially schools for Negro and rural children. Expenditures from federal funds, made available to and controlled by the States, could be made for teacher's salaries, purchase of necessary supplies, school library service, health, welfare and recreational activities, services for handicapped pupils, pre-primary training, educational and vocational guidance, transportation of pupils, and other operating and maintenance activities. Furthermore, the Committee recommended "that public schools receiving federal aid be authorized to make their health and welfare services available for pupils attending non-public schools." The Committee also recommended that "States using part of the federal grants for books, transportation, and scholarships be authorized, if they wished, to make such services available for the benefit of pupils attending both public and private schools."

With reference to states which maintain separate systems of white and Negro schools, the Committee recommended that in the case of those states, "the responsible officials be directed by law to provide for an equitable distribution of federal funds between white and Negro schools, without reduction of the proportion of state and local funds already being spent for Negro Schools."

General Federal Aid for Elementary and Secondary Education Amounts of Federal Funds Recommended

Starting with $49,000,000 in 1939–40, which would be increased by $20,000,000 each year until 1944–45 for a total of $140,000,000.

Supplementary Grants to States

- For improved preparation of teachers:
  $4,000,000 for 1940–41; and increased to $6,000,000 annually for the next four years.
- District reorganization and improved housing:
  $20,000,000 for 1939–40 and increased to $30,000,000 for the next five years. Chiefly for consolidation of schools, especially in rural areas, the new buildings and the transportation of pupils.
- Vocational education:
  The Committee recommended no new grants for vocational education apart from the almost 22 million dollars being made available under the new legislation. The Committee was generally supportive of the results of previous expenditures for vocational

education. They made a number of critical observations, however, on the administration of previous funds and they made several recommendations for improvement.

• Adult Education:

The key to recommendations on adult education derived from the dismal statistics on the state of education of adults. The facts were these: "Most of the 75,000,000 persons who make up the adult population of the United States were given only limited educational opportunities in childhood. Over 36,000,000 did not finish elementary school; at least 3,000,000 are unable to read and write." A pattern of federal grants of five million dollars for the first year; ten million in the second year and fifteen million annually for the next four years was recommended as supplementary to emergency programs under the Works Progress Administration, Civilian Conservation Corps and the National Youth Administration, which had proven their usefulness particularly in literacy programs and vocational training for youths. Reeves was particularly interested in this program for reasons related to his own background of work in this field.

• Rural Library Service:

Although library service was generally available in urban areas the Committee estimated that the 40,000,000 people in rural areas had no public libraries. Accordingly, the Committee proposed grants totaling thirty million dollars to the States over a six-year period with the prediction that "few fields of educational service grants as small as those recommended for rural library service will bring about results so large." Reeves had a special feeling for the importance of this recommendation, which was consistent with his earlier experiences and his later direction of a rural development program at the University of Chicago.

Research, Planning and Demonstrations

Stemming partly from the good results achieved by the grants to land-grant colleges for research, extension and demonstration in agriculture and related fields and also to aid States to make good use of the funds granted, the Committee recommended a total of $17,000,000 over six years for research, planning and demonstrations in fields in which grants were made. The United States Office of Education was suggested as the granting agency for research and planning activities throughout the whole educational system.

The Committee concluded its analysis of the needs for additional support for education in these far-sighted words:

- The inequalities of educational opportunity that characterize the educational system today constitute a challenge to American statesmanship. For millions of children the opportunity for anything more than the smallest amount of meager and formal public education is largely determined by place of birth.
- If, for a long period, each succeeding generation is drawn in large numbers from those areas in which economic conditions are poorest, if the population of the Nation continues to be recruited largely from economically underprivileged groups, and if the inability of the depressed economic areas and groups to provide proper education for their children is not corrected by aid from areas and groups more prosperous, the effect on American civilization and on representative political institutions may be disastrous . . .
- Education can be made a force to equalize the conditions of men. It is no less true that it may be a force to create class, race, and sectional distinctions. The evidence indicates clearly that the schools of the United States, which have hitherto been regarded as the bulwark of democracy, may in fact become an instrument for creating those very inequalities they were designed to prevent.
- During the years of increasing strain and social instability since 1914, it has become more and more certain that our country cannot succeed if a majority of the citizens are indifferent to the public interest. Democracy depends upon patriotism, but merely sentimental patriotism is not enough . . .
- The people of America are our most important resource. Whatever may happen in the conservation or the destruction of our material resources, nothing completely disastrous is likely to happen to a healthy and intelligent people, and nothing but disaster can happen if we are unable to meet successfully the strains and problems of our world.
- The Nation's future depends on the quality of the American people.[4]

The Committee was cognizant of the fact that Congress had the responsibility for actions on the Committee report. The dollar amounts recommended were offered as suggestions on the general magnitude of support required—not as definitive figures. But the scope and magnitude of the recommendations were at the time bold, forthright and well documented. The "anatomy" of the staff research and Committee deliberations on the problems of education which supported their recommendations constitute the next section. It reveals the genius Reeves had for organizing and directing research and decision making on the part of committees made up of persons of varying backgrounds.

Anatomy of Staff and Committee Work

The principal procedures which Reeves demonstrated in his chairmanship of this Committee and which were typical of his work other committees follow:

- Define the broad problems to be addressed, and break down the major problems and issues into their component parts which can be dealt with comfortably and objectively.
- Organize and assign work to subcommittees in terms of their interests and special abilities.
- Keep discussion of the Committee on track and sense when differences of opinion need to be acknowledged sensitively and sometimes postpone further discussion until tempers are cooled or relevant facts brought to bear on the issues.
- Communicate relevant information from outside sources regularly and objectively.
- Define areas of relevant research and select staff and consultants to conduct the research and to prepare their factual reports in language that lay persons in the subject can understand.
- Prepare drafts of interim reports of Committee recommendations to test for differences of opinion and the basis for resolving such differences and ultimately achieving consensus.
- Finally meet anticipated or imposed deadlines.

Details of the workings of the Committee and Reeves's strategy and leadership follow.

The first five meetings of the Advisory Committee, which stretched out from November 1936 to May 1937, were largely focused on understanding the charge to the Committee, on the issues to be faced and resolved, on defining areas to be researched, operating procedures to be followed and staff and consultants to be appointed. An important agreement was reached, in accordance with the President's wish that members of the Committee would function as individuals and not as representatives of organizations to which they belonged.

At the first session, lasting three days, Reeves opened the meeting by quoting the language of the President's letter of appointment of the Committee as follows:

> At the time I approved HR 12120 (the George Deen Act) which authorized additional appropriation for the Federal aid for vocational education . . . I indicated my belief that before the Act goes into effect on July 1, 1937, the whole subject should be reviewed by a disinterested group. It is my thought that such a group should study the experience under the existing program for vocational education, the relation of such training to general education and to prevailing economic and social conditions . . . I take pleasure in inviting you to accept membership on a committee to make such studies and to make recommendations which will be available to the Congress and the Executive . . .

And then Reeves expanded on this charge to the Committee as follows:

> We should keep in mind the deep interest expressed by the President in providing our young people with adequate opportunity for vocational training. The President's statement implies that the immediate occasion of the appointment of the Committee did not arise out of any feeling that there wasn't a need for adequate vocational training, but rather from a concern felt by the President over the particular provisions of the George Deen Act.[5]

Reeves followed with a brief history of vocational education and cited various issues and suggestions which had been made to him. Open discussion of the background material presented resulted in many pages of notes which Reeves summarized at the end of the discussion. The full Committee approved the appointment of a conference committee of six members who sorted out and classified 22 key issues, and approved the appointment of Paul T. David, who, as indicated above, was the key staff member assigned to prepare reports and provide leadership to the Committee—especially when Reeves was back at the University of Chicago. Additionally, the conference committee outlined a tentative series of activities which would bring the full Committee's deliberations to a successful completion with their major recommendation to the President in a report not exceeding 2000 words in length.

The next three meetings of the Committee moved its work along to a point where the initial Presidential charge to the Committee was enlarged to include the needs of education in all aspects of education instead of being limited to vocational education. Before advocating the change in the scope of the Committee's assignment to the President, however, Reeves reported to and consulted with Frances Perkins, the Secretary of Labor under whose jurisdiction vocational education was organizationally located. She recommended that the President enlarge the terms of reference of the Committee, closing her letter in which she made her recommendations to the President in these words:

> Dr. Reeves would be willing to undertake to develop a broadened program for Committee activity if you should feel that this procedure would afford the best facilities for meeting the present situation. He suggests, however, that an alternative procedure which might well be given consideration would be the appointment of a new committee to make a general study of Federal relations to education. If this were done, it should be understood that the present Committee on Vocational Education would have to restrict its report to a considerable extent, as there would be certain points as to which it would be impossible to arrive at conclusions without considering them in the light of recommendations pertinent to the wider field. It seems, therefore, that additional clarification as to the terms of reference to the existing Committee will be needed whether or not its functions are to be expanded as suggested.
>
> For my own part, I believe the work of the present Committee has been developed in a most effective manner and that it could well serve as a nucleus for the larger enterprise, which in my opinion must be undertaken in the near future, if not at once.[6]

Reeves met with the President shortly thereafter and presented a memorandum, the first paragraph of which described the need for expansion of the Committee's charge:

> At the present time there is an unprecedented number of bills before the Congress proposing Federal aid to education. Great legislative pressure is being placed behind the Harrison-Black-Fletcher Bill. A situation of administrative complexity exists due to the number of Federal agencies dealing with education. There is a recognized need for a reorganization of the entire field of secondary education, including both the vocational and the non-vocational fields. Vocational education at the secondary school level cannot well be considered in isolation from non-vocational education. Furthermore, it is difficult to arrive at sound conclusions as to the need for Federal support for an expanded program of vocational education without considering at the same time all aspects of Federal relations to education.[7]

Reeves also gave the President a report which provided him with a run-down of the activities of the Committee; organization and key personnel consulted; a summary of the nineteen days of conferences with educational and community leaders in six major cities; research reports in process; and an analysis of bill pending in Congress which would greatly expand the financial obligations of the federal government for vocational education.

As a result of Secretary Perkins recommendation for enlarging the scope of the assignment to the Committee and for increasing the size of the Committee, both of which Reeves strongly supported, the President agreed to both of the recommended changes.

The President, doubtless reflecting on some of the political and fiscal consequences of the expanded responsibilities charged to the Committee, expressed his cautionary view in a letter to Reeves:

> I have been giving thought to the general system of the relationship of the Federal Government to education. Many bills are now pending in Congress all of which seek to a greater or less degree to aid the Federal Government in future extensive programs costing very large sums of money.
>
> Inasmuch as the Committee of which you are Chairman, appointed last Fall to study vocational training, is also charged with considering the relation of such training to general education, it occurs to me that you already have considerable information at hand.
>
> I am, therefore, asking your Committee to give more extended consideration to the whole subject of Federal relationship to state and local conduct of education and to let me have a report. I appreciate that this will take more time than that allotted to your Committee.
>
> May I suggest to you that in the conduct of this study, your Committee should consider among other things the definite danger that an entering wedge of Federal expenditure in any system of taxing to state or localities might easily expand in a very short time to the point where the treasury would be gravely embarrassed and financial burdens now resting on the states and localities would tend to be cast on the Federal Government.[8]

The Committee was apprised of the developments noted above and reviewed a tentative formulation of guiding principles which they had requested Reeves to submit. These guiding principles were elaborated into thirteen general principles which provided the framework of the Committee's final recommendations.[9]

Members of the Committee by this time had become sufficiently acquainted with each other to function as colleagues. They were ready to move into high gear in formulating their recommendations, with the help of Reeves and his staff.

Final Activities of the Committee (Sixth to Ninth Meetings, November to January 1938)

To expedite the work of the expanded Committee, an executive committee was appointed to review the research underway, identify further interest groups to be consulted and to prepare further drafts of recommendations with consultants. Detailed records of the deliberations of the executive committee were sent to the full membership of the Committee for their information and reactions. Further refinements were made in the style of the reports and in contacts which staff members and researchers would have with outside groups to protect the Committee from premature leaks of their recommendations. Coordination of the Committee's work with the U. S. Office of Education, which was not officially represented on the Committee, was intensified to avoid conflicting policy positions on the level of federal support for education. After six months of intensive work of the executive committee on matters indicated above the full Committee was convened for the final four meetings. For these meetings Reeves was relieved of his duties at the University of Chicago to spend substantially full-time on the Committee's work until the final report was submitted to the President.

The last three months moved at a highly accelerated pace: Committee meetings were convened at approximately three-four week intervals and Reeves was relieved of chairing the meetings at his request, in order to participate more freely in discussion of the remaining policy questions and for intensive discussion of drafts of the final report which he prepared at the request of the Committee. Members of the staff and special consultants participated in these discussions.

A conference with Marvin McIntyre, a Presidential assistant, led to the President's approval of a slightly extended period for the completion of the report but this did not slow up the pace of the work of the executive committee or the full Committee. The President reviewed a preliminary draft on December 7, 1937 and a final draft of the report on February 1, 1938. He approved the report and ordered it being printed for submission to Congress on February 23, 1938. The President's letter of transmittal simply stated:

> I transmit herewith for the information of the Congress, the report of the Advisory Committee on Education appointed by me in September 1936 to study the experience under the existing programs of federal aid for vocational education and to prevailing economic and social conditions, and the extent of the need for an expanded program.

The President was very aware of the fact that the mood of the Congress was divided on further expansion of the federal government in education, which doubtless prompted him to make this rather bland transmittal.

The reaction of educational organizations such as the National Education Association, American Association of School Administrators, The American Federation of Teachers, American Library Association and other organizations such as the C. I. O., Committee on Legislation and of the P. T. A. and many other organizations and prominent leaders, however, were highly supportive. Many of the leading newspapers, including *The New York Times* and educational journals gave excellent coverage to the report. Thirty-five thousand copies of a brief digest were authorized by the Committee and distributed to city, labor and local newspapers and journals throughout the country. The executive committee continued to meet for the final review of the nineteen special research reports on various aspects of the Committee's work, which were also given wide circulation. Other organizations such as the American Protestant Defense League, Friends of the Public Schools of America, Peoples Lobby and a few other organizations and journals including the leading Catholic journal *America*, expressed negative reactions, chiefly on the issue of federal aid to private schools. The stage was thus set for extensive Congressional debate and the introduction of ten bills over the next few years. Reeves made many speeches to educational conferences and other groups, answered numerous letters, participated in radio programs, wrote several articles and otherwise aggressively sought support for the Committee's recommendation. He testified before several Congressional committees, including one chaired by Senator Thomas who said:

> . . . May I say this in connection with Dr. Reeves's report . . . I believe firmly that in the history of education in our own country probably no more significant report, based as it was upon honest research and investigation, dealing with the relationship of education and the government, has come from any group of persons.[10]

But the President persisted in his official neutral position, which reflected his objections to putting overt pressure on the Congress to enact supporting legislation. Eleanor Roosevelt explained the President's position in terms of his policy that only bills that were "must legislation got full administration pressure." These measures were largely addressed to measures for defense. But in a letter in which the President thanked Reeves and the Committee for their work he properly characterized the report as a "truly monumental work." There is little question that the report opened a new chapter in federal support of education.

The Advisory Committee Report and related studies of education associated with the name of Reeves will, hopefully, be remembered by students of education as among the major forces which greatly expanded the role of the federal government in education—whether applauded or condemned!

Chapter IV

Major Organizations and Programs to Meet the Needs of Youth

The roots of Reeves's enduring interest in a variety of programs for youth are doubtless buried in his own youth and upbringing. The principal activities were with: (1) the President's Advisory Committee on Education with particular reference to the Committee's recommendation to improve educational and work experience for youth; (2) the American Youth Commission (AYC), a non-governmental organization, which engaged in a wide variety of research projects and which coordinated and expanded the active participation in youth activities which were members of the AYC; (3) the National Youth Administration (NYA), the government program for youths from ages 16–25 years which involved collaboration with the Works Progress Administration (WPA) and the Civilian Conservation Corps (CCC); and (4) the student movements and White House Conferences in which Eleanor Roosevelt was also very active. Some of the conferences and demonstrations were militant in tone and spirit. Mrs. Roosevelt, however, was instrumental in getting the President interested in the concerns and needs of youth and in setting up numerous committee meetings and several conferences in the White House. Reeves served as an advisor to Mrs. Roosevelt and active participant in several activities in which she was personally involved. Joseph Lash, one of the most active and talented youth leaders, described the relationships which Reeves had with the youth organization and Mrs. Roosevelt:

> I remember Floyd Reeves quite well. He was one member of the educational establishment to whom we in the youth and student move-

> ments turned with a sense that his welcome mat was always out and that our ideas were taken seriously. That was true of the international Student Service (which Lash headed) but it was also true of his willingness to hear the views of the representatives of the American Youth Congress and the American Student Union . . . I know that Mrs. Roosevelt who feared the educational bureaucracy trusted him and did what she could that his work with the American Youth Commission was brought to the President's attention.[1]

It is doubtful if there is a parallel to the impact of these interrelated research and action programs in defining the needs of youth and in formulating relevant programs to meet their needs. In all of the four major activities on youth, Reeves was the person with the facts about needs of youth and with the energy, organizational skill and motivation to design and defend policies and practical activities to improve opportunities for youth. He literally shuttled back and forth between meetings of policy advocates at the highest levels of private and governmental organizations, who urgently requested his participation, and with professional and administrative persons who were on the "firing line" of activities and who, likewise, sought his guidance and dynamic interest in helping them accomplish their goals.

President's Advisory Committee on Education[2]

The President's Advisory Committee on Education, previously described in Chapter III Part I made numerous recommendations for the improvement of the organization and programs of the federal government in education and for expanded funding of these activities. Those recommendations which are related to the needs of youth are summarized here.[3] They were for: (1) student aid, provided by the NYA to the extent of 467 million dollars for high school age children and 169 million for college student aid; (2) occupational outlook service to provide data and projections for job opportunities; (3) vocational guidance to provide counseling and placement services to youth by the U.S. Employment Service as a part of the job placement service; (4) expansion and vocational training in industry through the revival of apprenticeships; and (5) work camps and work projects for young persons until they were absorbed in regular employment. Efforts to increase the educational values of the work camps and projects of the CCC and NYA were included in this last recommendation to place the leadership of CCC camps entirely on a civilian basis with a requirement that camp directors be qualified to provide educational leadership. Housing, feeding and other logistical support would continue to be provided by the Department of the Army.

American Youth Commission (AYC)[4]

The mandate of the AYC was to: "consider all the needs of youth and appraise the facilities and resources of serving those needs; plan experiments and programs which will be most helpful in solving the problems of youth, and popularize and promote desirable plans of action through publication, conferences, and demonstrations."

Reeves was appointed Director of the AYC (following Homer P. Rainey) on a part-time basis effective June 1, 1939, with a salary of $15,000, "less any amount which you may receive as a result of your continued connection with the University of Chicago." The appointing officer, George F. Zook, President of the American Council on Education and Chairman of the Executive Committee of the AYC, went on to write:

> I am very glad indeed that you have already indicated your willingness informally to accept the position. I feel that the Commission is going to render a very great service in the solution of the complex problems facing American youth and I am sure the Commission joins me in feeling that as Director of the Commission you can contribute very powerfully to this end.[5]

Reeves also received a number of other congratulatory letters from other members who had served with him on the Advisory Committee on Education. Included with these letters was one from Luther Gulick which demonstrated the close functional relationships between several important organizations focused wholly or in part on the problem and needs of youth.

> Your assumption of this task not only binds together the President's Committee (on Education), the New York Regents Inquiry and the American Youth Commission, but guarantees that the whole enterprise will make an important contribution to American life.[6]

Members of the AYC Commission during Reeves's tenure as Director, who was preceded by Homer P. Rainey, included Owen D. Young,

Honorary Chairman of the Board, General Electric Company; Rev. George Johnson, Director, Department of Education, National Catholic Welfare Conference; Henry C. Taylor, Director, Farm Foundation, and George F. Zook, all of whom except Owen D. Young were members of the President's Advisory Commission on Education. Other members of the Commission who were closely associated with Reeves in prior or subsequent activities included: Will W. Alexander, Vice President of the Julius Rosenwald Fund; Clarence A. Dykstra, President of the University of Wisconsin; Dorothy Canfield Fisher, author; Willard E. Givens, Executive Secretary of the National Education Association; Mordecai W. Johnson, President of Howard University; and Matthew Woll, Vice President, American Federation of Labor. Paul T. David, who served as Secretary of the President's Advisory Committee on Education served as Associate Director and Chief Economist of the Commission.

This was not a "paper committee" of endorsers of the program but active participants in the deliberations and in their recommendations for policy formulations and practical programs of action. The AYC, in brief, served as a research and judgment basis for guidance of the extensive programs of the NYA; for helpful assistance to the interests and activities of President Roosevelt—largely through the energetic participation of Mrs. Roosevelt in youth organizations; and for White House conferences on children and youth.

Reeves took the responsibility for the organization of all research projects, the selection of staff, and the approval of staff reports which merited publication. The Commission was responsible for the determination of the general areas in which research was conducted and for published statements which represented the conclusions and recommendations of the Commission.

The extensive research program, and the publications and recommendations resulting therefrom, constituted the visible core of the Commission's work. They generally—but not wholly—elaborated on the topics and issues briefly identified in the research and publications of the Advisory Committee on Education. For example, disparities in educational opportunity for rural and Negro youths, need for broader employment opportunities, vocational training, recreational needs of youth and related topics constituted the hard core of the research.

Seven publications focused on Negro youth; five on work camps; thirteen on jobs, health, leisure, secondary education and other programs (most of which were of book length). Monthly bulletins with circulation of over 3,000 and several pamphlets on "how to do it" or on policy recommendations were also published.

Brief notes on some of the principal publications illustrate the content and flavor of the reports.

- Howard Bell's "*Youth Tell Their Story*" (1938).

This publication, one of the first of the AYC, provided first hand information on opinions of more than 13,000 youths in a survey in Maryland and provided the Commission with a framework for the agenda for other research projects.

The study emphasized the following: The necessity of equalizing educational opportunities between the richer and the poorer states to offset, in part, the fact that those who enjoy the richest cultural resources are failing to reproduce themselves, whereas those who have the lowest income have the highest number of children per family. (2) The need to find employment for youth as they complete their school experience. Bell's research found that the "gap which now exists between school and employment is reaching ominous proportions." (3) The fact that a very large percentage of youth surveyed asserted that economic insecurity resulting from unemployment was their most urgent need. (4) The absence of adequate vocational guidance programs made necessary by the increasing complexity of modern life. (5) The lack of appropriate vocational training, especially for rural youth. (6) The need for a thorough reorganization of secondary schools, the programs of which as now operated are ill suited to a large percentage of youth attending them. (7) The lack of employment opportunities and the reduction in hours of labor created a leisure time social problem resulting from unemployment or under-employment which required that recreation and education programs be construed as being parallel needs of youth. (8) The need for more attention to health education. (9) The need to give greater attention to "youth's indifference to the ballot and other civic responsibilities." (10) The inadequacy of community organizations for planning to meet the needs of youth.

- Franklin Frazier's "*Negro Youth at the Crossroads*" (1940). Frazier pointed out that "Negro youth are at the crossroads." Many face dilemmas that are part of the transition from a southern rural to a middle states urban way of living which are related to Negro youth's new economic freedom . . . The study showed the many ways of determining the socio-psychological effects of being a

Negro upon the personality development of the individual boy or girl.

- Kenneth Holland's "*Youth in European Labor Camps*" (1939). Holland studied labor camps in Bulgaria, Germany, Poland and other European countries, and related his findings to the American CCC.
- Howard Bell's "*Matching Youth and Jobs*." Bell's study revealed that each year about 1,750,000 boys and girls in the United States offer their services as beginning workers, most of whom, however, have very little information about themselves as workers or about the world of work because they have had no vocational guidance or counseling; they know no basic skills because their schools offer either unattractive types of vocational preparation or none at all; and they are not guided to whatever suitable jobs may be available because no placement office or counseling services are available to them.
- C. Gilbert Wrenn and D. L. Harley's "*Time on Their Hands*" (1941). The needs of youth for constructive use of leisure in peace time as well as in periods of national defense was highlighted and the charge that youth are "soft" and must be "toughened" was examined and related in part to the poor use of leisure time.

Reeves elaborated on the above point to emphasize that:

> In a period of national emergency like the present, the use of leisure by youth is of special importance to our country. The American Youth Commission has frequently pointed out that only as youth feel they have a stake in our democracy will they be eager to defend it. They can hardly be expected to respond with enthusiasm to demands for special effort in creating and maintaining our defenses if no attention is given to their own pressing needs, one of which is healthful recreation.

The response of the AYC to the need for involving youth in the national defense effort was difficult on which to reach agreement. The records show that some members of the Commission felt strongly that the United States should avoid getting actively involved in the war, as reflected in the following illustrative excerpt from the minutes of one of the Commission meetings.

> I should like to impress on you my very strong feeling that the Commission should adopt a resolution that the United States should avoid

> getting into the European conflict at any cost. In view of what it means to the youth of this country and their future, I think it is the duty of the American Youth Commission to adopt such a resolution. Personally, I have never felt more strongly on any subject in my life . . . While I dislike the totalitarian form of government and should certainly not like to live under a Hitler regime, I feel that it would be the height of folly for the United States to enter into an alliance with the Western allies or become embroiled in any way.

Nevertheless, the Commission, after considerable debate, decided to give Reeves permission to concentrate on taking a leading role in setting up policies and procedures for accelerating training programs for defense.

The recommendations of the AYC on "Youth, Defense and the National Welfare" was one of the results of Reeves's efforts to clarify policy in this area. A special meeting of the AYC held on July 22–24, 1940 to "consider again the momentous relationships between youth, defense and the national welfare" concluded that: (1) "No one should be called for full-time military training before reaching the degree of maturity represented by the age of 21" and the "number called should be limited strictly to those needed for military reasons . . ." (2) Unfair discrimination in the operation of any system of selection must be answered . . . (3) The increasing mechanization of the military service shows that many new skills are needed and that the problem of making the best assignment of duties is becoming increasingly complex . . . (4) "The concern of the American Youth Commission is for youth, for it is youth who will bear most of the burden of selective compulsory military service . . ." and (5) The necessity for some form of work and training program for unemployed out-of-school youth is now widely admitted . . ."

The final report of the AYC, entitled *Youth and the Future*,[7] was issued in 1941 following the review of preliminary drafts and recommendations. The writing of Dorothy Canfield Fisher and of Paul T. David was specifically acknowledged by Reeves, who closed his foreword with these complimentary and prophetic words: "If this report proves to be a document which lives and has influence, it will be because it expresses the final outcome of the group thinking carried on over a period of six years by one of the most outstanding groups of men and women in America."

Owen D. Young's Introduction to the 291 page final report emphasized the thoughtful assumptions and forthright projections of the Commission that:

- The successful prosecution of the war is the most important problem confronting the American people.
- In the post-war period, economic reconstruction to achieve sustained full employment under peacetime conditions will be the most difficult problem and the most urgent objective of the American people.
- The changes in the basic structure of the American economic system which have taken place during the last fifty years will not present insuperable barriers to the achievement of peacetime full employment.
- For some years after the war, efforts to achieve sustained peacetime full employment through the expansion of private employment will be only partially successful, and meanwhile it will be necessary to carry on substantial programs of public works for the unemployed.
- Under democratic government and without giving up the liberties we prize, the American people will have it within their power to bring about a continuing abundance of available employment opportunity in future times of peace, with a rising standard of living for all who contribute to the productive effort of the nation and
- In stating these assumptions, the Commission does not assume either that we are completely at the mercy of fate or that we shall reach our desired goals without sacrifice and effort. It is assumed that the American people will continue to exercise their native qualities of good will, courage, and foresight, and that progress will thus continue toward the realization of the American dream of universal opportunity in a land of peace and freedom.

Before the completion of the work of the AYC, Reeves made a 29-page report on the work of the organization to the American Council's Committee on Problems and Plans in Education. The report summarized and reiterated his basic convictions and liberal values, which were shared by the distinguished Commission. Highlights of the summary: (1) emphasized the research base for and repeated deliberative sessions of the Commission on the first draft of the research; (2) repeated the central importance of "full and remunerative employment for which individuals are qualified by aptitude and training" which is to be provided by public works programs where necessary; (3) reiterated the need for a drastic revision of the curricula for secondary schools and increased financial support for schools in impoverished areas; (4) included previous references to a "national health program on a scale never attempted in this country which would be directed to the needs of citizens of all ages—with special emphasis on youth;'' (5) advocated that Congress pass no legislation for military conscription without provisions for adequate economic, educational, health and recreational needs of youth; (6) pointed out that the AYC demonstrated its ability to influence ''locally controlled secondary schools and federally controlled youth programs without being identified with either;'' and (7) finally provided procedural, personnel and financial ways and means to carry out the Commission's recommendations.

As a result of further considerations and reflections by the American Council on Reeves's final report a Committee on Youth Problems was established with Henry L. Harriman as Chairman and including some other former members of the Commission and some new members and consultants including Edmund Ezra Day, President of Cornell University; Robert Watt, an official of the American Federation of Labor; J. E. Sproul, National Council of the YMCA; E. L. Kirkpatrick, Director of the Rural Project of the American Council and others. Floyd Reeves served as a consultant to the Committee.

The Committee met on several occasions and conducted several conferences on defense related and post-war problems. It secured an additional grant of $25,000 from the Field Foundation and authorized the expenditure of funds from the sale of publications of the AYC. Furthermore, it published eight additional updated copies of the Bulletin on topics previously publicized.

A simple, poignant reflection of Lotus D. Coffman, former President of the University of Minnesota and a member of the first group of Commissioners, in a note written a week before he died, epitomizes the spirit of the AYC and the thoughtful and stimulating environment in which Reeves worked. Coffman wrote:

> The point to which I am moving is this. Men like to earn for themselves the things in life that bring them satisfaction. They like to provide the furnishings of their homes, the clothes for themselves and their families, for food for their table, and they like to provide, too, for more than subsistence needs. Men like to buy pictures for the walls, flowers for their gardens, wholesome amusement and a list of other items and services that every reader can extend indefinitely from his own experience. Men do not want these things given to them. They want to participate in acquiring them. Young people are no exception to this universal principle. They, too want, above all else the opportunity to work to the end that from income of their labors they may acquire those things that contribute to the enjoyment of life. I do not mean that there should be fewer parks,

> fine libraries, fewer orchestras and concerts and less opportunity for recreation. What I am saying is that if the report of the American Youth Commission is to be accepted and believed, that youth of this country want the chance through work to help pay for those things and those services by exercising their own earning capacity. The youth problem is still essentially a work problem. Education and work, out of which develop the sound utilization of leisure, are the twin stepping stones to the kind of life most people and especially young people want to live.

Although the outbreak of the war practically eliminated the unemployment problems of youth, many of the other problems and lost opportunities, dramatized by the research findings and publications of the Commission, persisted. The American Council on Education dealt with some of these problems through other committees and commissions and their recommendations.

But during the seven years of existence the AYC and its Director, Floyd Reeves, profoundly influenced thinking and actions of educational and governmental officials, and citizens interested in the problems of youth. Some of these "spin-off" influences are briefly described in the next section.

National Youth Administration (NYA)[8]

The NYA was created on June 26, 1935, by Executive Order, and came to an end on June 30, 1943. The organization was a part of the Works Progress Administration (WPA) for four years under the immediate supervision of Aubrey Williams, who continued as its chief executive throughout the life of the organization. On July 1, 1939 it became part of the Federal Security Agency after its mission was "no longer a purely relief organization, but was given the broader functions of extending to needy young persons opportunities for continuing their education and providing employment and training to needy unemployed persons." These functions were to be carried out within an administrative structure, the major purposes of which were to promote social and economic security, educational opportunity, and the health of the citizens of the nation. On September 17, 1942 the NYA became a part of the War Manpower Commission, which was under the Office of Emergency Management in the Executive Office of the President. This change was made because "Pearl Harbor had ended the depression period for youth. In fact, it completely altered the circumstances surrounding the life of everyone, no matter what his age. The times had changed. Unemployment was no longer a national problem. Total mobilization for war was in progress and the nation was concerned with manpower shortages rather than surpluses."

Aubrey Williams, as Administrator, was advised by two committees,[9] the members of which had all been associated with Reeves in one or more organizations. The relationship between members of the Committee to Reeves and of Reeves to Williams and to C. H. Judd were particularly helpful to Williams.

The two programs of the NYA were basically to: (1) provide work and financial assistance to needy young persons desirous of continuing their education, and (2) to provide for out-of-school youth and for needy unemployed youth work experience through a nation-wide system of work projects and to prepare these young people for private employment.

Programs for out-of-school youth included 16 so-called "manual" projects including construction, conservation, vocational farm and foundry projects, electrical and auto mechanic shops and similar fields. The so-called "non-manual" projects included clerical and stenographic, hospital assistance, ceramics, music and other similar subjects. Five experimental resident projects were also funded. A principal one of the so-called residence projects to which Mrs. Roosevelt and her close friends gave particular attention was at Passamaquoddy, Maine. There were also a variety of services for out-of-school youth including guidance, placement, aptitude testing, health, recreation and other such services. The magnitude of these programs was substantial as indicated in the following facts: expenditures for wages for the student work programs and for the unemployed youth program for producing useful goods and services totalled more than six hundred million dollars; and more than fifteen hundred colleges, universities and secondary schools participated in the program.

NYA-WPA (Works Progress Administration)-AYC Formal Relationships

The first document on the relationships between these organizations, dated May 23, 1938, is a letter from Reeves to Williams who then served as Deputy Administrator of the WPA, which then supervised the NYA program. Reeves was then involved in the AYC. The letter was written at Williams' request to "reduce to writing certain suggestions that Reeves made concerning the educational activities of the WPA and reflected his views and those of members of Reeves's staff." The suggestions, spelled out in detail, in a three-page letter, focused on: the need for a consolidation of the Education and Recreation Divisions of the Works Progress Administration and the need for more complete educational reports from the states.

A second communication titled, "A Suggested Plan for a Survey of the Effectiveness of the WPA Education Program" was prepared by a subcommittee of the Advisory Committee for the WPA Education Committee chaired by Reeves. This report took cognizance of the work of the Division of Education Projects of the Federal Emergency Relief Organization (FERA) which preceded the Education Division of the WPA. During a five-year period these organizations had spent more than one hundred million dollars for more than one hundred thousand unemployed plus more than four million persons who had been enrolled in WPA classes. The communication expressed the opinion of the Committee that "the need for a program of this type is still great, and there is little reason to believe that the program can or should be discontinued in the near future. In view of this situation we believe that the time has arrived for an intensive survey of the WPA educational activities, in order to evaluate the effectiveness of the program and to devise means whereby it may be improved." The report went on to suggest that the programs of three or four states be intensively studied in terms of such factors as: the quality of the administrative personnel of the state WPA program, of the State Department of Education and of the local schools; the type of state administrative organization established to administer the WPA program, and the extent to which cooperative relationships exist between the office of the WPA Administrator and the chief school officers of the several states.

Somewhat later, when Paul McNutt became the Administrator of the Federal Security Agency (which became the cabinet headquarters for the NYA), he invited Reeves, as Director of the AYC, to attend meetings convened by the Secretary, to serve on committees and to otherwise provide advice on a number of aspects of the Agency's work including a conference of some leaders in business, industry and education to discuss "problems of youth and unemployment; CCC leadership training; and to advise him on an assignment by the President to coordinate all health, medical, welfare, nutrition, recreation and other related fields of activity affecting the national defense." The Secretary went on to indicate that he would also "welcome any suggestions which you would care to make at this time regarding the organization of this work and the contribution that the American Youth Commission might make to this part of the defense program''—an open invitation to get the research findings and policy thinking of the AYC into the thinking and policies of the top government organization responsible for action programs on a number of areas of interest to the AYC.

The account of NYA-WPA-AYC day-to-day operating relationships would not be complete without some reference to Reeves's extensive organizational connections and speaking and conference leading activities. Among his organizational memberships having common interests with the WPA-AYC in youth were: the American Country Life Association, Work Camps for America, Youth Guidance Institute, American Committee for Democracy and Institutional Freedom, Council for Democracy and others. Furthermore, Reeves accepted numerous speaking and conference engagements with NYA state and regional organizations and other educational organizations too numerous to mention, and even a commencement address when given an honorary degree at Kent State University in 1940 on the not surprising subject of ''The Future Is Yours.'' Reeves's earlier youthful debating and speaking experience stood him in good stead for his back-breaking schedule for speeches for which there are many commendatory letters in the archives.

Interpersonal Relationships—Reeves-Judd-Williams

It is a commonplace observation—but no less important—that much of the work of organizations and particularly large governmental agencies is conducted on the basis largely of formal hierarchial relationships, formal memoranda and formal reports. But there is another dimension of perhaps equal—if not greater importance—namely, the non-formal, more personal, less structured relationships based on mutual respect, confidence and trust. These relationships were possibly even more important in the fast-moving, quickly changing period of the New Deal, confronted as it was with new economic, social and political problems on a massive scale which called for new creative experimental and rapid solutions to the problems. The relationship of researchers, advisors and consultants of the AYC (Reeves, Judd, *et. al.*) and officials of the NYA and WPA (especially Williams) was anything but a hands-off, arms-length, bureaucratic relationship. No complete enumeration of specific activities such as committee meetings, telephone calls, dinners, luncheons and related information is available. The extensive collection of material in the Reeves files in the MSU Archives and Historical Collections clearly indicate, however, that the personal relations were relaxed but highly professional. A few comments illustrate the nature of the relationships.

Reeves-Judd Relationship

The relationship of Charles Hubbard Judd, who was a members of the National Advisory Committee of the NYA, and Floyd Reeves went back to 1925 when Reeves was a graduate student at the University of Chicago. They were both interested in organizational and administrative matters, educational surveys (on several of which they joined forces) on broad questions of educational policy and social issues, the then new educational programs such as adult and rural education, innovative curriculum developments especially in the social sciences and other aspects of education. Reeves probably persuaded Judd to serve on the National Advisory Committee and to join the NYA staff and to get into the somewhat "topsy-turvey" world of government in the depression years in contrast to the more tranquil environment of the University of Chicago campus. Apropos of this point a story went around—probably apocryphal—that Judd was asked how he got along in Washington in the bureaucracy in which he was in the unusual situation of being under a "supervisor" who could assign him work, etc. He was reported to have responded somewhat shyly, "Well it is different to be on the receiving end of a buzzer." Anyway they turned out to be collaborators in an NYA-NYC relationship and had frequent formal and informal meetings and discussions between themselves and with Williams and other government officials. The records show that Judd quite frequently invited Reeves to attend meetings called by him, to serve on committees, exchange critical correspondence, review proposed speeches and related activities. Judd did not hesitate to suggest studies and research projects which should be undertaken by the AYC which would be helpful to his work as head of the secondary school educational program of the NYA and doubtless on other areas of collaboration between the two agencies.

Reeves-Williams Relationship

In addition to the formal communications and meetings between AYC and NYA, Williams invited Reeves to be closely involved in policy and program issues and choices facing the NYA. A letter from Williams to "My dear Floyd" on September 30, 1939 characterizes the tone of their relationship:

> I am calling together a small group of eleven for the purpose of discussing in an intimate way during a period of two or three days the problems of the National Youth Administration and the general problems which must be solved if young people are to be dealt with adequately.

Since the nature of this meeting was clearly informal and probably off the record, no minutes or other documents are available. There is further evidence, however, that the two men were in frequent communication through exchange of correspondence, copies of speeches and doubtless many telephone conversations on strictly NYA-AYC matters and other matters as well. One significant—if not unusual—task, which Reeves performed at the request of Williams was to investigate a major scandal in the administration of NYA funds in Louisiana. The scandal involved top officials in the state government, the University and in the schools which resulted in one suicide, many firings and even more resignations.

Although contemporaries in age—both born in 1890—Williams was "junior" to Reeves in formal education and in high level experience as, I believe, the tone of the correspondence shows. Williams graduated from a small sectarian college in Tennessee. His extensive experience in social work, public welfare and civil works and early depression educational relief work plus his interests in rural problems, however, provided a basis for shared values which were enhanced by mutual concern for youth. Their closest association, however, came through their numerous activities with Mrs. Roosevelt. The description of the relationship would not be complete, at this point, however, without reference to a letter from Williams to "My dear Floyd" written on January 1, 1940 in which he wrote:

> I am sitting here on New Year's Day thinking of the people who have made a real contribution to the future of our Nation and I find myself placing you in the forefront.
>
> I am sure that your taking the (American) Youth Commission job and what you have latterly done has made a real dent in the national thinking.[10]

Mrs. Roosevelt, Reeves and the Student Movements

Reeves's association with Mrs. Roosevelt and the student movements of the 30's cannot be accurately understood except by briefly noting the activities with which they both were prominently associated. These relationships started back in 1933 when Reeves became an active participant in FDR's New Deal. They continued with his work with the Advisory Committee on Education, the AYC, NYA and other organizations described above. The work of all of these organizations were of great interest to Mrs. Roosevelt and led naturally to close association with Reeves and their mutual interest in the youth movements of the period.

Inherent in all that follows was, of course, the compatibility of Mrs. Roosevelt and Reeves's basic set of values which put the needs and development of people, especially youth, as having the highest priority; of education as a principal instrumentality for helping people meet their needs and to reach their highest potential; and of a positive role for government—especially the federal government—in helping provide the kind of educational system and framework of policies which was realistically attuned to societal problems, needs and opportunities. Reeves's penchant for assembling facts, creating consensus among national leaders as to policy positions for government and private action, and for creating and guiding largely in the role of an advisor, implementing programs to give effect to the ideas, policies and convictions based on facts, were appreciated by Mrs. Roosevelt. He was a good listener and coordinator of ideas, as well as a dynamic catalyst in group deliberative processes.

Youth Movements and Organization[11]

Because of the closely related work of the AYC and its many publications and recommendations and the action program of the NYA, it is not difficult to see who the youth movements found it relevant to collaborate with these organizations and with Reeves, Aubrey Williams and Mrs. Roosevelt, who were conspiciously sympathetic to their needs, especially on economic and some educational issues. A quick run-down on some of the highlights of the history of student movements in the United States will probably be helpful in sorting out their organizations, major policies and affiliations.

By the end of 1935 the National Student League, which was pro Communist, merged with the Socialist Student League for Industrial Democracy to form the American Student Union. Joseph P. Lash, the National Secretary of the Student Union, and James Wechsler, who had headed the National Student League, were Editor and Associate

Editor respectively of the *Student Advocate*.[12] The *Student Advocate* was a well edited journal which was somewhat satirical in tone with reference particularly to issues of war and autocratic administration of universities—the latter under the series title of "Academic Napoleons." Lash and Wechsler were both members of the Communist party at this time but left the party in 1939 and 1937 respectively.

The American Student Union had a large number of campus chapters (200 by 1938) in leading U.S. universities and some high school organizations (100 by 1938). Their four annual conferences held at Columbus, Chicago, Vassar College and New York City in the years 1935–1938 were the rallying grounds for their highly motivated programs. Joseph Lash made comprehensive and brilliantly worded reports at the last three annual meetings which were printed and made available for the price of 5¢ each. Annual membership of the Union was 25¢.

Columbus, Ohio Conference, 1935

The Conference at Columbus was the site of the consolidation of the two radical campus organizations. The content of the speeches and policy pronouncements was very strident anti-war and anti-ROTC. Student anti-war strikes were reported at Syracuse, Johns Hopkins, Harvard, California and the University of Michigan and at Springfield, Vassar, Wellesley and Amherst Colleges.

Chicago Conference, 1936

Lash's report of the Chicago meeting, published under the title of "Toward a Closed Shop on Campus," was much more restrained than the rhetoric of the Columbus conference. Lash also reported that there were 20,000 members of the student union out of a total seven hundred fifty thousand College and 5 million high school students. Lash further reported that the union expressed support for the NYA, student cóops, better support for Negro students, for a free city college in Philadelphia, and for support of dismissed liberal professors from several universities, e.g., Jerome Frank of Yale, and for Presidents and Deans who supported Spanish rebels and anti-ROTC activities. Linkages were reported to be had with foreign student groups in Cuba, China and Spain. These countries sent representatives to the "International Socialist Student Congress" in Oxford, England and the "Anti-Imperialist Student Conference'' in Mexico. At Oxford, Lash reported that the amalgamation of the Communist and Socialist Movements in the U.S. (which created the Student Union) contributed toward bringing similar movements together in Belgium and other European countries.

Vassar Conference, 1937–38

The masthead of the Vassar Conference was ''The Campus—A Fortress of Democracy.'' The Conference was greeted by a warm endorsement by President Roosevelt in a letter to Joe Lash, excerpts from which follow:

> It is encouraging to find that there are students sufficiently socially minded to devote four days of their brief Christmas holiday to a discussion of our country's social and economic problems . . . The fact that large groups of students, on their own initiative, are taking up national problems is evidence that our institutions of learning are getting results . . . The freshness of point of view of youth should make your discussions especially valuable not only to the youth of the country but to the country as a whole.

Aubrey Williams also commended the Student Union for contributing to:

> . . . the growing interest which American students are taking not only in their immediate campus problems, but also in the larger issues so vital to our future.

Some of the highlights of Lash's moving report to the Convention follows:

> It used to be said that college and school, instead of being windows through which the student looked out upon the world with sharpened eyes, were really feudal walls that shut him off from the world. If the depression and the distant threat of war sapped the barriers between school and society, the developments of the last few months have not only breached those barriers, but engulfed the campus with a plenitude of problems. Students were once smug; they were indifferent; they made a pose of their cynicism. Today they are worried . . . We shall not try to enumerate all the historical facts that have caused this profound change in the temper of the student body. Two, however, are basic: The formation

> of the Rome-Berlin-Tokyo alliance for war and fascism, and the economic recession . . .

He then went on to enumerate actions taken by student members to boycott Japanese goods, fight fascism in Spain, conduct peace strikes against the ROTC and similar actions—but he supported the NYA.

The convention considered problems related to the limited availability of education to many children, and the content and control of education. The tone of the deliberations regarding education was expressed in the following: ". . . The American Student Union is not a philistine organization. We do not in our efforts to achieve peace and life of greater security, ignore the cultural heritage of contemporary American civilians. Indeed, without smugness we declare that we are the upholders of the best in the American educational system. We take the values expressed in our textbooks seriously . . ."

In the interim period before the fourth and last convention in New York in October 1938, Lash wrote a pamphlet, which was widely circulated to members of the Student Union, under the title of "The Student in Post-war Munich." The document vividly portrayed the military actions, consequences and aftermath of the "Munich Peace" concocted by Neville Chamberlain and Adolf Hitler. The sordid events which followed led the Union to advocate: support for FDR's intervention in the war, continued support for Spain under the slogan "No Munich—Peace for Spain;" cessation of sending war material to Japan; continued provision of humanitarian aid to Spain; and strengthening our good neighbor policy to Latin America.

New York, December 1938

The theme of the fourth and last convention was "Keep Democracy Working by Keeping it Moving Forward." This overall theme had three components:

- The university we want to live in
- The America we want to live in
- The world that will give us peace.

Postscript to the American Student Union and the Student Advocate

George Rawick in his Preface to volumes 1–3 of the *Student Advocate*, which is part of a series published by the Greenwood Reprint

Corporation of "Radical Periodicals in the United States 1890–1930" published in 1968, provides the following succinct summary of the demise of the *Student Advocate* which was basically concurrent with basic changes in the policy, posture and program of the Student Union as described above:

- The American Student Union and the *Student Advocate* were probably the most important popular fronts entreprenured in the 30s. . . .
- The New Deal itself fully recognized this and utilized the pages of the *Student Advocate* as propaganda for President Roosevelt's policies.
- Mrs. Eleanor Roosevelt became the champion of the American Student Union and of the *Student Advocate's* Editor, Joseph Lash.
- The leading American Student Union officials were guests at the White House and were consulted on matters dealing with youth in the activities of the federal government's National Youth Administration, and the American Student Union had an official and important position on the National Advisory Committee of that Agency.
- In the first part of 1938 the *Student Advocate* was abandoned, as the popular front as the United States moved to disband any institutions that might be seen as conflicting with or disagreeing with the New Deal. It was obviously felt that the *Student Advocate* provided too close a link with that period of the American student's history when it was presumed to be a united front of Socialists and Communists. . . .
- The main significance of the relationships of the (ASU) American Student Union and the *Student Advocate*,—was the fact that, through the manipulation of the Communist party, these organs became conveyor belts that carried young Communist and young Socialist students from these commitments to official liberalism. The function of the A.S.U. was therefore not that of making Communists out of liberals, as has been charged by many, but precisely the opposite. It made liberals out of Socialists and Communists. . . .
- Thus it was no accident that both Communist James Wechsler and former Socialist, Joseph Lash . . . were to refuse to go along with the Communists in the American Student Union when they later sharply abandoned the collective security line at the time of the Hitler-Stalin pact in late 1939 . . . The *Student Advocate* was based

no longer on the tactical needs of the Communist Party and the Soviet Union, but upon genuine advocacy of the New Deal at home and collective security abroad. . . .

- Wechsler resigned from the Communist Party in 1937 and Lash in 1939 at the time of the Nazi-Soviet Pact.
- The American Student Union and *Student Advocate* were not simply somewhat isolated parts of the American Left; they were part of the mainstream of official governmental and political life.

Lash's experiences with Mrs. Roosevelt (and to a much lesser degree with President Roosevelt) and others prominently identified with the Roosevelt years in the White House, including some references to Reeves, are vividly and poignantly described in his *Love Eleanor—Eleanor and Her Friends*.[13]

American Youth Congress

Reeves's association with the American Youth Congress began while he was still serving as Chairman of the President's Advisory Committee on Education. William W. Hinckley, the Chairman of the Congress, had apparently been following the news about and publications of the Advisory Committee. In a letter to Reeves he wrote:

> Because of the vital importance of education as a youth problem, the American Youth Congress, representing more than ten million young people in national and local organizations, is deeply interested in the work of the Advisory Committee on Education. For this reason we wish to place before the Committee the point of view and the proposals of young people themselves concerning the future of American education . . . We have drawn freely upon existing source material; but we have one additional source which is youths' alone: The experiences and needs of young people themselves who face this problem directly and personally. We are confident that the Advisory Committee will give serious attention to the proposals herewith submitted.

There is no record in available files of the proposals submitted by Hinckley or of Reeves's response. However, a letter from the Executive Secretary, Joseph Cadden on May 25, 1939 urged Reeves to join the "Congress of Youth" which was expected to attract "more than 2,000 delegates from national and youth organizations (councils) from all parts of the country and with every type of interest." He also went on to indicate that he was also very anxious to see Reeves and have a talk with him about the possibility of developing a closer working relationship between the American Youth Commission and the American Youth Congress during the next year. Cadden offered to help implement the recommendations of the AYC and to offer the Youth Congress for experimental purposes as well as a medium through which implementation could be accomplished. An attachment to the letter spelled out interests of the Youth Congress which were, indeed, common to the AYC and including employment, health, recreation, interfaith and interracial cooperation and national and international affairs.

Reeves's long-hand note on this letter stated that "At a later date (about 1941 or 42) Cadden stated that he had been a Communist when he helped organize the American Youth Congress." The creed of the Youth Congress, as passed by their Senate, and a resolution adopted unanimously by the Joint Sessions of the American Congress on July 4, 1939, do not, however, reveal evidence of any Communist infiltration, except perhaps of the most subtle type. In the resolution indicated above the second item specifically indicated that: "This Congress of Youth records its opposition to all forms of dictatorships, regardless of whether they be Communist, Fascist, Nazi or any other type or bear any other name."

Reeves continued to cooperate with the Congress. A letter to Frances Williams, Administrative Secretary, on February 23, 1940 indicated that he had sent them six additional copies of the AYC's basic research publication *Youth Tell Their Story*, which Frances Williams referred to as "our Bible" in the office and is much in demand by old and young people working on the youth problem. She also reported that Joe Cadden would be looking forward "to keeping in contact with you because your advice is of great assistance to us." Frances Williams wrote to Reeves again on March 2, 1940 to report two columns which Dorothy Thompson had published in the *New York Herald Tribune* which purported to quote a speech by Williams and to criticize policy positions taken at a then recent meeting of the Congress. In this exchange Dorothy Thompson was quoted as reporting that Williams had said: "The American Youth Congress will welcome Communists within its ranks because the recent history of Italy, Germany, Austria, France and Canada proves that the suppression of Communists is always the opening gun in a general campaign on civil liberties." Williams countered by pointing out that: ". . . Communists are represented in the Congress . . . and they are there, though in a minority, because they are part of the youth of the United States . . . to help get better wages, jobs and security for young people. We welcome them because they would rather work for the betterment of American youth than sit around wringing their hands spouting long, pious phrases.'' Williams also quoted the American Youth Commission reports which indicated that one-third of all unemployed in the nation, about 4 million, were among young Americans 10–25 years of age.

Reeves also participated on a panel in an institute conducted by the Congress, as did President and Mrs. Roosevelt; James Carey, President of the United Electrical Radio and Machine Workers of America, Attorney General Jackson, Senator James Murray, John L. Lewis, President of the Congress of Industrial Organizations, and others. Reeves's speech was reported under the heading, ''A Generation Cannot Wait.'' In addition to pointing out publicly the basic compatibility of the interests of the Congres and the AYC, Reeves reiterated the critical need for jobs for youth.

> The American Youth Commission does not believe that American youth is asking for a handout . . . As I examine the basic principles that this Congress has been standing for, and I look at the recommendations of the American Youth Commission, with reference to jobs, with reference to health, with reference to recreation and with reference to education, I realize the fact that basically the things you are asking for are the same things that the American Youth Commission has been asking. The American Youth Commission has said that it believed that there should be no out-of-school unemployed youth, and it has asked that until private enterprise finds out the way and provides the opportunity for youth that government must provide opportunities for youth to have jobs. Now the Commission isn't stopping there . . . Youth cannot wait. This generation cannot wait. They must have an opportunity for jobs, an opportunity for education, an opportunity for health. For those youths who want jobs and need jobs they should have jobs.

Mrs. Roosevelt on the same occasion fielded open questions from the group under a title given in the report as ''Youth Becomes Professor Quiz.'' She frankly commented on a wide variety of queries including the Russian invasion of Finland; the passage of the ''American Youth Act,'' (the administration's program for putting unemployed to work) and on the question of how we can ''prevent the United States from being drawn into war.'' Her remarks included defense of Aubrey Williams's release of names of NYA personnel to the Army recruiters (which did not include the right to solicit on projects); of the President's preparations for possible involvement in the war and other remarks which were not wholly satisfactory to the youths. In closing she said:

> Now having told you honestly what I think on many things, I want to congratulate you on your fairness, on your ability to listen to other points of view. I want to urge upon you in the future that you always try to have all points of view presented because they will make your decisions much more important . . . I have every respect for the interest and sacrifices all of you have made. I am very, very fond of many of your leaders and I am sure I would like to know all of you personally. I can't do that, but I hope that you will carry back into your community the determination to know the conditions of your community, to get the organizations together that can improve that community.

Washington Youth Council

Reeves was invited to participate in 1939 and 1940 in several meetings of the Washington Youth Council, which was affiliated with the American Youth Congress, and to serve with Mrs. Roosevelt on the Adult Advisory Board of the Council. He served as the opening speaker in a major conference on January 20, 1940 which was based on discussion of the recommendations of the American Youth Commission which paralleled those of the Advisory Committee on Education. The press release from the Commission on his speech showed a very uncharacteristic criticism of the President for back-tracking on his earlier concurrence with the previously described recommendations of the Advisory Committee on Education for a six-year program of increased expenditure of the federal government to "close the gap in the standard of education (and for health programs) between the richest communities and the poorest communities, not in any way by decreasing the facilities of the richer communities but by extending aid to the less fortunate."

Reeves went on to emphasize that there are three major steps that are necessary if education, and probably other social services, are to be placed upon a sound basis of finance and administration: first, the amalgamation of small school districts must be vigorously pushed; second, some states must increase their aid to local school districts and other states must distribute their present state-aid funds in a manner much more nearly designed to reduce the educational inequalities that result from the lack of taxable resources in many parts of many states; and third, as the White House conference itself agreed, federal aid to the states for educational purposes, safeguarded against federal interference, is essential.

Reeves also cooperated with the leaders of the Washington Youth Council in a variety of activities, which were organized by committees of youths and youth serving organizations convened by Mrs. Roosevelt at the White House. By 1941, however, as he became more directly involved in the National Defense Advisory Commission and possibly in the changes of leadership in the youth movements, he resigned his membership on the Adult Advisory Committee of the Council in a letter dated November 8, 1941 to Anne Gordon, Secretary of the Council:

> I have given careful consideration to the request in your letter of November 5 that I permit my name to be used in the list of sponsors for the annual convention of the Washington Youth Council, I have decided that I do not want my name to be so used. My reason for this decision is the relationship that appears to exist between the Washington Youth Council and the American Youth Congress. I have no faith in the direction of the American Youth Congress, and this naturally raises a question in my mind concerning the Washington Youth Council. I herewith tender my resignation as a member of the Adult Advisory Committee of the Washington Youth Council.[14]

Reeves—Mrs. Roosevelt—White House and Youth Activities[15]

The relationships and friendships of Mrs. Roosevelt and Reeves centered on their mutual interest in youth in 1933 but was most active from 1939 to 1946. As their relationship developed Reeves became in a sense an unofficial consultant and "staff" to Mrs. Roosevelt although there was no formal relationship. A brief record of the most important meetings and correspondence on youth problems on which they collaborated during 1934–46 includes:

- Several references to private lunches with Reeves and other meetings at the White House with leaders of youth serving agencies (such as Boy and Girl Scouts, YMCA, Jewish Welfare Board, C10 and others) to plan agenda and for conferences of youth. With references to planning one such conference, Mrs. Roosevelt said: "If enough people wish to discuss Communism in the youth led group we might limit their part of the discussion to a half hour. I will tell Dr. Reeves that I am amenable to any change, and if he will draw up an agenda, I will attempt to follow it closely."

- Reference to a full-day conference at the White House presided over by Mrs. Roosevelt. Reeves made a presentation on "Youth and Jobs," prepared a statement of conclusions of the conference leaders of youth serving agencies and appeared with Mrs. Roosevelt on several programs of organizations of youth following the conference.
- References to correspondence between Mrs. Roosevelt and Reeves regarding the publications of the AYC, and of the work of the Office of Civilian Defense—in which she served as Assistant Director and Reeves as a member of the Executive Committee at Mrs. Roosevelt's request.
- Reference to a copy of a letter from Mrs. Roosevelt to Reeves when she represented the United States at the United Nations General Assembly in 1946. She invited Reeves to come to Hyde Park for a luncheon discussion over the weekend.

Mrs. Roosevelt also had meetings with Reeves, McCloskey (staff associate in the AYC) and with Aubrey Williams and referred to Reeves in at least two issues of her "My Day." Joseph Lash in his "*Love Eleanor*" also refers to a weekend gathering at Campobella to discuss youth problems which included Mr. and Mrs. Archibald McLeish, Justice Frankfurter, Dr. and Mrs. David Levy, Mrs. Albert Lasker, Mrs. Morgenthau, James Roosevelt, Aubrey Williams and Reeves.

White House Conference on "Children in a Democracy"[16]

Floyd Reeves participated actively in the planning, reporting and follow-up activities of the White House Conference on "Children in a Democracy." He considered it essential that the cooperation between the AYC and the Conference be developed and accepted responsibility for pulling together the viewpoints of the more than six hundred conference participants who came from all states of the union and from numerous youth serving educational and religious and community organizations.

The key planners of the conference—Secretary Perkins and Miss Katherine Lenroot, Head of the Children's Bureau of the Department of Labor, recognized the relevant background of Reeves for a key role in the White House Conference. His close association with Mrs.

Roosevelt on the NYA, student organizations, CCC and other action agencies related to youth were also known to Secretary Perkins and Miss Lenroot. The availability of the comprehensive studies of the AYC on youth problems (which were frequently cited in the Conference planning sessions) led the Conference Planning Committee to conclude that additional studies were not needed, but that emphasis should be given to interpreting the meaning and implications of these data as a basis for designing an action program.

The initial session of the Conference was officially opened by President Roosevelt on April 26, 1939. He made a characteristically stirring speech.

> In providing for the health and education of children, for the formation of their minds and characters in ways which are in harmony with the institutions of a free society, democracy is training its future leaders. The safety of democracy therefore depends upon the widespread diffusion of opportunities for developing those qualities of mind and character which are essential to leadership in our modern age . . . The success of democratic institutions is measured, not by the extent of territory, financial power, machines or armaments, but by the desires, the hopes, the deep-lying satisfaction of the individual men, women and children who make up its citizenship . . .

After a few other opening speeches including a "folksy" speech by Mrs. Roosevelt on Children and the Future, Reeves as chairman of the Committee on Report, specified the tasks of the Conference: (1) to determine and define minimum needs for the suitable rearing of children to be adequate citizens of the American democracy; (2) to measure the extent to which these services are now being actually rendered and where they fall short in volume, quality or distribution; (3) to find out the causes for such shortcomings as may be found, and (4) to ascertain and recommend how such causes can be removed, and how suitable provision for child health, training, and development may be adopted to every type of condition and circumstance, and be effective for every child in the United States.

Four sectional discussion meetings were held—one of which (Section 4) was attended by Reeves on "The Child and Community Services for Health, Education and Social Protection."

In the discussion of this section Reeves was called upon to make a few observations, in which he said:

> It seems that we have available in the field of education a wealth of information that goes beyond anything we have ever had before. It can

> give us a picture of the situation as it exists in all parts of our commonwealth. We have the facts. We know what the educational picture is; we know what the obstacles are that are standing in the way of a sound program of education.
>
> This is a group set up in an ideal manner, it seems to me, to attack that problem and to look at the entire situation with reference to children in a democracy; to utilize the results of these expensive studies that have been made in the several fields and to propose a program of action.

At a dinner session devoted to reports of the four sections and general discussion of particular interest to legislative follow-up on the work of the President's Advisory Committee on Education, George F. Zook, former U.S. Commissioner of Education and President of ACE and Frank Graham, President of the University of North Carolina made confirming remarks about Reeves's observations.

At the first general session of the Conference—after appropriate opening statements by the Secretary of Labor, the Chairman of the Conference and the Chairman of the Reports Committee, were five statements by members of the Planning and Reports Committee, including one by Reeves. The purpose of these reports was to highlight some of the major points which were included in the General Report which was formally adopted on January 19, the second day of the Conference.

Reeves reiterated the familiar themes and major conclusions reached by the AYC and Advisory Committee on the problems and needs of youth. The net effects of Reeves's report was to provide specificity to the conference findings and to give him an additional large audience of educational, business and community leaders to implement the findings of the conference and thus improve the opportunities for youth about which he felt so deeply.

Further sessions on January 18, 19 and 20 were devoted to major speeches by President and Mrs. Roosevelt, Paul V. McNutt, Federal Security Administration and others. More significantly, perhaps, were section by section discussions of the General Report and its ultimate adoption and to translating the conference report into action. An eight-five page General Report[17] covered topics already referred to plus additional sections on Public Administration and Financing, Government by the People and Call to Action. A brief report of twenty-six pages covering only the final "Recommendations"[18] was also published for even wider distribution.

Involvement in Further Follow-up on the Conference

A press release issued by the National Citizens Committee of the White House Conference on Children in a Democracy, headed by Marshall Field, was issued on January 8, 1942. The recommendations of the White House Conference and the AYC were interrelated with the added consideration of the effects of the war and post-war adjustments of children and youth. In the words of the press release, "The reports in the main deal with different age groups but since the welfare of children and youth are closely related cooperative action furthering public consideration of these two most important long-range programs seem both logical and imperative. They represent, we believe, recommendations which can prove of greatest value in avoiding much of the disruption which war-time activities might otherwise produce." Floyd Reeves was named as Chairman of the National Citizens Committee, the membership of which included several of Reeves's colleagues in the AYC plus Marshall Field and a few other civic and educational leaders.

Katherine Lenroot, Chief of the Childrens' Bureau, U.S. Department of Labor, also requested Reeves to be a member of the "Childrens' Bureau Advisory Committee on Children in Wartime"—which he agreed to do.

Some years later Reeves, in what appeared to be lecture notes which he left in the MSU Archives, containing undated reflections on the five major reports of projects which he directed which were concerned with children and youth.

> I am considering taking these five basic reports and comparing them in detail (with) all aspects of the present "Great Society" program of President Johnson's and pointing out that during the quarter of a century since these reports were made about half of the recommendations have been adopted . . . and all of the remaining recommendations are now included in one form or another in the "Great Society" program. Either I or President Johnson or some key man in his administration such as McGeorge Bunday might write a foreword for this document. If that is done the entire document could be written in the third person entirely from published reports. I estimate that this could be published in a book of about 300 pages in length.[19]

It is regrettable that the history of these significant landmarks of concern for the problems and needs of youth has not yet been written but perhaps this account will, at least, remind its readers of these water shed efforts to enhance the availability of educational and economic opportunities for youth.

Reeves was somewhat harassed by several newspapers, particularly *The Chicago Tribune* for his liberal views and advocacy of expanded federal programs for education and youth activities but he was cleared of allegations regarding Communist connections, as evidenced by approval of his appointment to serve as a consultant to the U.S. Atomic Energy Commission, which required security clearance.

Chapter V

Activities to Reduce Discrimination and Expand Educational Opportunities

Floyd Reeves's deep interest in expanding educational opportunities for youth and for those who are discriminated against for reasons of race, religion, and national origin was expressed in a number of activities, particularly during the nineteen forties and fifties. The basis for his involvement in a variety of practical measures to widen educational opportunity and to diminish discriminatory policies and practices was laid in activities described earlier. His motivation derived in part from early poignant experiences with discriminatory attitudes and actions against Indians and Negroes, as will be indicated in the following excerpts from insights which he described in his later years.[1] Later on he expanded his understanding of and sympathies for all manner of discriminatory practices affecting all persons of different ethnic, social, religious and economic backgrounds who were not part of the "WASP" culture. He affiliated himself with committees of colleagues at the University of Chicago; engaged in activities of the American Federation of Teachers; and served as Chairman of the American Council on Education's Committee on Discrimination—all of which were dedicated to eliminating or diminishing discriminatory policies and practices. Reeves also served on the Boards of Trustees of Howard and Roosevelt Universities, which opened their doors to students who may not have had as good an opportunity to demonstrate their capacities to learn as might otherwise have been the case.

Basic Motivation in His Early Life[1]

The earlier years of my life were spent in close contact with the Crow and Sioux American Indians. Two or three years before my birth in 1890 the Battle of Wounded Knee took place in the Badlands of South Dakota which was a part of the Indian territory where my father ranged several hundred head of cattle and horses. Discriminating against Indians during my childhood was very great. Aside from members of my own family all white children and adults with whom I associated were frequently heard to say, "The only good Indian is a dead Indian."

When I was ten years old my parents moved to a ranch farther north near Gann Valley . . . During the two-year period that we lived on this ranch, a regular stopping place of Indians traveling from one reservation to another was a valley on our ranch with a flowing spring. Here I associated with Indian children, accepted their hospitality of delicious food made from a mixture of dried powered Indian turnips and well fattened puppy dogs.

There was a deserted one room school building about five miles from our house which was used by the White Protestant ranchers and their employees for Sunday church services. One Sunday our visiting pastor was a Methodist Negro who my grandmother . . . told me was a highly educated man and a graduate of a Methodist Seminary associated with Northwestern University. This is the first Negro that I had ever seen. I remember nothing of his sermon but I do remember that following his sermon he shook hands with everyone including the children. I recall looking at my hand to see if the black had rubbed off from his hand and asking my mother why some people were Black and others White . . . When we returned home she found a passage in the Bible which made it clear to her that Negroes were the descendants from Cain, the dark-skinned son of Adam who had murdered his light-skinned brother Able with the result that he was banished to Africa.

The next Negro, whose name was Abbot, I met when I was twenty years old and a senior in high school . . . He held the state high school record in the mile run. I met him again during my senior year at college. I was captain of a debating team that went from Huron College to South Dakota State College at Brookings to compete for the state championships in debating. On the way from my hotel to the College and where the debate was to be held I decided to get a shoe shine. I recognized that man who shined my shoes as Abbot, the long distance runner who was working his way through college. Abbot was the only Negro on the College football team, basketball team, and the baseball team. In fact, he was the only Negro attending State College. He was captain of all three teams and undoubtedly the greatest athlete in the state at that time . . . When he graduated from college, he became athletic director at what was then

> Wilbur Force, then a private school for Negroes in southern Ohio.
>
> In 1923 I went to Transylvania University at Lexington, Kentucky, the oldest university in the United States west of the Allegheny Mountains. There I learned a number of things that I had not known before. A Negro man must be addressed either by his first name or as "boy" unless by chance he might have some kind of doctor's degree where he might be addressed as doctor. A Negro woman must be addressed by her first name. Under no conditions must a Negro be addressed as Mr. or Mrs.

The first organized effort in which Reeves actively participated to diminish discriminatory policies and practices began with his cooperation in a Chicago School System and University of Chicago collaborative effort. Largely under the active leadership of Herold C. Hunt, Superintendent of the Chicago Public Schools, and Louis Wirth, a distinguished sociologist, and several other senior members of the faculty and Reeves, sustained attention was given over several years (1948–52) to the problems broadly associated with the assimilation of Negroes and other minorities in the public school system. The program involved studies, research and seminars on policies and practices related to such aspects of the problem as: teacher attitudes and behaviors toward minorities; specific discriminatory policies and practices; application of the merit system to salaries, promotions, transfers and other personnel actions without reference to race, religion or nationality; school boundaries; and needs for revision of curricula and teaching materials to foster integration. Reeves's principal contribution to the research and seminars was as an active member of the University's Technical Committee on Education, Training, and Research. The University also had a Center for the Study of Intergroup Relations funded for five years by the National Conference of Christians and Jews. In addition to the seminars for teachers, conferences were held with the Citizens Advisory Committee of the Chicago Public Schools.

American Federation of Teachers (AFT)

Reeves was an active member of Local 255 of the American Federation of Teachers from some time in the late 1930's until June 1941 when he resigned from the local union and became a "member at large." He declined to run for election as Vice President and a member of the Council in 1940 when he became Director of Labor Supply in the Department of Defense under Sidney Hillman, a prominent labor leader. He renewed his membership in the union after completion of his work with the Department of Defense. The letterhead of the AFT summarized their purpose as: "Democracy in Education—Education for Democracy."

For nine to ten years, Reeves found his association with the AFT supportive for his interests in expanding educational opportunities for economically and otherwise disadvantaged youth as previously described in the recommendations of President Roosevelt's Advisory Committee on Education; and in the work of the American Youth Commission and the NYA. Reeves was in great demand as a speaker and conference leader with unions on the recommendations of the organizations indicated above. For example, he was asked to speak to the National Education Policies Committee of the union in these words: "The main item of business will be a reappraisal of the work of the Advisory Committee in light of recent events. All of us want to learn from you concerning developments in Washington and throughout the country as you see them from your vantage point." He declined many invitations to speak because of his many other activities and responsibilities at the University and elsewhere. He also addressed the 1946, 1947 and 1948 annual conferences of the union. After the 1946 annual meeting, the secretary-treasurer wrote Reeves as follows: "Allow me to thank you most sincerely for your address at the annual convention of the AFT in St. Paul last week. The program was one of the best in the history of AFT and we sincerely appreciate your splendid contribution of the program."

The union's publication, *American Teacher*, provided Reeves several opportunities to publish articles on his research and views on the current educational issues. In fact the editor of the *American Teacher* urged him to prepare an article on federal aid to education in these words: ". . . I hope you realize that it would be a minor tragedy to publish this issue without at least a short statement from you on the whole problem of federal aid." Reeves contributed four articles during the years 1943–46 on "Schools and Manpower," "Demobilization and Readjustment," "Senate Bill 717" and "Current Educational Problems and Work of the AFT's Commission on Educational Reconstruction." The journal also carried articles by other educational and public affairs leaders such as William Heard Kilpatrick, Paul Hanna, Robert Lynd, Franz Boaz, Robert Morse Lovett, Colston Warne, Ernest O. Melby, George Axtelle and Mike Mansfield. The AFT also published and gave wide distribution to brochures on topics which were also treated in the *American Teacher*.

The union campaigned for the passage of Senate Bill 717 to implement the recommendations of the Advisory Committee on Education, which bill was strongly supported by Reeves.

AFT Commission on Educational Reconstruction

The activity of greatest interest and involvement was the Federation's Commission on Educational Reconstruction which Reeves chaired. The members of the Commission included prominent educators such as Robert Weaver.

The Commission at its first meeting concluded that "the function of the Commission was to furnish leadership to the AFT rather than to follow it, but it was also a policy-forming body designed to influence the action of the AFT, the American Federation of Labor (AFL) and the public." Further on in the same meeting Reeves was reported to have said, "I raised the question three years ago as to whether we might formulate statements of policy which might or might not accord with the official position of the AFT. We must now think it through."

After discussion of the issue of relationships of the Commission to the AFT and the AFL, Reeves summarized the discussion as follows:

> It would be wisdom on the Commission's part to act responsibly. The function of the Commission is to increase the knowledge and effectiveness of the AFT . . . As a Commission, we have freedom of expression and we are free to deal with any problem (as) we see fit. As individual members we also have freedom of expression but as a responsible Commission we should very carefully consider whether we should lay our findings before the Council, the convention or interim statements to the public. We should be guided by the opinions of the Council . . . The Commission favors joint meetings from time-to-time with the AFL Messrs. Green, Meany and Woll and with other groups if desirable.

The archival records suggest no major problem in pursuing the policy of basic independence of expression but with an operating mode of consultation with groups having wider responsibility for union policies and positions on controversial issues. Unresolved differences of opinion were reflected in the publications of the Commission. Reeves took this position in all of the committees or commissions which he chaired or directed—which was a source of his leadership and effectiveness.

The members of the Commission discussed the pros and cons of many possible topics or potential areas of study, including the following: federal legislation for support of education, universal military training, international relations, mental health, merit rating related to teachers salaries, democracy in and for the teaching profession, loyalty tests, the relation of civil rights to totalitarian governments and several similar subjects. One of the most controversial policies on which the Commission made a daring policy pronouncement concerned teacher membership in the Communist Party at a time when "McCarthyism" was rampant:

> The Commission on Educational Reconstruction of the American Federation of Teachers believes that membership in the Communist Party is not compatible with service in the educational system of the United States. It holds that we misconceive the real nature of the Communist movement in this country when we regard it as a political party organized in accordance with the principles inherent in the democratic system of government. The Communist Party has demonstrated by its deeds over a period of years that it functions as a disciplined and conspiratorial agency to advance the interests and the policies of the Soviet Union . . .
>
> The Commission recognizes the right and the obligation of our government at this time to take due steps to assure itself of the loyalty of those engaged in public service, including education. It believes, however, that the public interest as well as justice to individuals requires that all such investigations be undertaken with real regard for the high values at stake, and under procedures that will adequately safeguard he rights of individuals . . .

Reeves, in a long-hand note, in his personal copy of the statement, refers to a book by Sidney Hook, who expressed the belief that this was the first published statement by any national education association expressing "opposition to employing or retaining Communists in educational positions."

Pamphlets on "Federal Aid and the Crisis in American Education" and "To Provide for the Common Defense" and a small book on "Goals for American Education" illustrate the nature of the Commission's work. In the Foreword to the pamphlet on Federal Aid, Reeves reported on the work of the Commission in preparing the pamphlet as follows:

> After three years of most careful consideration of all aspects of federal aid to education and services for children the Commission on Education Reconstruction of the AFT has by unanimous vote adopted this report. After thirty-six months of deliberation, however, the areas of disagree-

> ment have been narrowed down to three specific points which, in my opinion, are relatively minor in relation to the very great importance of finding ways and means through which the federal government may assist the states in providing an adequate program of education and welfare services for children and youth.

The minor dissents were published along with the full Commission report.

Another pamphlet by three members of the Commission, including Reeves, was focused on the hotly contested issues related to preparations for war. The title of the pamphlet was "To Provide for the Common Defense." Topics treated included: The Darkening Prospect; False Roads to Peace: Appeasement. Let Europe Go; The Big Stick; Foreign Policy as the First Line of National Security; Domestic Policy and Security; Military Policy; For the Education of the Young—Health, Recreation, Work-study Projects and Travel.

The concluding statement of this Commission report affirmed that:

> The critical state of the world and the complexity of our problems allow of no simple solution. American democracy is being tested as never before in our history, and to meet this test we will need all the strength we can call forth. But it must be a strength appropriate to the need. The simple conception of national defense in narrow and traditional military terms can serve only to lull us into a false sense of security. The safety of our country—and of democracy throughout the world—demands a sweeping and comprehensive defense, on many fronts. It calls for a firm, consistent and principled foreign policy; for a domestic program that will assure us of economic stability and remove the discriminatory practices that divide and weaken us as a people; for a highly trained and mobile fighting force designed for modern warfare; and, above all, for an educational system that will give all our children an abiding belief in democracy and the willingness and ability to defend it—physically, morally, and intellectually. In the final test we can only defend what we understand and deeply cherish.

The major publication of the Commission was a book on *Goals for American Education* authored by Lester A. Kirkendall, Irvin D. Kuenzli and Floyd Reeves published in 1948. Reeves wrote the Preface and contributed, as one of the authors to the final product, which included six chapters headed as follows: The World We Face, Goals for American Education, The American School System, Major Deficiencies in American Education, A Program for American Education, and Can We Afford the Program. Examples of major deficiencies cited were:

- Lack of democratic administration of schools which has contributed to making teaching an unattractive profession. "One of the most unethical and undemocratic of all procedures—a procedure followed in many schools from coast to coast is that of bringing pressure upon teachers to join teachers organizations not of their own choosing."
- "Curricula and methods have failed to keep pace with demands of times." Among specifics the following were mentioned: failure to include subjects which would aid students to meet the tempo of modern life; prevention of aggression through sanctions of international law; and failure to incorporate psychological studies of human behavior.
- "The present system of school district organization is confused, wasteful and inefficient"—110,000 local school districts."
- "A majority of state departments of education are politically controlled and many of them are hotbeds of intrigue and favoritism. Appointments are often made in response to political pressures without regard to the best interests of the school system and the welfare of children."
- And, of course, low salaries, restrictions and lack of appreciation of the problems of teachers.

Some of the farsighted correctives to the deficiencies follow:

- The American educational system must be democratic in its organization and practices . . . The teachers should be organized, and should select representatives to negotiate with the administrative officers. The teachers should have the right to approve, disapprove or support modifications of policy recommendations by the superintendents and to advance policies desired by the teaching staff . . . In any democratically organized school, teachers should always have direct access to the board so that the faculty viewpoint may be presented directly to the board on important matters of educational policy on which the faculty and administration cannot agree.
- The schools and community should develop an interacting relationship of mutual value . . . The community should be used as a laboratory for social sciences, vocational agriculture, home making and other courses.
- The curriculum must be carefully organized to embody important objectives for which American democracy is striving.
- Modernization of the curricula of teachers colleges.

- Personnel policies should be improved in order to strengthen the educational profession and to build a stronger morale among teachers." Specifics included: "Salaries for men and women teachers should be equal when the work is of an identical or equivalent nature; sex, marital status and religious affiliation should never be factors in the selection, promotion and retention of teachers."

Similar progressive recommendations were made with reference to buildings and equipment, financial support, reorganization of school administrative units and other areas.

The report was given wide publicity capped by a highly positive appraisal by the educational reporter of *The New York Times*, and many inquiries and requests for copies from many schools and interested persons throughout the United States. The Japanese Teachers Union ordered 20,000 copies. The book was also reviewed very favorably by the International Bureau of Education in Geneva, Switzerland and many other journals. The impact was widespread and was a high tribute to Reeves's leadership of the Commission.

American Council on Education (ACE)

Reeves accepted the Chairmanship of the American Council on Education's Committee on Discrimination in Higher Education on September 3, 1948. The President of the ACE was George F. Zook, a colleague of many years with whom Reeves had worked on several surveys of colleges and universities in the American Youth Commission and other organizations. The Chairman of the Executive Committee of the ACE at that time was James B. Conant. Members of the ACE Committee on Discrimination included Arthur Adams and Francis J. Brown, officials of the ACE; and Professors Kenneth Benne, University of Illinois; R. Fred Thomason, University of Tennessee; Karl Bigelow, Columbia University; and Irvin Kuenzil from the Anti Defamation League. Reeves resigned after five years as chairman when he left the University of Chicago to become consultant to John A. Hannah, President of Michigan State University. He was succeeded as Chairman by Algo Henderson who had served as Reeves Associate Director of Studies for the State of New York Temporary Commission for a State University.

Major funding of the work of the Committee was provided by the

Anti-Defamation League (ADL) of the B'nai B'rith. Key officials of the ADL actively participated in the work of the Committee but the ACE was fully responsible for the policies, activities and recommendations of the Committee. Reeves encouraged wide participation and cooperation but was highly sensitive, as was the ACE to keeping lines of authority straight and responsible.

In order to get a factual basis for their deliberations the Committee, early on, engaged the Elmo Roper organization to make an extensive study of seventeen thousand high school seniors including over five thousand high school graduates from all over the country. The study, entitled "On Getting into College," provided data on such questions as to how far admissions to colleges were being controlled, consciously or otherwise, by the tested interests and aptitudes of the candidates rather than by such personal and social factors as sex, age, family background, religious affiliation, interest in extra curricular activities and the like.

A later survey by the Roper organization on discriminatory practices in admission to graduate and professional schools also provided important data for review and use by the Committee.

The first national conference on discrimination sponsored by the Committee was held in Chicago on November 4–5, 1949, attended by nineteen college and university presidents, twenty-four college and university deans and registrars, and representatives from public school systems, and government agencies. The problems addressed included: admission procedures in undergraduate, graduate and professional academic programs, regional problems and economic factors. The conference was divided up into four sections in terms of the problems indicated above—each of which reported their findings and recommendations separately but was reviewed by the whole conference in plenary sessions. The reports were adopted unanimously.

Conferees were supplied with studies and reports which were published by four agencies which had made extensive studies of barriers experienced by youth who desired to secure a higher education as follows: President's Commission on Higher Education; the New York State Commission on the Need for a State University, for which Reeves served as Director of Studies; report of the Connecticut State Inter-Racial Commission; and the ACE's own report on Discrimination in College Admissions.

Reeves was designated to be the opening speaker with responsibility for summarizing the findings of the above studies in terms of basic questions, covering such subjects as the extent to which: (1) restructured curriculums constituted barriers to youth desiring to secure higher education in certain fields; (2) geographic barriers which stood in the way of college admissions; (3) policies and actions of admissions officers which were discriminatory; (4) race, religion or national origins which were barriers to admission; and (5) types of control of public or private colleges and universities which were related to discriminatory admission policies and practices.

Reeves then went on systematically, in twenty-seven double-spaced pages, to summarize and to interrelate the findings of each of the four basic studies. For example, with reference to the criteria for selection he reported that:

> The President's Commission found that most colleges tend to select as their special clientele those persons who possess verbal aptitudes and a capacity for grasping instructions; they tend, on the other hand, to neglect the development of youth with other aptitudes of great social importance such as social sensitivity and versatility, artistic ability, motor skill and dexterity, and mechanical aptitude and ingenuity.
>
> In New York state the greatest shortage of educational facilities was found to be that of facilities for both general education and technical training for youth who either did not desire or did not need four years of college, but who could profit by one or two years of general education and technical training beyond the high school level.

With reference to the relationship of financial resources to college attendance Reeves cited several studies as follows:

> One investigation . . . shows that the probability is between two and three times as great that a high school graduate will attend college if his father is engaged in a professional or managerial occupation than if he is a farmer or an unskilled worker. A second investigation, reported by the President's Commission . . . showed that in families in which the father's occupation was "professional-technical," 12 out of 13 children advanced beyond the eighth grade, where as in the "unskilled-labor" category only 1 child out of 3 advanced beyond this grade.

As to discriminatory admission practices the following excerpts from a New York study were cited:

- Of the 206 private non-sectarian schools and colleges in New York reporting, some of which were separate institutions and others parts of universities, 7 institutions stated that the admission of students was restricted on the basis of race, and 18 stated that students were restricted on the basis of creed. From other information secured in this study, however, it appears almost certain that many more schools and colleges in New York actually restricted admissions on the basis of race or creed or both than the number that reported such practices.

With reference to the further extend of discriminatory practices, including quota systems, Reeves brought the following data to the attention of the conferees:

- A total of twenty-four schools and colleges in New York stated that they placed some restrictions on the admission of Negroes, Jews, Catholics, or Protestants. Of these, three Catholic, 2 Protestant, and 2 non-sectarian institutions reported restrictions on the enrollment of Negroes; 11 Catholic, 1 Protestant, and 6 non-sectarian institutions reported restrictions on the enrollment of Jews; 1 Protestant and 7 non-sectarian institutions reported restrictions on the enrollment of Catholics; and 11 Catholic and 5 non-sectarian institutions reported restrictions were in the form of quotas and others represented complete exclusion of all members of a particular group.
- The New York Study also reported that some institutions asked the applicant directly about his racial, religious, or national origin background; others obtained this kind of information indirectly by asking questions about the applicant's nationality, race, birth place or parents, or mother's maiden name, or by requesting a photograph. The mother's maiden name or the birth place of the parents sometimes serves to identify the applicant's national origin or to give a clue as to his religious affiliation.

The situation with reference to discrimination specifically of Negroes was reported by Reeves in this excerpt from his summary:

> The problem of discrimination against Negroes at the undergraduate level is largely a regional problem. The President's Commission points out that in Southern states having segregation in higher education facilities, so-called "separate and equal" education for whites and Negroes does not actually exist. The report states that "Whether one considers enrollment, overall costs per student, teachers' salaries, transportation facilities, availability of secondary schools, or opportunities for undergraduate and graduate study, the consequences of segregation were always the same, and always adverse to the Negro citizen . . . A major factor limiting the training of Negro doctors is the practice of barring

> Negro students from clinical facilities. This takes place even in tax-supported hospitals in the North.
>
> The New York Study further showed that less than 50 Negroes were graduated from the five New York City medical schools during the entire twenty-five year period from 1920 to 1945. In the fall of 1946, there were only 15 Negroes enrolled in these five schools.

Reeves summarized his remarks and pointed out the need for further detailed studies to document the varied policies and practices of discrimination as a basis for designing and implementing corrective actions.

A Statement of Policy was adopted unanimously by the Conference:

> All institutions of higher learning should re-examine their philosophies in the light of the dignity of every human being, and his right to equality of educational opportunity, and make sure that the procedures instituted in their admissions programs are administered in such a way that the specific human worth and the dignity of no individual are violated because of his membership in any cultural, racial or socio-economic group. It is never justifiable in our democratic society to discriminate against an individual for any reason which minimizes his stature as a member of the human family.

These excerpts are quoted at some length since they became the hard core of factual material considered in subsequent conferences.

In accord with Reeves's recommendation that grass roots deliberations were essential to positive actions on the findings, three regional conferences were held in 1950 and 1951 as follows: (1) The East coast conference was attended by eighty-five educators and students from twenty-eight institutions in Virginia, Maryland, Delaware and the District of Columbia. (2) The Middle West conference was attended by 170 educators from seventy-five institutions in Illinois, Indiana, Wisconsin and Michigan assembled for a second conference in Chicago. (3) In the Mountain States eight representatives from fourteen colleges and universities in Colorado, New Mexico and Utah convened at the University of Denver with particular focus on "quota systems."

Discrimination in Medical and Other Professional Schools

A subcommittee of the American Council's overall committee on discrimination focused on discrimination in medical and other professional schools. Reeves met with the subcommittee and helped it plan the conference, which was attended by medical school administrators and administrative officials of other professional schools. Dr. Kenneth D. Beene, a member of this subcommittee described what happened in a letter to the author:

> I was impressed both by Reeves's ideas about strategy of changing practice and by his effective way of directing committee work. He managed to help the committee maintain direction and yet supported all members in the expression of their views. I had expected Robert Hutchins to be the idea man on the committee but Reeves excelled him by far. Incidentally, Hutchins had a high respect for Reeves, as, indeed, all committee members came to have.
>
> It was Reeves' idea to get deans into our conferences, along with admission officers and faculty chairmen of admissions committees. This proved effective, since the deans, in most institutions were in positions of power with respect to admissions policies.
>
> We built the conferences around data from ADL and other studies of admissions practices and policies and encouraged participants to go home and do their own self-surveys. We did little preaching but did talk about the consequences of barring able brains from training and education. Incidentally, the roots of discrimination in prejudice as well as unexamined traditions were explored.
>
> The effects of the conferences were evident in some cases. Dr. Andrew Ivey, Dean of University of Illinois's medical school was genuinely shocked about the quotas which his admissions committee used and changed both committee and policy the day after his discovery.

Student Conferences

Earlham College was host to a conference of 230 students from ninety-five colleges and universities from twenty-seven states. The ACE Committee on Discrimination took special care in planning this conference to focus on students' interest in discrimination and to avoid other interests of students in other aspects of their collegiate life. Data on discriminatory practices revealed by the several studies already referred were made available to the conferees.

Reeves was the keynote speaker at the conference. Resolutions passed by the students were similar to the resolutions passed by other conferences but included some additional points of particular relevance to student affairs and organizations. For example, the preamble to the section on social, honorary and professional fraternities read as follows:

> The problem of discrimination and prejudices in student organizations are not isolated problems, but are aspects of the broader problems of interpersonal and inter-group relations. Any student organization creates poor human relations when . . . it places such high value on prestige and status which emphasized inequality between man rather than equality, resulting in disharmony and tensions in interpersonal relations. . . . The resolution continued: Its values become distorted to the extent that it places a high premium on the symbols of power and prestige such as high economic status, class, race, or appearance, thereby losing sight of the essential human values involved in respect for individual worth and dignity . . . This conference urges all student organizations in institutions of higher education to eliminate tacit or gentlemen's agreements restricting membership in these organizations.

The students stated about what they thought about interscholastic and intramural athletics in these words:

> This conferences opposes unsportsmanlike and discriminatory tactics in the field of athletics. Minority group players should enjoy nonsegregated housing, dressing rooms and eating facilities. Institutions should engage in athletic contests with only those schools which allow minority players to participate in the contests. A firm stand should be followed in awarding athletic scholarship, using athletic ability and scholastic ability as the only bases. Athletic groups which include minority participants should not be excluded from the use of off-campus athletic facilities.

With reference to faculty employment the students were equally forthright:

> All institutions of higher learning should institute a policy of nondiscrimination on the basis of race, religion, creed, national origin, sex or political views in the hiring, firing and promotion of faculty (except that sectarian schools may give preference on the basis of creed and religion) . . . The signing of loyalty oaths should not be used as a criterion for the hiring, firing or upgrading of faculty.

The students had this to say with reference to federal aid to education:

> This conference believes that in cases where there is federal aid to education, such aid should be given only to those states which do not

> discriminate on the basis of race, color, creed, national origin or religion (except for sectarian schools, which may give preference on the basis of sect) . . .

Resolutions of a similar tone and content were passed with reference to scholarships and loans, student employment, and facilities (owned and operated by institutions as well as those not controlled by the institutions).

The ACE printed the resolutions of the conference and made them available widely throughout the country. The records show a great deal of correspondence with Reeves on follow-up activities of the regional and student conferences. He attended many meetings and made numerous speeches before interested groups.

A partial summary of reports of the Committee on Discrimination, renamed the "Committee on Equality of Higher Education," for the period 1948–53 indicated the following accomplishments, for which much credit is due for the work of the ACE.

- Negroes had been admitted to graduate programs in Arkansas, Virginia, North Carolina, Tennessee, Texas and Louisiana—also to technical and professional schools in most of those states. No administrative problems have arisen by virtue of such admission of Negroes.
- The Municipal College for Negroes in Louisville, Kentucky was abolished in July 1951 as a separate institution to become part of the University of Louisville.
- Several junior colleges—particularly in West Texas have admitted Negroes on a completely non-segregated basis.
- The Texas Association of Colleges, which include Negro colleges in its membership and members, attend meetings on an unsegregated basis.
- The Commission on Colleges and Universities of the Southern Association of Colleges and Secondary Schools is restudying all of the Negro colleges and is applying the standards of the Association in the same way they are applied to all institutions.

Although these brief indications of progress are focused on southern institutions and only a few discriminatory practices, it is reasonable to believe that a complete inventory of changes in policy and practice would reveal many changes which we now know have occurred. The work of Reeves and his many colleagues in this vineyard have certainly paid large dividends and he received many tributes to his leadership.

But the letter from Arthur S. Adams, President of the American Council on Education, provides an impressive appraisal of Reeves's contribution to anti-discriminatory policies and practices in colleges and universities.

> You will understand, I am sure, my regret that you wish to relinquish the chairmanship of the Committee (on Discrimination); but I do understand your request and want you to know that I appreciate keenly the distinguished leadership which you have given this Committee. I earnestly hope that you will be willing to remain a member of the Committee, in order to bring the benefit of your own experience and wisdom to the group as it gives continuing consideration to its appropriate role . . .

Reeves's Membership on Boards of Trustees

Roosevelt University

Reeves was a member of the initial Board of Trustees of Roosevelt University in possibly its most critical year—1945–1946. The initial board was chaired by Edwin Embree of the Julius Rosenwald Fund and included Marshall Field and Lyle Spencer, who later created the Spencer Foundation, and several other prominent liberal Chicagoans. The College—later renamed Roosevelt University—epitomizes many of the values of extending opportunity to economically and socially disadvantaged youth and older persons which consumed much of Reeves' time and effort for many years of his professional life. The dedicatory address on November 16, 1945 by Mrs. Eleanor Roosevelt, which follows, sums up the mission of the College/University in clear and warmly human terms:

> It is a great pleasure to be here to dedicate Roosevelt College, which is a memorial to my husband, and which perpetuates the American ideal he and all other great Americans have supported and do support. The ideal is, of course, equality of opportunity for all, without regard to race, creed or color . . .
>
> I believe in Roosevelt College as an institution of learning for more than one reason. I believe in it first because its application forms do not ask students or faculty to state race or creed. I believe in it secondly, because of its democratic Board of Directors. On this board sit representatives of organized labor, management, cooperatives, the press, education, and the faculty of Roosevelt College itself.

> The faculty boasts—and I (use the word advisedly), a Negro scientist of great distinction, a Hindu philosopher, who is a friend of Mahatma Gandhi's, a Chinese-American, German refugees, and an Italian, Jewish, Catholic, and countless other religious groups are represented . . . Although some of the students are eighteen and nineteen, they represent a picture of an unusually adult group of people . . . The veterans, particularly, are being helped to get an education by this low cost, centrally located, yet fine institution of higher learning . . . They must work to earn a living . . . Roosevelt College, known as "an around the clock" college, makes it possible for them to work and to go to school at the same time.
>
> Roosevelt College was born in 1945 . . . a fitting year. For it was in 1945 that men who preached the myth of the super race, the men who believed in the divinity of their emperor . . . the men who called their neighbors "inferior" and democracy "decadent" . . . the men who built a vast structure upon a nationalism born of prejudice and hate . . . were ground to earth.
>
> And it was in 1945, too, even on the home front, men sought to destroy democracy by attempting to circumscribe it . . . by trying to limit education to a system of quotas and authoritarian rule.
>
> But knowledge is essentially democratic and universal. It knows no borders, boundaries, color, creed, or cultures.

Reeves felt obliged to resign from the Board when he accepted a major position with the North Central Association of Colleges and Schools in order to avoid a conflict of interest in determining accreditation for the University. The Board's resolution regarding his resignation documents his critical contribution to helping establish the University.[2]

Reeves continued his interest in the development of the University by participation in two major activities: (1) an effort by a federation of thirteen private and public colleges and universities and private and governmental coordinating bodies in Illinois to sort out objectives and possible areas of collaboration in which the President of Roosevelt University played a leading role, and (2) a reexamination, after twenty years, of the mission and program of the University in which Lyle Spencer, Philip Hauser and Ralph Tyler of the University of Chicago, Frank Bowles of the Ford Foundation and others participated. A brief statement of the mission of Roosevelt University reaffirmed the original objectives and missions so well described by Eleanor Roosevelt but took account of new problems which faced disadvantaged students.

Howard University

Reeves was a member of the Board of Trustees of Howard University and Vice Chairman of the Board from 1948 to 1964 and an honorary trustee thereafter until 1969. The University was predominantly an institution for Negroes during much of the time he was associated with it. The first major activity in which he engaged was to chair a special committee of the trustees to study the structure and organization of the University. Associated with him was Lloyd K. Garrison, a prominent liberal lawyer, and other distinguished trustees. After an examination of the somewhat glaring organizational and operational faults which had accumulated over time, Reeves and his committee made a number of major recommendations to improve the organization and operations of the Board.

At a meeting on June 7, 1963 Reeves was named to the Chairmanship of the Committee on Instruction and Research. The minutes of several meetings indicate that this Committee, which included the President and a few other top administrative officials as well as trustees, reviewed reports of deans and faculty of schools such as social work, engineering, medicine and others and reported back to the whole body of trustees their observations and recommendations, which included: a new freshman curriculum for the College of Medicine, a statute for patentable inventions, a new Ph.D. program for the graduate school, a policy for outside employment of teachers, and statements of aims and general purposes of the University.

A brief treatment of some aspects of policy as to aims of the University, with particular reference to its special responsibility for its major clientele, Negro students, is of special interest.

On March 31, 1960 the Council of the University Senate unanimously voted the following:

> The educational facilities and opportunities of this University should be primarily devoted to analysis and amelioration of the problems of the American Negro. This must remain our first objective for an indeterminate period . . . Thus the fundamental role of Howard University has been and remains the training of Negroes in scientific, medical, dental, engineering, legal and other professional and learned areas.

On April 26, 1961, President Nabrit, who argued the Negro position before the Supreme Court in Brown vs. the Board of Education, put the above policy in a somewhat broader context in his inaugural address:

To speak of Negro colleges or of an institution of higher education for Negroes in the United States in 1961 is to speak of an anachronism in a truly democratic society. But racial segregation and discrimination are also anachronistic in America and the one begets the other. The institution of segregation has been severely weakened but it has not been destroyed—racial discrimination has been restricted but it has not been eliminated.

The devastating effect of these twin evils upon the Negro people is so catastrophic that even if segregation were effectively ended today, if racial discrimination ceased completely and immediately, and all political, economic and educational leaders in the country whole-heartedly supported these actions, it would be fifty years at least before the crippling effects of the segregated system could be entirely alleviated.

It is to the everlasting credit of our Government that it has seen this, for it has sensed the critical importance of creating at least one center in America in which the primary purpose is searching for and salvaging valuable talents among the Negro people, talents which are vitally needed by the United States . . .

I would venture to suggest that Howard University is the only complex institution in higher education in America which, as a matter of policy, concerns itself with the handicaps and disabilities suffered by Negro students, as a consequence of being segregated by law or custom. If we must apologize for this anachronistic feature in higher education in America it must not be for the Negroes role in it, but it must be for an America which makes these institutions necessary.

My initial message to you, therefore, is that as we approach our 100th anniversary, we are still committed to the primary function conceived by our founders.

By January 22, 1963, when Reeves was Chairman of the Committee on Instruction and Research, the Committee recommended the following restatement of the aims and objectives of the Institution, retaining as it did its historical commitment to the education of Negro students, but broadened to include other disadvantaged students as well:

Howard University is committed to the philosophy of the publicly-supported university which holds that all persons, irrespective of race, creed, color, sex, religion or national origin, who are capable of successfully pursuing a higher education should be given the opportunity to do so.

Howard University is dedicated to the task of educating its students for a socially intelligent and a morally responsible life.

As a matter of history and tradition, Howard University accepts a special responsibility for the education of capable Negro students disadvantaged by the system of racial segregation and discrimination, and it will continue to do so as long as Negroes suffer these disabilities.

Howard University also accepts a special responsibility to make a continuous and comprehensive study of disadvantaged persons in American society, so as to contribute to the prevention, amelioration and removal of disabilities caused by race, color, or social, economic, or political circumstances, by (a) extending and intensifying its research efforts in the field of race and collateral areas, (b) helping its students as potential leaders and effective citizens to develop a basic understanding of and some critical intelligence in dealing with these problems, and (c) increasing its current efforts in the dissemination and preservation of knowledge in these special fields.

Chapter VI

International Activities: Philippines and Pakistan[1]

UNESCO Mission to the Philippines

Although Reeves was internationally oriented in his thinking and in making various recommendations regarding the need to foster knowledge of international affairs in educational curricula, his first assignment abroad was to head the "UNESCO Consultative Mission to the Philippines" in January 1948.[1] The mission was formally requested by the Government of the Republic of the Philippines. In addition to the primary purpose of the mission to examine the educational needs of the Republic of the Philippines and to suggest ways of meeting them, UNESCO was also interested in this first mission of its kind in providing valuable information that might be used by other nations in solving specific educational problems. These included literacy education, rural education, teacher education, information for planning and conducting future educational missions, and more generally to open up channels of communication between the Philippines and other member states.

The initial scope of the mission was to focus on administration, finance and elementary education, to which was added secondary education. The addition of secondary education was applauded by a UNESCO official, J. Guiton, who wrote to Reeves:

> We are all delighted by the good news that no one objected to including secondary education (excluding technical education) among the fields to

> be covered by the mission. May I congratulate you for this victory which I feel sure, is largely due to your diplomatic action.

The UNESCO team of consultants associated with Reeves included Paul Hanna, Professor of Education at Stanford University, Archie C. Lewis, Dean of the Ontario College of Education at the University of Toronto and Viriato Vargas Camacho, head of the Latin American Bureau of Education in Costa Rica. In addition, two Fulbright scholars and six professional Filipinos, all of whom had advanced degrees from United States universities, were members of the team. The United States State Department was also interested in the findings of the mission and in follow-up activities. The mission was funded by UNESCO for the salaries and travel of the consultants and by the Philippine Government for their housing, feeding and other local expenses. Reeves was paid $1500 per month, which under the University of Chicago salary policy, was returned to the University.

The record of policy and procedural orientation with Dr. Beeby, the UNESCO Director General for Education is interesting for insights into UNESCO strategy for missions of this character—with particular reference to use of the report outside of the country being surveyed. The highlights of Dr. Beeby's instructions on parts of the report:

> The report should comprise two distinct parts: a straight forward report on the general findings, both good and bad of the mission, which would be available for ultimate publication by UNESCO and an addendum to include criticisms and suggestions as to the institution and individuals, which would not be for publication. Division of the report thus would have the advantage of allaying any fears that might arise of publicity given to matters of concern only to the Philippines.

However, there is no evidence that the report as suggested contained two such parts. As was characteristic of Reeves's policy and practice, the findings were discussed with the responsible officials involved in draft form before publication.

Reeves submitted a draft report of the mission to the President, E. Elpidio Quirino, and completed the final report in Paris enroute back to Chicago. After an introductory chapter which noted relevant facts about the history, geography, population, natural resources, government and culture of the Philippines the report made a number of specific recommendations which are partially summarized in the report by Dr. Isidro which follows.

In addition to his overall responsibilities as Mission Director, Reeves had major responsibility for preparing recommendations in the area of organization and administration. Because of the critical and somewhat controversial nature of creating recommendations for dealing with the unique problem of the organization, governance and role of public and private educational institutions in the Philippines, the recommendations are given priority in this account.

- The Department of Education and its bureaus and divisions in the nation capital be relieved of the detailed operation of educational institutions in order that more of their time and energy may be devoted to the major function of providing educational leadership to the nation.
- In light of the large number of private proprietary schools, the Bureau of Public Schools and of Private School be converted into a single Bureau—The Bureau of Education. Coupled with this recommendation was another that consideration be given to establishing a national consultative committee on education which would meet to consider matters of general policy pertaining to public-private education. The members of the consultative committee would be non-political and serve without remuneration.
- A Board of Education be established for each province with members elected by the people to serve for overlapping terms without remuneration. The boards would serve transitionally in an advisory capacity for a number of years but would ultimately be given the authority, within the framework of national policies to make final decisions in matters pertaining to the operation and financing of schools.
- Other recommendations were addressed to matters of finance, including authority to levy taxes and impose collection of taxes to finance the salaries of teachers and administrators, buildings and equipment, and for extension of free, public secondary education.

Congressional Committee on Education

Upon the conclusion of the UNESCO mission report, a "Congressional Committee on Education" was established in 1949 by concurrent resolution of the two houses of the Philippine Congress. The scope of the Congressional committee included elementary, secondary, vocational and adult education in the forty-three provinces, and various aspects of the operations of one hundred ninety private institutions.

The scope of this inquiry was thus considerably broader than the UNESCO mission.

Dr. Antonio Isidro, a former graduate student of Reeves at the University of Chicago, compared the recommendations of the UNESCO mission and those of the Congressional Committee. The comparison was published in the April 1950 edition of the Philippine *Journal of Education*.

Both studies:

- Recommended "further experimentation" as a means of determining national policy relating to language teaching.
- Agreed on the need for improving the elementary curriculum, "by stressing Philippino ideas and character comparable with our new political status and utilizing community resources for the improvement of barriors and towns."
- Agreed that "secondary schools should provide opportunities for training in productive work to help meet the country's need for greater economic development."
- Concurred in the restoration of grade 7 and "the extension of compulsory education until the completion of elementary schooling."
- Stressed the importance of adult education, the eradication of illiteracy and "the total education of the common man."
- Agreed on the need to expand teacher training institutions and the creation of a Teacher Education Division to "provide professional leadership and insure better preparation of teachers." Also for the need to decentralize administration in order that "officials in the lower bracket may enjoy greater freedom and exercise more authority commensurate with their responsibility."
- Agreed generally that the Division of Superintendents should have "greater freedom and authority to insure educational leadership" and "would even have the superintendents to supervise private schools in their divisions."
- Agreed on the need for the creation of Boards of Education. "They differed, however, on the governance of the schools: the UNESCO mission recommended a provincial board for each province to deal with local schools, the Congressional committee would have a board for private schools for the entire country."

Isidro pointed out that the UNESCO and Congressional recommendations were generally compatible. However, they were quite far apart on how to deal with the private-public question. The Congressional committee noted that from 1941 to 1948 the number of private schools, colleges and universities increased from 884 to 1581 and enrollments from 170,000 to 325,000. The UNESCO mission reasoned that: "So long as public and private institutions operate under the general direction or supervision of separate bureaus, it will continue to be difficult, if not impossible to provide equality of educational opportunity." The Congressional committee, however, took account of the great increase of private schools; and the "political pressure" arising therefrom, often resorted to because of the alleged undemocratic process of accrediting private schools and the commercialization of private education—which led to their recommendation of raising the rank of the Director of Private Schools to the rank of Commissioner. This was not done, however.

The gains for education generally, however, were significant and the mission was, accordingly, quite successful.

Follow-up surveys in specific areas were made by members of the Philippine staff with observations and recommendations recorded for further study. Reeves was invited back in 1950 to advise on implementing legislation. He agreed to serve but was unable to go because of the serious illness of his wife. He did, however, return to the Philippines in 1958 as a part of a Michigan State University mission to study and make recommendations regarding higher education.

University of the Philippines[2]

Ten years after Reeves headed the UNESCO consultative mission to the Philippines he returned as a member of a Michigan State University team to make a study of the University of the Philippines. Heading this mission was Dr. John A. Hannah, President of Michigan State University and it included Dr. William T. Middlebrook, Vice President of the University of Minnesota and Dr. Thomas Hamilton, Vice President of Michigan State University. The study was requested by the Board of Trustees of the University of the Philippines and financed by the International Cooperation Administration of the U.S. government.

The study came while the Philippines were still struggling from the devastation of World War II, during which many buildings and much equipment of the University were destroyed and academic programs were severely disrupted. Although the focus was on the leading University in the Philippines, the study had to take into account the multiplicity of public and private post-secondary educational institutions. For example, there were eighteen public institutions, in addition to the University of the Philippines, which offered the bachelor degree, four which offered the master's degree, nine had their own Boards of Trustees while thirteen were under the supervision of the Bureau of Public Schools. In addition there were eight normal schools and five arts, trades and agricultural schools. In light of this complexity and the limitations of sixty days for examining the various problems with which University officials were confronted, the study team made it clear that they were not prepared to make an exhaustive study or detailed series of recommendations. Such an action by outsiders, wrote the committee, "would have bordered on the presumptuous and the superficial." Furthermore they observed that improvement comes only when those with responsibility take stock, give thought to ends and devise appropriate means. If the report helps to stimulate such stock-taking, thought and devising, it will have served its purpose well." Additionally, the recommendations would need various kinds of implementation—some only administrative action, others would call for code and charter revision, and still others would need Congressional action. The sorting out of which measures were appropriate to implement each of the recommendations would be the responsibility of the administrative officials of the University.

In light of the diversity of public institutions of post-secondary education in the Phililppines and the unusual number and strength of private, proprietary institutions it apparently seemed desirable and appropriate to the study team to define the attributes of the key public university, the University of the Philippines. Excerpts from that definition contained in the introduction to the report which clearly reflected Reeves's views regarding the special characteristics of public universities were:

- Too little, careful in nature and sympathetic in purpose, has been said concerning the nature of the public university. Too often, the fact has been ignored that it has distinctive features more important than the nature of its control. All universities share a dedication to the proposition that truth and knowledge are preferable to error and ignorance and that the university must be free to preserve the wisdom of the past, discover new knowledge and disseminate both. Without this base there can be no true university of any kind. But the public university in a free society has the additional responsibility of devising ways in which this knowledge can be utilized to improve the lot of all the citizens.
- The relationship of a public university to the rest of society is symbiotic: the public university must be free and it must be critical; at the same

> time, it must ever be aware of the fact that the health of the society and the health of the university are being weighed in the same balance. Thus, the public university takes note of the social needs it may properly and uniquely serve. Private institutions of higher learning can justify their existence by reference to the fact that knowledge is valuable for its own sake; a public university cannot. The public university has the responsibility to use knowledge to help solve the problems of the citizens who support it. This does not deny the validity of the proposition that knowledge should be sought for its own sake, but affirms rather that this by itself does not embrace the total mission of the public university. The University of the Philippines must not become so concerned with the narrower, traditional concept of a university that it avoids its proper responsibility for emphasizing the utilization of knowledge to improve the lot of all the people—laborers, small farmers, and small business operators, as well as the professional and the influential classes.

The report of the four-member team to the University did not specify the contribution which each member made to the final report. However Dr. Hannah has confirmed that Reeves and his former student and colleague, Thomas Hamilton, gave particular attention to the governance, internal organization and administration, agricultural extension, research and the academic programs of the University. William Middlebrook focused on the business and financial aspects of the University. Dr. Hannah coordinated the team effort on a part-time basis while serving as President of Michigan State University.

Recommendations on sections of the report which were primarily authored by Reeves and Hamilton follow:

Organization of Public Institutions

- All institutions which grant bachelors degrees be governed by the Bureau of Public Schools or the Board of Regents of the University of the Philippines.
- All graduate work be given by the University of the Philippines but in cooperation with other institutions.

Governance and Internal Organization and Administration of the University

The principal recommendations with reference to these central aspects of management of large, modern universities followed very closely those which Reeves had generally recommended to other universities in his numerous surveys. The basis for his recommendations in this study, however, were derived from an analysis of minutes of the Board and in his consultation with Board members and administrators. They were:

- The Board of Trustees be freed of detailed operations of the University so that they could focus on policy matters and general surveillance of the University.
- The President should be the top administrative officer with responsibility for implementing board policies; prepare the agenda for board meetings and serve as the communication linkage to and from the Board with the faculty.
- Reduce the number of administrative officers reporting directly to the President by the appointment of Vice Presidents (or equivalent titles) for academic, business, agriculture, and health science areas of University operations and for a logical delineation of functions within each of these areas plus increased decentralization.

Agricultural Extension and Research

- The central importance of agriculture to the Philippine economy was regarded by the team as being "taken too lightly—with a tendency of preferring to look with greater pride to the more traditional scholarly fields."
- Primary responsibility for agricultural research to be undertaken by the University of the Philippines combined with the transfer of agricultural extension from the Department of Agriculture to the University.
- The appointment of extension agents (as in the USA land-grant model) to be appointed cooperatively by the University and local governmental agencies.

The report not only chartered a course for the modernization of the University of the Philippines but provided a framework for large amounts of external assistance by the U.S. government and private foundations in subsequent years. Unfortunately, the follow-up on the recommendations of the team report were not as satisfactory as the team had probably hoped to have occurred. Nevertheless, Case and Bunnell's study of the University of the Philippines, made in 1962 indicated that long-term impact of the study, was more favorable:

A large number of recommendations of the Hannah Report have been carried out. In general, the report has had more influence on the administration of the University than on its academic program. However, the creation of the University College for lower division general education resulted partly at least as a result of the emphasis upon early specialization as contained in the report. Unfortunately, many of the benefits of the administrative reorganization which followed submission of the report have been lost or negated by special delegation of specific authorities which do not follow the lines of administrative responsibilities as indicated in the overall organizational plan.[3]

Pakistan Academies for Rural Development[4]

Pakistan became a sovereign nation in 1947 after the bloody partition of India and Pakistan over unresolved religious, political and cultural issues between Hindus and Moslems. The United States, shortly thereafter, started a massive aid program—mostly military but partly economic—to this new nation. As part of United States interest in Pakistan, but independent of the official U.S. aid program, the Ford Foundation in 1951 established an Overseas Development Program—largely focused on technical assistance training and institution building. Under this program the Foundation contracted with a number of American universities to perform specific advisory functions in Pakistan: Harvard University for work with the Planning Commission; Johns Hopkins University for a family planning program; the University of Chicago for teacher training; Oklahoma State University for polytechnic trades training; the University of Wisconsin for home economics training; and Michigan State University for the development of academies for rural development.

In April 1956, George F. Gant, who had served as an educational consultant to the Government of Pakistan and the Harvard Advisory Team, and later as the Ford Foundation Representative in Pakistan, got in touch with Floyd Reeves with reference to the possible interest of Michigan State University in providing advisory assistance for the development of two Academies for Rural Development—one in West Pakistan at Peshawar and the other in East Pakistan at Comilla—approximately one thousand miles apart. Gant was then Director of the South and South East Asia program of the Foundation. His association with Reeves went back to 1934 when he was a staff member of the Social and Economic Division of the Tennessee Valley Authority.

An 1956 exploratory meeting was attended by Gant, Reeves, Carleton Wood and William Lightfoot (staff members of the Foundation) and Said Hasan, the Minister for Economic Affairs of the Government of Pakistan. Other meetings at this time were held with Rowan Gaither, the President of the Foundation, and F. F. Hill, who was the principal staff member of the Foundation for agriculture and rural development.

General information was exchanged on developments in Pakistan and on the anticipated purposes of a possible project which included assistance to the Government of Pakistan in preparing specific plans for establishing the academies and getting a program underway as soon as possible.

Gant's review of these tentative plans with Pakistani officials and other Ford Foundation officials led to a contract with Michigan State University to send a team of four faculty members to Pakistan headed by Reeves. The team included Reeves; Cole Brembeck, an educator, Wilbur Brookover, a sociologist, and Edward Weidner, a political scientist and public administrator. Subsequent missions included Lawrence Boger, an agricultural economist and William Ross, an anthropologist. The substance of the discussions with Pakistani, International Cooperation Agency (ICA), Ford Foundation and Michigan State University officials led to an agreement on the advisability of proceeding with the project. An innovative governance plan emerged in the creation of a Central Board of Governors headed by the Minister responsible for supervision of the Village Agricultural and Industrial Development (V-AID) and principal officials from each of the ministries which had responsibility for programs designed to improve agricultural production and rural living—Agriculture, Education, Community Development and related ministries plus the Ministry of Finance. Provincial boards were later established which were chaired by the Provincial Chief Secretaries with membership comparable to the Central Board. The Directors of each of the Academies were responsible to the Central Board. The Directors of each of the Academies were responsible to the Central and Provincial Boards. The Chief Advisor of the Michigan State University staff in Pakistan served as advisor to the Boards of Governors. In addition, the Central Board had a secretariat for a few years which provided some evaluative and other services. The secretariat was later disbanded after the Academies became better established. The principal trainees of the Academies were to be high level officers of the government who had responsibility for the V-AID and other rural development programs which the government had devised for improvement of the citizens living in the rural sector—sometimes characterized as programs for "rural uplift."

The innovative organization and governance structures, as projected, had several important features which contributed to the later success of the Academies. The principal value was to focus and integrate all of the government resources allocated to rural development under Boards, as indicated above, which were composed of high level officials (Secretaries and Joint Secretaries) who had responsibility for different aspects of rural development. For example, although the projected purpose of the Academies was clearly educational, the program exceeded the scope of persons conventionally involved in formal education. Similarly, although the Academies were to be concerned with the improvement of agricultural production and the welfare of farmers, the focus went beyond the scope of the Ministry and Department of Agriculture. Although the creation of this novel organizational arrangement was clearly a joint product of the thinking of the Pakistani and Ford Foundation officials and the MSU team of advisors and it is thus impossible to assign credit for any specific features of or for the total organizational plan, the final "scheme," as the Pakistan Government called it, was consistent with a number of principles which Reeves had come to embrace as a result of his then long lifetime experience in education, organizational analysis and resource development. Education, for example, to him embraced more than formal "schooling" and the problems of rural development were more complex than those normally considered by agriculturists. Furthermore, Reeves had a distinguished record of fostering consensus among persons of differing backgrounds and purposes and in the creation of organizational forms which integrated their collective efforts for a common purpose.

The final outcome of the deliberations was the preparation of the "scheme" which included the provisions indicated above. The scheme was approved by the Government of Pakistan, the Ford Foundation and Michigan State University and a contract was entered into for a three-year period starting in September 1957. Twenty Pakistanis with backgrounds in social science, education and public administration were selected on a world-wide search to serve as faculties of the two Academies under the direction of two Directors from East and West Pakistan. They were brought together in Pakistan from England, the United States, and Pakistan for a short orientation period to their new tasks and for a specially designed non-degree training program at MSU for nine months before returning to Pakistan to take up their new duties. In the meantime, the architectural firm of Doxiadis was selected to design and supervise the building of campuses at Peshawar, in West Pakistan, and at Comilla in East Pakistan. The story of what happened in the first ten years of the fifteen-year period during which the Ford Foundation provided funds for the MSU advisory services, the training of the Pakistani staff, architectural services and importation of some building materials and equipment is fully documented, with special reference to the Academy in Comilla, in "*Rural Development in Action: The Comprehensive Experiment at Comilla, East Pakistan*"[5] by Arthur Raper, assisted by William Ross, Harry L. Case and Richard O. Niehoff and published in 1970 by the Cornell University Press. Raper, Ross and Niehoff had served on the advisory team. Case was Representative of the Ford Foundation in Pakistan from 1960–62. Niehoff served as Chief Advisor from 1960–1975.

In addition to serving as the principal advisor regarding the organization and basic initial policies of the Academy, Reeves was particularly instrumental in identifying Akhter Hameed Khan as the best possible Director of the Comilla Academy and in persuading the key Pakistani and Ford Foundation officials to appoint him to the position. Khan was a highly regarded person—a member of the prestigious Indian Civil Service before partition—but a maverick in disposition and outlook with reference to how best to direct the Academy. These were characteristics which Reeves appreciated and supported for the novel and creative mission of the Academy. As the Academy program evolved and matured David E. Bell, Vice President of the Ford Foundation, in a Foreword to the previously cited book on the project, wrote:

> For the last ten years a sustained and impressive effort has been made to bring radical change to a rural area in East Pakistan. This book is a report on that effort. It is an interim report, for the effort is continuing, and the story is far from ended. But enough has occurred to shed much illumination on a baffling problem of great importance in the developing countries; how to help rural families live at the ragged edge of survival to acquire power—the power of knowledge and of organization—to lift themselves toward a better life.
>
> The scene of this particular effort is Comilla thana, a county-size rural area of about one hundred square miles, named for and centering on the small city of Comilla. The thana lies at the eastern edge of the delta of the mighty Brahmaputra River, 80 miles north of the Bay of Bengal. This is rice-growing country, green, hot, cut up by waterways, in the rainy season soggily wet. About a quarter of a million people live there. They

> are Bengalis, small, shrewd, inured over centuries to the overpowering vagaries of natural disasters in the form of floods, typhoons, epidemics. The land is beautiful, and the Bengalis add to its beauty with their graceful boats and their lyrical songs. But their life is excruciatingly hard . . .
>
> The conditions in Comilla thana are not at all unique. These are the conditions of hundreds of millions of people in many countries around the world. The problem of development is to change those conditions, and many good men have poured their energies into fruitless efforts to accomplish this.
>
> The efforts being made in Comilla thana are plainly not fruitless. It is too soon to claim great success, but not too soon to assess what has worked and what has not worked at Comilla, and to think about what lessons may be learned for application in other places. That is the purpose of this book.
>
> The Comilla story centers in a more important sense around a man—a remarkable man—Akhter Hameed Khan, who except for a brief interlude has been director of the Academy since its inception and is the prime cause of its success . . .
>
> The central concept of the Academy from its beginning therefore has been to regard Comilla thana as a laboratory for social and economic research, and to enlist the people of the thana, the staff of the Academy, and the local officers of government in a joint program of research and experimentation. And the staff members of the Academy—Pakistani and foreign alike—had to start by listening to the villagers, because that was the only way to find out where the process of change had to begin, and—furthermore—the only way to persuade the villagers that the people from the Academy might be worth listening to.[6]

All of the essential ingredients of success for rural development set forth by Bell: purposes and programs geared to the need of the villagers; the basic wisdom of the villagers about their needs and programs which might be helpful; an organization and policy framework to support experimentation; and the selection of a leader who found creative and pragmatic measures to meet the complex challenges of rural development in third-world countries were wholly consistent with the values and outlook of Reeves which he had advocated in somewhat more sophisticated environments.

University Study Center

From September 18, 1945 to November 16, 1945 Reeves took a leave from his teaching and research at the University of Chicago to participate as a member of the faculty at the "University Study Center" in Italy. The Italian Center, like others in France and England, was operated for personnel of all branches of the armed forces. More than two thousand were enrolled in courses taught by almost two hundred instructors including professors from the Universities of Chicago, Nebraska, Princeton and personnel from other educational institutions and foundations. Reeves had earlier declined to participate in an educational rehabilitation program in Japan under General MacArthur. He taught three courses: Adult Education, Introduction to Education and Principles of Administration. In addition he used the occasion of being in Italy with trips to Florence, Venice and other places to study Italian education and politics and to become well acquainted with several Italian professors.

Chapter VII

Michigan State University: 1943–1969

Floyd Reeves's association with Michigan State College (MSC), which became Michigan State University (MSU) in 1955, cannot be disassociated from the career of John A. Hannah, who served as President from July 1, 1941 to his retirement in 1969. Before becoming President, Hannah had served as Specialist in Poultry Extension from June 1923 when he graduated from MSC with a B.S. degree, until January 1935, when he was named Secretary of the State Board of Agriculture, the governing body of the institution.[1]

He was named President in 1941, with an uncommon zeal to make MSC a leading—if not the leading, land-grant college. At age thirty-nine he was one of the youngest presidents of a land-grant or other major college or university. Although MSC was highly respected among land-grant colleges it had to play second fiddle especially as compared with the older and more distinguished University of Michigan. He had several problems which had to be solved before it could become the kind of high quality institution which he had envisioned. At the top of the list of problems was the selection and retention of a competent and diversified faculty, which could only be accomplished by the recruitment and selection of bright young scholars at lower salaries than were being paid elsewhere. He saw the solution in terms of developing institutional policies and practices which were conducive to their growth and which would encourage them to stay and grow with the institution. There were also problems of focusing the efforts of the faculty to recast the curriculum to reflect new and expanding opportunities and for establishing effective organizational and communication arrangements to encourage and stimulate the faculty to move from the important, but limiting, framework of a college into a modern university.

Greatly expanded enrollments of women and returning veterans were anticipated at the end of the war, which would necessitate building additional classrooms, laboratory and housing facilities and to create academic programs which were attractive and pragmatically functional to meet the needs of an older and more experienced post-war ("GI") college clientele. Hannah's view of creating a first rate university, against the background of these constraints, led him in his early years as President to seek help from a person with broad experiences in university development and administration and whose motivations and outlook for public service were compatible with his. Floyd Reeves, whose record of experiences and accomplishments in the prestigious University of Chicago, other educational activities and the federal government (described in Part II) was the person selected for this exciting challenge.

John Hannah was aware of most of the major aspects of Reeves's background in government and in several nationally important educational activities. Most, if not all, of these activities formed a useful background of experience and contacts with educational, governmental, business and civic leaders which Hannah could tap in his ambition to develop a first-class university. The results of this unusual administrator-consultant relationship—a kind of symbiotic relationship between a vigorous and ambitious and highly competent younger man and his consultant, twelve years his senior in age and experience in university organization and administration, is expressed in Hannah's responses to several questions which were put to him by two of his senior associates in the preparation of *A Memior*[2]* about his relationship to and the influence of Reeves on the development of MSU.

> What about the movement to liberalize the curriculum at Michigan State? . . . What influence did Professor Floyd Reeves have on your thinking in this respect? Would you like to comment generally upon his services to you and to Michigan State?
>
> Hannah Responded: First, I am happy to give Floyd Reeves full credit. If I were to identify a single person for his contribution to making Michigan State move from what it was in 1941 to the kind of institution it

* Published in 1980 by the Michigan State University Press.

> was in 1969, I would put Floyd Reeves at the head of the list. When I first came to know him he was Dean of Education at the University of Chicago, with a distinguished academic record. He had played a key role in government during the Roosevelt administrations and had been called upon to do many important things. He was also a very practical fellow. He had been born and raised in a sod house in South Dakota, in an area where there was no primary school. Taught as a boy by his mother, he secured an education in the hardest way and early in life achieved the distinguished reputation he fully deserved. (Page 48)

Hannah did not act precipitously in his early relationship to Reeves. But by a series of "testings" which demonstrated his usefulness and by Reeves's increasing immersion in the problems and potentiality of MSC, the relationship of mutual professional respect deepened and the frequency of involvement increased.

Hannah expressed the growing relationship:

> I first persuaded him to come to East Lansing as a consultant in 1943, first for one day a month, then one day a week, and eventually for a few months at a time. Finally I succeeded in persuading him to leave his tenured position at the University of Chicago and come to Michigan State full time. I told him that I thought he could have a more profound effect for good on the lives of more people, and bring about more improvements in the world as a full-time member of the staff at Michigan State than he could at the University of Chicago or anywhere else. (Page 48).

Reeves served as an experienced staff officer, who was very cognizant of his role as a consultant. He was comfortable in being a catalyst, "devil's advocate," advisor, and consultant. As one senior official of the University commented to the author about Reeves's work method: "He was a bit mysterious. Everyone knew he was close to Hannah and somewhat powerful but he never pretended to be President." Hannah too was comfortable in this relationship. Hannah described Reeves's work method as follows:

> Floyd Reeves's greatest strength was his ability to take a group of people who did not agree on much of anything, start asking questions and keep asking them, and listen to their answers. He kept the questions and answers going, so that over a period of a few hours, days, or weeks they would change their thinking and become full participants in dealing with the problems at hand.[3]

As to the timing of Reeves's work as consultant Hannah said:

> During the early days of my presidency the war was on and our faculty had few regular students. We had women students, some men who could not qualify for military service, and large numbers of military students from the Army and Air Force. All of our facilities were fully used, and our dormitories, fraternities, and sororities were taken over for military personnel. Many members of our faculty were teaching courses designed for the military, rather than university courses of the prewar type. This was a good time, I believed, to begin to look at Michigan State and to plan for the kind of university that we hoped it was going to be after the war. No one knew, then, that the federal government would institute the G. I. Bill and provide subsidized education for all returning veterans. So we started looking at what we had been doing. Here we involved Floyd Reeves and some of our best faculty who were interested in making Michigan State better than it had been before. We used a technique that we later used very widely, that of appointing a committee of bright people from all of the colleges across the whole University. Some were academic conservatives and some were progressives, but their first objective was to figure out what we were trying to do educationally. It is relatively simple to accomplish an objective if you understand what the objective is, but very difficult to accomplish much that is constructive if you are uncertain what it is you are aiming at.[4]

Part-time Consultancies: 1943–1953

From this ten-year period there are sixteen official minutes[5] of meetings of the Administrative Group[6] and of the State Board of Agriculture (the governing Board of MSC,) which show how Hannah used Reeves's consulting services. It is clear from these records that Hannah involved Reeves in most, if not all of the important problems and developments during this period. The first meeting with the Administrative Group, held on December 14, 1943, was devoted to plans for using Reeves during his quarter off from the University of Chicago focused largely on rural education. A follow-up meeting with the Board on February 17, 1944 discussed Reeves's early impressions of his informal discussions with Hannah and members of the faculty concerning the organization, policies and procedures of other institutions with which he was familiar from his extensive experience in making surveys and in accrediting of colleges and universities. Another meeting was held shortly thereafter when Reeves was called upon to give a more specific report on several developments at other institutions, including data and forecasts on enrollments and their implications for Michigan State College. Reeves made a number of critical observations of present programs of the College and also made specific recommendations for the College of Engineering as related to enrollment forecasts. He also made his first reference to the desirability of creating a "General College." He extended his remarks about general and vocational education at a meeting two days later when he also mentioned for the first time the possibility of putting Business, Police and Hotel Administration under one of the existing divisions.

Hannah suggested at the end of this meeting that the deans discuss with their faculties the various observations and suggestions made by Reeves, and that a general meeting of all members of the faculty be convened in two weeks. A summary of Reeves's remarks was made which became the program for the general faculty meeting, which was held as planned.

Less than a month later another meeting of the Administrative Group was held devoted largely to the possibility of unifying student personnel services and to the feedback from the faculty on reactions to the creation of a General College. With reference to the latter subject, at a follow-up meeting of the whole faculty, Madison Kuhn in his hundred-year history of the University reported:

> In that faculty meeting of March 1944, President Hannah called upon Professor Reeves of the University of Chicago, who had been on the campus for several weeks studying college policy and suggesting changes. Reeves proposed a program of basic general education, required rather than optional, for all freshmen and sophomores rather than those of a particular division, and taught by a distinct faculty rather than by those within specialized departments. He suggested a board of examiners to prepare comprehensive examinations which would encourage integrated rather than disconnected learning and would permit the mature veteran to accelerate his education. The faculty agreed that such a program should be worked out in time for the fall term, which would allow a year or more in which to perfect the instrument while enrollments were small. With breath-taking speed the program was formulated and begun.[7]

The Basic College

Within the time frame indicated by Kuhn, Reeves on his first major assignment to follow-up on his recommendations, consulted with a college-wide faculty committee composed of members who had already shown some commitment to curricular changes and who were generally comfortable with the idea of a new organizational framework to achieve a better integration of instruction for general rather than specialized education. During an eight-week period committee members were relieved of other duties to attend thirty-three work sessions to develop the program. Reeves, on invitation, met several times with subcommittees and the full committee to raise questions and to offer suggestions on developments at other colleges and universities. Hannah also participated in the discussions at intervals. With a keen sense of the importance of public understanding and support for the developing program Hannah vigorously responded in writing to questions of reporters who were assigned to follow the progress of the plan. In one public statement he described the serious educational problems with which the new College was being created to deal. He pointed out that "many freshmen could neither speak or write forcefully or intelligently; they could not spell; their knowledge of mathematics, history or basic science was generally rudimentary; they had no conception of their place in nature or human society and they were unprepared to become citizens in the broadest sense."

Periodic progress reports were made to the full faculty and a final report was presented for their review and approval. Six weeks later Hannah secured approval of the State Board of Education for the creation of the Basic College and the appointment of a dean, from the faculty of agriculture. Reeves was invited to attend the State Governing Board meeting to add his prestige to the recommendation and to respond to questions by members of the Board. He told the Board that the proposed courses, instructional and evaluation methods, and other aspects of the program were well received by the students, including many returning veterans. The Basic College prospered for several years with relatively minor revisions and brought considerable prestige to MSU. Special curricular material was widely sold and members of the faculty were also invited to numerous conferences and meetings on and off-campus to discuss questions which had arisen in the experience of creating the College and to offer suggestions to the colleges and universities which were in the process of planning similar programs.[8] Although the program resembled, in several features, the two-year College program at the University of Chicago to which Reeves had contributed ideas, there were several curricular modifications which were more appropriate for a large public university.

Hannah's aims for the program, his interpretation of what happened in this accelerated period of planning, and his appraisal of Reeves's contribution to the innovative structure and program for general education follows:

The aim of the . . . Basic College was to establish what kind of education the average Michigan State student—from Detroit or some other Michigan city, or from a Michigan farm or small town—would need. What kind of an education was he or she going to need to fit him or her for a useful and satisfying role in the life of the postwar years? Obviously, all of our graduates would need to know much more than before about the kind of world they would be living in, but that was a secondary consideration. Our first was to give the student the best education we could for a full, useful life.

Out of this effort, out of all the discussions and committee meetings, came the notion that we needed a program that was all inclusive, one in which all freshmen and sophomores would be exposed to the kinds of knowledge that every education person should be exposed to. Then, if they went on to be agricultural scientists or engineers or teachers or home economists or medical students or business persons or whatever, they could then specialize. First, though, we believed they all should be generally educated. . . .

After months of diligent effort the faculty committees under Reeves's leadership, came up with recommendations for a required two-year program common to all freshmen and sophomores. Originally, there were seven basic courses, of which all students were required to take five.

It was remarkable that our diverse faculty voted, without a single no vote, to create a new Basic College . . . under the supervision of a separate faculty. Each student had the opportunity, while completing Basic College requirements, to enroll in the prerequisite courses required for those seeking degrees in the upper colleges. . . .

To return to Floyd Reeves. He played a major role in creating the Basic College but he had good material to work with. If the faculty and administrators of Michigan State had not been forward-looking and open-minded and dedicated to building a university designed to achieve its own objectives without reference to what was being done at Ann Arbor or Ohio State or Harvard or California-Berkeley or somewhere else, we would not have been able to do what we did . . .[9]

Other Organizational Changes

At the next several visits to the college in 1944 Reeves met frequently with the President and informally with faculty members and on invitation, with the Administrative Group. These discussions laid the ground work for a number of organizational changes which were formally approved by the Board, on recommendation of the Administrative Group and President Hannah. Among these were: the creation of a School of Business and Public Service which included Public, Police and Hotel Administration, Social Service, Journalism, Physical Education and two-year terminal curricula in secretarial, clerical services, merchandising, salesmanship and real estate. A School of Science and Arts which included languages and literature, fine arts, social, physical and biological sciences and education was also created. Student personnel services were also recognized to include counseling and guidance services.* With reference to teacher education Reeves's recommendations mirrored the policy of the University of Chicago which placed primary responsibility for teaching subject matter courses in the respective Colleges for teachers preparing for teaching positions in these fields. Education courses such as History of Education, Educational Psychology, Educational Measurements and other related general courses were taught by the Department of Education with methods courses to be jointly taught by the Department of Education and the respective subject matter departments. With further reference to programs for the preparation of teachers, Reeves recommended that these programs be under the supervision of an Advisory Committee made up of the deans of the subject matter areas under the chairmanship of the Dean of the School of Science and Arts with the Head of the Department of Education serving as Executive Secretary. Reeves was invited, in an executive session of the Board, to confer with them and President Hannah on personnel selections in connection with the approved reorganizations.

At the same meeting, the Board approved the retention of Reeves as a consultant to serve for at least twenty days per year on campus and be available for other consultation as necessary at an annual stipend of $1,500 plus travel.[10]

Cooperative Extension Service

In early January 1945, Reeves was involved in a second major assignment by President Hannah to work with a committee for a major reorganization of the Cooperative Extension Service.[11] Hannah, who knew the needs and problems of agriculture in Michigan from his long experience as an extension agent and Secretary of the Board of Agriculture "felt strongly that the whole land-grant system, including the Cooperative Extension Service, had become ultra conservative"

---

* For more details on these developments see Paul L. Dressel, *College to University, The Hannah Years at Michigan State 1935–69*, Michigan State Publications, East Lansing, Michigan.

(since its establishment in 1914) and that it needed a "shaking up to restore its vitality and maximum usefulness to society . . ." Hannah also had in mind readjustments in agriculture which could reasonably be anticipated as a result of the war effort and returning veterans to the farms and rural areas and of other legal and program changes in the Extension Service.

The committee entrusted with this complex task differed from most comparable committees in that its members were chosen from within the organization but did not include the administrators of the program. Hannah wanted a "bottoms-up" rather than a "top-down" review. He had strong convictions about the way to go about this somewhat delicate, if not radical, business of shaking up the well established and complex organization which was funded from federal, state and county sources and administered by some officials who had been in leadership positions since the beginning of the service. Hannah's motivation for the reorganization, however, was in no way to be construed as negative with reference to the value of the service, as evidenced by his earlier public statements and proposals for expanded financial support for budgetary increases in the number of home demonstration agents, assistant agents, and 4-H Club agents. Hannah charged the committee to address such basic questions as: "What is the program basis for an expanded extension service; is a single link of authority to the counties essential for optimum extension administration; how assign agricultural and other specialists to the college departments; how bring all fields of University academic offerings to all of the people of the state; how establish a career service or services within the organization; and how create organizational, personnel and other policy and procedural changes to reflect answers to the above and other questions?"

The work of the committee started at the annual conference of state extension personnel with an opening lecture by Hannah on the "Place of the Land-grant College in the Public Education System of the Future." In Hannah's opening remarks he directed the committee to "thoroughly analyze our whole Extension set-up, particularly in view of the changing program which confronts us in the immediate future." Furthermore, he urged them to forget their specialized organizational connections and to "concentrate objectively on what should be done to improve the Extension Service for the State." He indicated that the committee would have a free hand to consult administrators and others in carrying on their deliberations and made it clear that the committee was directly responsible to him.

Reeves delivered three lectures on "Rural America—Yesterday,

Today and Tomorrow," "Elements of a Sound Program of Education through Extension" and "Organization and Administration of the Extension Service." At the time Reeves was director of the Center for Rural Education at the University of Chicago. In these lectures Reeves propounded his philosophy and principles of administration around topics such as the purposes to be achieved, the structure through which to achieve the purposes, and the personnel and administrative processes necessary to do the job.

The Committee then adopted the procedure, suggested by Reeves, of having a subcommittee draft a report of the major points discussed and tentative recommendations formulated after each session for review by the whole committee; secured the services of an editor to keep a running record of their deliberations and started making a series of draft reports—the first of which was sent only to Hannah—although later drafts were shared with the Extension Director and other administrators, who sometimes reacted with emotion. Reeves met with the committee from time to time at its request; responded to their questions; and sought his counsel on the issues with which they were confronted; and even made impromptu lectures on principles of organization and administration.

After thirty-eight meetings and conferences lasting over a period of six months, the committee submitted its final report in November 1945, which was approved by Hannah and the faculty. Nine months later the State Board of Agriculture tentatively approved the report. Several measures to implement the report were taken, however, before final approval by the State Board including the central recommendation for organization of the Extension Service in five districts with line and staff responsibilities, established essentially as recommended by the committee. This key recommendation entailed the designation of a County Extension Director for each county with responsibility for supervising all phases of field work in the counties, including one or more agricultural, home economics and 4-H specialists. Furthermore, the Extension Director and his staff of Assistant Directors would determine the type of specialist help to be brought into the county from the state level in response to the requests of the farmers in the county. Subject matter specialists were recommended to be made members of the college departments in which their subject matter specialty was involved and to report administratively to the Director of Extension. These recommendations cut across previously established lines of authority and were strongly opposed by the officials, who would need to change their thinking and style of operation with which they had become, possibly, too comfortable. Others continued to be debated for several years thereafter. One of the recommendations to establish an all-inclusive, University-wide Extension Service which would include the College of Arts and Sciences and other colleges under the direction of an all-College Board was, however, not approved. The extensive debates which revolved around the provision of this somewhat novel approach to providing services for adult learning led, soon thereafter, to the creation of the "Center for Continuing Education" with an initial grant of a million dollars from the Kellogg Foundation—the first of such grants made by the Foundation for similar centers at other universities. Reeves actively participated in the preparation of the proposal to the Kellogg Foundation for the new Center.

An appraisal of Reeves's contribution to the establishment of the revamped Extension Service was provided by Lowell Treaster, who had served as editor of the committee reports. His reflections, eighteen years after his work with the committee, regarding Reeves's style and influence are expressed in a letter to the author:

> It was through these meetings that I became well acquainted with Dr. Reeves . . . His calm voice, his curved pipe that was always a part of him at each meeting, and the sweet aroma of the tobacco that he smoked gave everyone a feeling of tranquility and self-assurance . . . Through his remarks, always in a thoughtful manner, he led the group logically from one point to another. Nor was it a dull, heavy discussion. Some Reeves' humor surfaced just often enough to keep the meetings entertaining . . . One word seems to describe Floyd Reeves. That word is incisive. Few persons of my acquaintance, in fact none, could push aside the overlay and come to grips with a problem more quickly and more effectively. He was sharp, keen, penetrating and acute. His wealth of knowledge on so many subjects made him capable in every respect.

Reeves continued to serve as a part-time consultant to President Hannah, the Administrative Group and to the faculty, more generally, and on invitation of Hannah, to the Board on several less dramatic changes in the curriculum, organization structure and other changes. Among the recommendations which he did make included the establishment of a program for educational research; a seminar on the improvement of teaching; and a detailed college-wide analysis of curricular offerings which would lead to the fewer courses for larger amounts of credit and thus change the ratio of students to faculty from 17–1 to 20–1, which was the average of colleges and universities which enrolled 2,000 or more students. He also made some comments to the Administrative Group on his informal sampling of student reactions to their experiences with the Basic College which he found to be very favorable except for their reaction to the comprehensive examinations. Hannah arranged for Reeves to meet with the Board from time to time to repot on his observations and recommendations which were being acted upon.

He also continued to spend some time in various activities in Michigan such as a school redistricting project in Battle Creek and at several conferences at Wayne State, Western Michigan and the University of Michigan. But during the next few years he became involved in other activities such as serving as Director of Studies for the State of New York Temporary Commission on the need for a State University and other activities described elsewhere in this volume. Since he became involved in all these other activities he felt that he could not commit himself to further consulting time to MSC. Accordingly, he offered his resignation in a letter to President Hannah on July 19, 1950. Hannah promptly responded with a counter proposal:

> In response to your letter of July 19, I very much dislike to accept your resignation but recognize that if you are going to be out of the country and be fully occupied with your other responsibilities there is no alternative. Instead of accepting your resignation, I am making this alternative proposal. It is that we continue you on our role as a consultant but instead of paying you an annual salary as at present that we pay you $100 per day and expenses for whatever time you are able to spend on our campus, and it is our hope that you will find it possible to spend fifteen or twenty days each year here. Is this agreeable to you?[12]

Reeves agreed to Hannah's counter proposal.

Hannah was obviously pleased with Reeves's contribution as a part-time consultant to the development of the college and wanted to make the relationship more permanent after Reeves had completed other commitments referred to above. Accordingly, he recommended to the Board that the 62 year old Reeves be appointed to a full-time position effective September 1, 1953.

The components of Hannah's offer to Reeves included appointment as Professor of Administration in the School of Education for half-time and Consultant to the President for half-time on a ten-month basis at a salary of $14,000. Furthermore, it was understood that his employment could continue for five additional years after attaining age 65 if he remained in good health and with the option to reduce his responsibility with a proportionate reduction in salary. The Board approved Hannah's recommendation at its December 18th meeting.

Major Activities at MSC/MSU 1953–1962

The role played by Reeves between the time of his appointment to a regular staff position in September 1953 and his first retirement in 1962 was significantly different, reflecting major and maturing changes in the institution. Michigan State College had become Michigan State University in its Centennial year—1955, which epitomized a number of significant changes in which Reeves, as noted in the preceding pages, had played a major role. Among these, with varying inputs from Reeves, were: the reorganization of the structure of the institution, including the Office of the President; and the carefully planned enrollment of large numbers of returning veterans, which had brought the number of students up to almost 16,000, and a number of significant curricular changes, in addition to the creation of the Basic College. The other changes included the creation of programs in Food Technology, Nursing Education, and Veterinary Medicine. The Cooperative Extension Service had been reorganized and the scope of the program in continuing education, capped off with the building of the Kellogg Center in 1951, and the creation of the position of Dean of Continuing Education had been established in 1952. The number of foreign students and curricular offerings in languages and non-western cultures had increased substantially with several key faculty appointments. The policy of selecting, promoting and retaining bright young faculty members who were given every opportunity to develop was paying off with a teaching and research force of increased competence—including two former students of Reeves at the University of Chicago who rose to vice presidential positions. A six million dollar building program added significantly to residential, research and classroom facilities. And finally, but perhaps not less significantly in terms of the growing maturity and prestige of the institution, was its admission as a member of the Big Ten Conference, when the University of Chicago in 1948 dropped its membership with Hutchins' "ten-cent football."

The institution was so well organized and staffed, particularly at the administrative level, that the Board of Trustees acquiesced in the request of President Eisenhower and Charles Wilson, Secretary of Defense, to have President Hannah serve as Assistant Secretary of

Defense for Manpower for a period of twelve months (later increased to eighteen months) beginning in January 1953.* Because of the close professional relationship between Hannah and Reeves, it seemed appropriate for Hannah to write to Reeves, on January 6, 1953, while he was teaching at the Claremont Graduate School, to reassure him that his appointment did not modify his continuation as President of MSC. Excerpts from Hannah's letter:

> You may read in the next few days that I am accepting temporarily an important assignment in the new administration. I want you to know before you read it that this is in no way a violation of the understanding that I have with you that I am going to stay here for the rest of my active career unless our Board decides to terminate my services . . .
>
> As you know, this assignment is of such vital concern to colleges and universities and to all of education that it seems desirable to accept it on behalf of the best interests of education.
>
> Arrangements have been worked out that will permit me to be on the campus almost every weekend. I expect to continue to act as President with our regular staff carrying on as at present.
>
> It would be simpler for me if you were already on the job here. We are all looking forward to your being with us next September.[13]

Reeves's appointment on September 1, 1953 specified that he was to serve half-time as consultant to President Hannah and half-time as Professor of Educational Administration. The material which follows generally reflects this dual assignment, the first section of which will focus on his continuing work as consultant to the President.

As Continuing Consultant to President Hannah

For about four years Reeves occupied an office next to Hannah's until Reeves moved to the newly built Erickson Hall for the College of Education. Much of the consultation between the two occurred informally with a minimum of formal and other communications from which one can build a definitive record. It is clear from available records, however, that the following were characteristic: informal notes from Reeves to Hannah; direct assignments from the President; direct instructions to administrative officials to consult with Reeves on cer-

---

* This assignment from President Eisenhower and others which followed are described in: *John A. Hannah, Versatile Administrator and Distinguished Public Servant* by Richard O. Niehoff, published by the University Press of America.

tain matters including major decisions on personnel; participation in major committee assignments; participation in major conferences; and the more general and informal relationships in which Reeves could relate himself to ongoing projects and would be available to faculty members and administrators who wished to consult with him informally about their ideas, frustrations or whatever. Reeves continued to serve, also informally, as a two-way communicator and consultant between the President and the rest of the University. He also became increasingly involved in educational conferences in the state of Michigan and continued, particularly in his quarters off, to be active as a consultant and active committee member in national and international affairs which were fed back into the thinking and planning going on in the University and which to some degree brought prestige to the University. There were, however, no more dramatic developments such as the creation of the Basic College and the reorganization of the Cooperative Extension Service, the creation of basic organizational structure and staffing of key positions and other actions involved in developing Michigan State College to become Michigan State University. Rather his work and influence were more diffused and slower paced as befitted an increasingly mature institution and a person approaching retirement age. His title was changed to "Distinguished Professor of Education and Consultant to the President."

A poignant example of one result of informal consultations between Reeves and a member of the faculty was described in a letter to the author from Dr. Paul A. Miller, who was the first Provost of MSU. Miller later served as the President of West Virginia University, Assistant Secretary of the United States Department of Health, Education and Welfare and still later as Professor of Science and Humanities at the Rochester Institute of Technology where he still serves. The full text of Miller's reflections on his association with Reeves expressed in a letter to the author dated 8/23/82 is in Appendix C.

Temporary Committees

Another type of communication which resulted in several major changes was a letter from Reeves to Hannah dated January 5, 1956. Reeves recommended the establishment of three temporary committees, and proposed the members and functions for each of the committees. They were to report to the Administrative Group, which provided a vehicle for sorting out ideas and for preparing decisions which

Hannah could make while back on campus on weekends and other short periods away from his assignments in Washington. These included: committee for the Lecture-Concert Series; a committee on the organization of possible schools including nursing, music and fine arts and medical technology; and a committee for course and curriculum planning. The latter committee would focus on, among other aspects of the broad subject, reduction of course offerings and number of programs offered; increasing time available for faculty research and off-campus teaching; utilizing savings resulting from reduction of course offerings for salary increases for faculty. Hannah supported all of these recommendations.

Still other activities in which Reeves actively participated included: the creation of a national study of agricultural communications; an inventory and analysis of overseas programs of American universities; the establishment of the first Office of Dean of International Studies and Programs in any American university and in helping to secure initial funding from the Ford Foundation for a program of faculty and graduate student research and for the establishment of campus centers for international activities. He also worked with a faculty committee charged with the creation of a then controversial Labor and Industrial Relations Center in which his experience with labor leaders in national labor organizations and committees was useful. Another committee involved an initial discussion with the leaders of the osteopathic medical profession in Michigan which led several years later to the establishment of the first University-based College of Osteopathic Medicine in the country. Committee assignments in which Reeves also actively participated included: establishment of a Graduate School of Business; a committee on "The Future of the University;" and an all-University committee on the "Education of Women."

Although not linked directly to consulting duties in President Hannah's office but with Hannah's support and approval, Reeves participated as a speaker or resource person in a number of conferences which were beneficial to Michigan State University. They included: a conference at the University of Michigan's Institute on College Administration on the subject of "Institutional Self Studies" which Reeves had pioneered at the University of Chicago in 1929. He also spoke to the annual meeting of the North Central Association of Colleges and Secondary Schools on the "Role of the Consultant in Institutional Self Surveys" and at Harvard University on the "Economics of Higher Education" and at a similar conference sponsored for twenty invited guests by the Fund for the Advancement of Education at the Merrill

Center for Economics. He gave the "Inglis Lecture" at Harvard in 1942.

Likewise, he continued to be involved in other speaking, consulting and committee work the more important of which included: (1) Consultations with John Ivey, Vice President of New York University, the Presidents of the University of Puerto Rico, and the President of Ball State College; (2) Committee on Research Needs and Resources of the American Society of Public Administration; Committee on Planning of Howard University; Executive Secretary of a Committee of the Board of Trustees of Howard University to select a replacement for Dr. Mordecai Johnson, long time distinguished President of Howard, and (3) as Visiting Professor at the Universities of South Florida and New Mexico.

An aspect of Reeves's informal, open and friendly relationships to administrators, professors and others in the academic community is not subject to complete documentation. It is clear from letters and notes in the MSU Archives that his advice and counsel were sought by many persons in and out of the University. He received numerous letters of inquiry from persons requesting his views of persons considered for high positions in educational institutions (a veritable "personnel clearance" function) and he had several occasions to recommend able young persons on the Michigan State University staff to positions of greater responsibility—e.g., Thomas Hamilton to become President of the State University of New York. He numbered a host of educational leaders as good friends and professional colleagues including Alvin C. Eurich, President of the Academy for Educational Development and first President of the State University of New York; Herman Wells, Chancellor of Indiana University, Milton Eisenhower President Emeritus of Johns Hopkins University and several others from whom the author has received letters in connection with the preparation of this biography. They are quoted at the end of this Chapter.

Not all of the interactions with Reeves were positive in fact there is some evidence that some younger persons were "turned off" by his recital of experiences which they had no basis for understanding or appreciating. However, archival files reveal numerous instances of appreciation for his friendly and stimulating influence on their thinking and professional development.

Transition Years at MSU—Retirement and Post Retirement Activities: 1958–1962

At age 68 Reeves, having contributed substantially to the creation of a large, well organized, and significant university largely through advisory assistance to President Hannah and other key officials of the University, was named to the position of "Distinguished Professor of Education and Consultant to the President."

Post Retirement, 1962–1969

College of Education[14]

To head this section Post Retirement is in many respects a misnomer—for only six weeks after the official Board minutes showed him to be retired, Reeves received a letter from John Ivey, the newly appointed Dean of the College of Education:

> We sincerely appreciate your willingness to give us your counsel during this particularly important time in the development of the College of Education. We will be giving considerable time to examining our administrative policies, procedures, and coordinative relationships within the College and with other Colleges on the campus . . . We would like to have you, during the coming year, serve as Consultant to our administrative group—and to me, personally—on these and other matters.

Reeves agreed and continued his relationships on a part-time basis in the College. He was put back on the payroll for six different periods over a span of forty-two months until June 30, 1969. Ivey, twenty-nine years younger than Reeves, was one of the bright and able young men who had earlier come under the influence of Reeves and became, essentially, a protege of his. Ivey came to MSU with a distinguished academic record at the University of North Carolina in Sociology and Planning and in several major administrative positions. He had been a Vice President of New York University just before coming to MSU. He received the Freedom Foundation Medal in 1951 and an Eisenhower Exchange Fellowship for World Travel in 1956.

A unique resource for stimulation and high level collaboration in the College of Education was the presence of four distinguished educators—sometimes referred to as the "four wise men." They were Floyd Reeves, Carleton Washburn, a leader in progressive education, Ernest Melby, a leader in the field of counseling and university administration and George Counts, a well known liberal student of educational politics and of the relations of school and society. The participation of these men of wide experience in all aspects of education in teaching, committee work, special lectures and forums in informal discussions in the coffee lounge added a dimension to the thinking and writing of the faculty and students which was probably unmatched in any College of Education. Reeves fitted in with this team and contributed to the discussions and debates which ensued. He continued to be much involved in counseling students and administrators on a two-thirds time which he elected under his contract previously referred to.

Teaching

Reeves taught one graduate course each quarter, plus other courses in which he "team taught." The titles of the courses were "Current Problems in Administration of Programs in Higher Education" and "Theory and Practice of Administration." Students included graduate students in the College of Education and other colleges plus a number of young faculty members who occupied or anticipated occupying administrative positions. Although no data are available as to the reaction of students to his teaching, informal conversations with knowledgeable persons in the department provides a basis for believing that he was more influential with older students and faculty members and some outside of the College of Education than he was with younger and less experienced students and faculty members. His preoccupation with his dynamic experiences in education and public administration made him less effective in his personal relations with some young faculty members who were more eager for guidance in their personal careers than in his recital and interpretation of his own experiences in education and government.

Consulting and Advising

The principal consulting and advising assignment involved working with faculty committees and included: the preparation of a basic document entitled "Program Directions for the College of Education;" devising innovative measures to expand the recruitment of able students from the urban slum areas of Michigan—both whites and Negroes; and the preparation of a University-wide plan for the Provost's review for the creation of three four-year colleges for undergraduates focused on Science, Public Policy and International Affairs and Languages. Three separate degree granting colleges were later established.

Advisory Assistance to President Hannah and Other Activities (1962–1969)

Possibly the most important task assigned to Reeves was a request from the President in October 1963 to provide suggestions for "two patterns for the Office of the President of the University: first, the office as it might be organized one year from now, and second, as the office might be organized five years from now."

With reference to the earlier of the two organizational plans Reeves responded:

> Before any radical changes are made in the central offices of the University it seems important that careful consideration be given both to the effectiveness and the efficiency of present key personnel within the University, as well as to the probable availability of persons not now on the faculty or staff who might be recruited to fill important posts. This I have tried to do.
>
> I can now see few changes that need to be made before October, 1964, either in central office personnel or in the functions that they perform. Actions that should not be delayed, however, include: the appointment of a Provost; and a tentative assignment to the Provost of his duties and of adequate authority for him to act effectively in their performance. Also, it is important that the responsibilities that you will share with the Provost be made clear.

Reeves went on to recommend the appointment of Dr. Howard Neville to serve as Provost, who Reeves thought would be widely accepted throughout the University. Neville was appointed.

Reeves's recommendations with reference to a five-year plan for the organization and staffing of the Office of the President and the central administration was prefaced by some thoughtful observations:

> It seems to me unwise for any university to attempt to take its organization apart and try to put it together again at any one time, although a few colleges and universities at one time or another have attempted to do so. No matter how urgently changes in institutional programs or structures are needed, acceptance upon the part of many people is required before such changes can be brought about. A major factor involved in bringing about changes in universities is an effective personnel program for professional personnel.
>
> What is much needed within almost every large university with complex functions to perform is a greatly improved program for securing and retaining highly qualified professional, technical and administrative per-

> sonnel. Much more than money has been required in the past and will be in the future to recruit and develop such personnel. What is needed is a system whereby able people within a university are rotated in positions from time to time in order to broaden their experiences. Competencies develop through a variety of types of experience. As a whole Michigan State does well in this regard, but in parts of the University even more could and should be done.
>
> In addition to a developing personnel within the University, this institution needs to engage in more active recruitment of personnel. To meet the need for developing present personnel and recruiting new personnel, I have suggested that a faculty personnel office be established in the office of the Provost. This office would assist the central administration as well as all colleges and other units employing professional, technical and/or administrative personnel within the University, in securing and developing such personnel. It would do this through a program of active recruitment and of comprehensive in-service training. Although I have suggested that such an office be established in the Provost's office, it is possible that such a person (or persons) might operate as effectively if attached directly to the President serving in a staff relationship.[15]

Reeves also recommended in March 1968 that a new "College of Public Administration and International Affairs" be created. The suggestion was probably influenced by Reeves's work with the National Institute of Public Affairs (Chapter V Part II). The rationale for the suggestion included the fact that in recent years, under different titles, Harvard, MIT, University of Virginia, Syracuse University and Princeton had created organizations focused on those areas of Public Administration and Public Affairs. Furthermore, he went on to support his recommendation "that there is great need in Michigan for a strong program of public administration to deal with problems of research, teaching and service in the field of both state and metropolitan administration and "I am of the opinion that the Ford Foundation (which funded the NIPA) may be greatly interested in these problems. (This recommendation, however, was not implemented.)

Activities Reeves participated in which were interesting to him and useful for the University included: membership on the Advisory Committee on University Branches of the Michigan Council of State College and University Presidents; a review of a Report of the Committee on Undergraduate Education for Provost Neville; and the preparation of comments of several reports addressed to President Hannah on educational developments in the Philippines and Australia.

Reeves continued his extensive involvement in Michigan and national educational activities—although at a somewhat reduced rate. Requests for opinions about persons being considered for important positions and other matters continued at a high level. He also continued to attend meetings of the Cleveland Conference and to speak at an important conference of the North Central Association on "Appraisal of Changes in General Education;" and to a group of university administrators at the Center for the Study of Higher Education at the University of Michigan. His earlier association with the curricula of dental schools brought him back to review a proposal sent to him by the Secretary of the American Dental Schools to establish a Department of Educational Research. He also continued to engage in consulting services during this period to the presidents of the University of Georgia, New Mexico, and Puerto Rico and to the Superintendent of the Cleveland School System.

Reeves finally stopped working at the University in June 1969—with the title of Distinguished Professor of Education (Emeritus). He had experienced poor health in his last years of work and had to curtail his activities. His contribution to the University was gratefully acknowledged in March 14, 1971 by being awarded an Honorary Doctor of Laws Degree. The citation partially summarized his achievements and contributions to education and to the University.

> Your long and distinguished career in education and public administration has brought you widespread recognition. Between the beginning of your professional life as a rural school teacher and your present position as Distinguished Emeritus Professor of Education at this university, you served in many capacities, such as principal and superintendent of public schools, and professor at the University of Chicago. In addition to being an exemplary teacher, you produced a number of outstanding studies of American higher education. It was this rich and varied background which you brought to Michigan State University in 1953, and in the ensuing years you have contributed greatly to its educational policies and planning.
>
> The innovativeness and dedication which have marked your academic enterprises are also characteristic of your labors in public administration, where you have served as a Director of (Personnel at) the Tennessee Valley Authority, a member of President Roosevelt's Committee on Administrative Management, and consultant to such varied projects as the Pakistan Academies for Rural Development and the UNESCO Committee to the Philippines. Because of your eminent role in improving higher education and public administration both in this country and abroad, and in special recognition of your faithful and important service

to this institution, Michigan State University is pleased to grant you the degree of Doctor of Laws.

Other honorary degrees were awarded to Reeves by Albion College, Kent State University, Bethany College and Temple University.

Reeves died in East Lansing, Michigan on August 20, 1979.

Chapter VIII

Reflections and Appraisals

Reeves had a significant influence on several aspects of education during the thirty or more years of his active professional life. Three aspects stand at or near the top in any kind of general appraisal. In retrospect possibly his persistent, indefatigable advocacy of increased support—local, state and federal—for education should be listed as of first importance. He dramatized the marked variation of standards of support for education between rich and poor counties and school districts; states and regions; rural and urban areas; and between areas with large concentrations of Negroes and other minorities and areas of comfortably and predominately homogeneous white, middle and affluent classes of citizens. All of these variations he considered indefensible. He boldly advocated greatly expanded federal expenditures to provide a more equitable opportunity for all citizens to have the benefits of education. He interrelated the data from the Advisory Committee on Education to the deliberations and recommendations of the American Youth Commission, the Civilian Conservation Corps, National Youth Commission, White House Conference on Children in a Democracy, Regents Inquiry into the Character and Cost of Education in New York State and the interests of youth organizations, labor unions, professional education organizations, PTAs and other organizations interested in education.

He advocated an expanded role for the federal government in lessening the shock of readjustment to post-war vocational and educational conditions for those who had participated in the war effort. He made the case for the legislation commonly known as the G. I. Bill of Rights in his role as Chairman of the Conference on Readjustment of Civilian and Military Personnel.

For all of the above efforts to expand educational opportunity in various programs, Reeves was on a veritable tread mill of speaking engagements and radio programs to gain the support of educational and civic organizations, labor unions, business and other groups. Some of these were made at the specific request of the President of the United States. Committees of Congress called on him to testify and advise them on legislation. The correspondence load on the subject was also heavy.

Unlike many committee reports which are dutifully submitted, momentarily discussed and filed away, those with which Reeves was associated became headline stories in the press and other media and on innumerable conference programs. Not all were supportive of the recommendations but most of them were. Implementation was built into the research and policy recommendation as an integral part of the whole enterprise.

A second area of emphasis was concentrated on efforts to reduce discriminatory practices with reference to Negroes and other minority groups and overlooked or underfinanced programs for adults, women and rural citizens. These activities were closely related to the broader efforts to expand educational opportunity described above but focused more precisely on these problem areas. The work of the American Council of Education's Committee on Discriminatory Practices in Higher Education, for example, vigorously exposed overt and subtle discriminatory practices in admissions to colleges and universities generally and to professional schools in particular. The many discriminatory practices of fraternities and other student groups in colleges and universities were also exposed. A more particularized instance was in the research studies and testimony of Negroes, Catholics and Jews regarding the restrictions imposed by institutions of higher education in New York State. The impact of the data and the highly charged and pent-up frustrations of the victimized groups pressed the Governor of the State and the legislators to create greatly expanded opportunities for these and other disadvantaged groups. Reeves's convictions about this central problem and his ingenuity in devising practical solutions gave indispensable support to Owen D. Young and other members of the Committee, who as respected leaders in New York State wanted to correct the discriminatory practices of the educational institutions.

A third area in which Reeves did distinguished work involved the methods of surveying and evaluating educational institutions—especially colleges and universities. Having been involved in the examination of some two hundred educational institutions, he developed in his association with committees of one of the most influential accrediting bodies—the North Central Association—more flexible, less doctrinaire, and less primarily statistical standards of appraisal. The new and more functional standards, which included more room for judgment, were helpful to institutions with varying educational objectives and clientele in developing distinctive programs to meet their particular objectives.

Reeves also pressed for broadly oriented general education, rather than narrowly vocational curricula—especially in the first two years of college. The curricular pattern followed at the University of Chicago and other institutions was adapted to Michigan State University.

He was also influential in demonstrating the need for better organization and administration of educational institutions, especially the need for developing clear lines of authority and responsibility for instructional as well as administrative positions and between boards of trustees and administrative officials.

Reeves's Personal Qualities and Work Method

Reeves, possibly, had the widest first hand knowledge of American educational institutions and their leaders of any person in his generation. These contacts, plus those which he developed in government, business, labor, religion and other fields combined to give him an exceptionally practical grasp of the complex problems, resources, and needs of educational institutions as related to the broader societal needs and aspirations. His natural disposition to embrace and learn from these varied contacts was highly stimulating to him and was translated into what he thought about as desirable and achievable public policy for education and other public sectors of activity. He was comfortable in his work associations with persons of varying backgrounds and they with him.

One person who observed his work as a consultant characterized him as the "consummate consultant."

In order to keep himself free to spend more of his time on strategy, personal discussions, formulation of research designs and more effective working procedures he consistently chose competent young persons as associates to carry delegated responsibilities. These younger associates were usually made full partners in the work and they grew in their association with Reeves.

He was energetic and indefatigable, dedicated, optimistic, and of good humor, although his work intensity—often with more than one major activity being carried on concurrently—occasionally caused him to become ill for short periods of time.

Publications

Over his lifetime Reeves wrote over 25 articles,[1] and dozens of chapters in books and introductions to books, and edited over 50 research reports. To a very large extent the content of these publications and of his speeches was directly related to work in which he was involved. He was not much given to theorizing in the abstract, but based his conclusions and recommendations on facts and the logical implications and principles which could be derived from the facts. His persistent concern to relate education to social, economic and political realities, and to extend the benefits of education to the largest number, without artificial restrictions, was central in his motivation and drive and fully reflected in his writings. In a sense he put schools and schooling back into society. His philosophy of education went well beyond traditional concepts in that he saw formal schooling as only a part of the total lifelong educational process to which all institutions and all experiences contributed. With reference to the value of work experiences he wrote:

> Appropriate amounts of useful work are desirable elements in the experience of children and youth of all ages . . . After they have passed the point to which schooling should be their major occupation, young people should normally be able, without undue difficulty, to enter private gainful employment. When the opportunities to do so are not adequate in number, it is a function of government to provide the necessary additional opportunities . . . Any form of work or gainful employment may have educational effects. In this respect employment is not different from such other major aspects of life as those involved in marriage, citizenship, community participation, and at present, military service.[2]

Other reflections on Reeves's generalizations about education are expressed in excerpts from his Inglis Lecture in Appendix B.[3]

Reeves's pragmatic philosophy of education and his deep concern for expanding opportunities for those who were disadvantaged for reasons of sex were expressed in an article published in the Journal of the *American Association of University Women* in which he strongly advocated increased participation and appropriate compensation of women to persuade them to join in the war effort. He later expressed progressive views on an expanded role for women in all aspects of professional and social life—unrelated to conditions of war or peace.[4]

Reeves's deep convictions and values were further expressed in a speech entitled "Youth and the Future" which he applied to all persons. In this speech he quoted and shared the views of Dorothy Canfield Fisher when she wrote:

> The really searching, intimate problem for each one of us is that of how to develop, out of the new and changed conditions of modern times, a way of life satisfying and rewarding to the best and finest qualities we have—those qualities which deserve to be creative. For if the long recorded experience of our race proves anything, it proves that living may become intolerable to complex human beings, if it is wholly centered on material security, even when comfort is added to safety.[5]

Appraisals by Colleagues

Appraisals of Reeves's outlook on education and on his personal qualities as experienced by those who were closely associated with him in research and action programs are partially expressed in the following additional excerpts from a few of the letters sent to the author.

As a Director of Surveys

- There is no question that Floyd Reeves was an expert, perhaps *the* expert on institutional surveys. He always knew what he wanted to accomplish. He organized well for the field work and the collation of data . . . Floyd was a work horse . . . Floyd was creative in designing his course on administration. He was creative in redesigning the methods used by the North Central Association.[6] Dr. Algo D. Henderson
- More than anyone I have ever known Floyd Reeves was always ready to question established practices and entertain new ideas. In the area of evaluation and accrediting of colleges and universities, the area in which I worked closely with him, Floyd was one of the first to recognize the inadequacy of sole or even heavy reliance on

quantitative standards—faculty degrees, class size, student-faculty ratios, library holdings, income and expenditures per student and the like. He frankly recognized and accepted the importance in the evaluative process of judgment of institutional quality by knowledgeable persons.[7] Dr. Norman Burns

On Liberal and Adult Education and Post-War Planning

• Both Dr. Reeves and I were interested in broad liberal education. Our views coincided, though each (of us) approached the problem from a different point of view. I was deeply concerned by the fact that developments after World War II could place our nation in a position of world leadership, and for that we were not prepared. Our educational institutions, I was certain, should help produce men and women who not only used their education for personal, community, and national needs, but should also produce men and women of broad minds capable of self-education throughout lifetime and eager to be so well informed on national and international affairs that they would in fact constitute "new Americans." This view was an outgrowth of my own experience in World War II as well as (in) lengthy conversations with my brother (President Eisenhower). Doctor Reeves felt the same, but his views had been developed within the academic community. We both felt that life-long study by all able citizens was imperative.[8] Dr. Milton Eisenhower

On Relationships with His Colleagues at the University of Chicago and on the UNESCO Mission

• My association with Floyd Reeves from 1945–1968 added new dimensions to my understanding of education and society. His experiences with the TVA and with the reorganization of the University of Chicago had led to the development of a philosophy, as well as operational concepts, of educational and political organization and administration. His observations of life in the rural south and in the Philippines had whetted his compassion for the deprivations of the poor in his own and other societies and prompted him to seek remedies through social reconstruction. Perhaps, the two outstanding characteristics of Floyd Reeves, as I knew him were: (1) his empathetic response to the needs and ideas of others; and (2) his continuing search for ways to improve the human condition through the functioning of social institutions . . .

His contagious enthusiasm for the constructive ideas and plans of others encouraged students, colleagues and organization leaders to develop and implement their own concepts for educational and social reform. Floyd Reeves influence extended far beyond his published works and his formal lectures for which he was not especially noted. His major impact was on the lives of the thousands who were moved by his encouragement and his enthusiastic support for ideas with potential for the improvement of social institutions . . . His response to individuals and to social needs was never impeded by barriers of culture, creeds or race.[9] Dr. Francis Chase

- I knew Floyd Reeves as a very stimulating scholar who was fundamentally an intellectual or academic entrepreneur. He was highly motivated in advancing insights and ideas to give them practical meaning. He also saw the importance of the decisions that people make privately and that bodies make collectively if and when they would respond to the new insights that he and any of us could bring to bear on real issues. I would very much underline the word robust in characterizing Floyd Reeves as a dynamic intellectual human being. He was a member of a very rare breed. There are so few.[10] Dr. T. W. Schultz
- Floyd Reeves was a dedicated worker for the causes in which he believed. He was a tireless and hard driver of himself and those with whom he worked. His level of physical and mental energy was phenomenal. His vision of what education could and should do to develop the talents of the individual and enhance the conditions of the nation and world population were always central in his work, whether the cause was the improvement of the Tennessee Valley, the manpower requirements of our war effort, or the making of a new Asian nation, Dr. Reeves was in the leadership group.[11] Dr. Paul Hanna

From a Colleague in Several National Committees or Commissions

- He (Floyd Reeves) was outstanding in every respect as an educational leader especially in the fields . . . of organization and administration of university appraisal and related fields. His reputation was not only national but international. He was skilled as an organizer and director of educational research. He was a man of broad experience which enabled him to attract other people of talent. He was an important figure during his long and active life.[12] Dr. Herman Wells

A Colleague on the Temporary Commission on the Need for a University of the State of New York

- He was perhaps the greatest figure of empirical school of American social science.[13] Dr. David S. Berkowitz

Colleagues at Michigan State University

- . . . John Hannah sought out geniuses like Reeves and asked them to move MSU forward . . . He was a mover, a shaker, a hopeful man always and he frightened about half the people who heard him. But in belief in human potential, and the possibilities of creating human structures and institutions to unlock and unleash that potential, was boundless. The belief was sustained by a broad scintillating mind, utter fearlessness, and an apparent depth of spiritual and emotional resources that enabled him to go from crest to crest.[14] Dr. Stanley Irzerda
- First, I want to make an observation which, I believe is factual regarding Floyd's professional career. The facts are very clear that Floyd exerted tremendous influence in the field of higher education, nationally and most specifically at Michigan State University. The products of his influence have been documented and are visible. . .
  Second, let me indicate my personal sense about Floyd Reeves and his influence on my own activities in higher education and on many others, as I knew about them personally.
  In my case, there is no question about the fact that Floyd was a 'model' and consultant for me as I developed my own professional plans and as I worked on specific projects in the field of higher education. Not only was he always available for private discussion, they were personal, but he was highly visible in informal group discussions in places like the College of Education coffee lounge . . . Those informal discussions provided very fertile grounds for ideas which shaped the future of individuals and of the college.[15] Dr. John X Jamrich

The above comments, although short of a comprehensive philosophical appraisal, are indicative of the kind of influence which Reeves had on his collaborating colleagues and, with them, on innovative, progressive and broadly oriented educational policies and programs. There is little doubt that the factual record of his accomplishments and the high professional regard which his closest colleagues had for him constitute an important chapter in educational developments, particularly in the decades of the 30's to 50's.

Part II

Reeves in Government (Public Administration)

Chapter 1

The Tennessee Valley Authority (TVA)

Floyd Reeves joined the Tennessee Valley Authority on June 16, 1933, two and a half months after the inauguration of Franklin Delano Roosevelt and one month after the passage, on May 18, of the TVA Act. He served as the first Director of the Personnel and Social Economic Divisions until January 1, 1936, when he returned to the University of Chicago. No treatment of his work with the Authority, which launched him into national prominence, would be meaningful without a brief sketch of the conditions which confronted the country in the early thirties; Roosevelt's New Deal's response to these conditions in the Tennessee Valley; and the long history of federal legislation to improve those conditions.

The approximately seventeen years of Congressional debate and struggle to deal with problems of national and regional development of natural resources led to the passage of several predecessor acts of Congress which were vetoed by the then incumbent Presidents. But the legislative record also shows the emergency and contribution of strong advocates of comprehensive natural resource development. Senator George Norris of Nebraska was the key influence in the evolution of a national policy to achieve this purpose. He had the deserved reputation of being the "Father of the TVA."

FDR became President at a propitious time in the country's history to give administrative leadership and support for the TVA Act of 1933. The Act not only prescribed some innovative engineering and other technical features but several organizational and administrative policies which made it possible for TVA to demonstrate a better way of accomplishing comprehensive regional development. Some of the key points of the history and administration of the TVA Act follow.

FDR's New Deal

FDR's famous inaugural speech delivered on March 4, 1933 set the tone and pace for the first hundred days of his historic first term. The key words of the speech centered on a renewal of faith on freedom from fear and on actions to correct an accumulation of critical national problems which Herbert Hoover had documented by a variety of surveys but failed to take appropriate steps to correct.

Arthur M. Schlesinger, Jr., in his *The Coming of the New Deal** summarized not only the economic problems faced by millions of people in all walks of life, and the political consequences of not solving those problems within the framework of the capitalist economic system, but also of the international ramifications of the problems.

> The national income was less than half of what it had been four short years before. Nearly thirteen million Americans—about one quarter of the labor force—were desperately seeking jobs. The machinery for sheltering and feeding the unemployed was breaking down everywhere under the growing burden. And a few hours before, in the early morning before the inauguration, every bank in America had locked its doors. It was now not just a matter of staving off hunger. It was a matter of seeing whether a representative democracy could conquer economic collapse. It was a matter of staving off violence even (at least some so thought) revolution . . .[1]

FDR tackled the problems with extraordinary vigor. At the heart of his attack were his successful efforts and pressures on Congress to pass fifteen basic legislative Acts between March 9 and June 15, 1933 before an exhausted Congress adjourned. These Acts were all addressed to deal with such economic problems as bank and farm failures, unemployment and other social problems. Among the Acts was also the Tennessee Valley Authority Act.

The President had a special and dedicated interest in the passage of the TVA Act as interpreted by Arthur Schlesinger when he wrote:

---

* Excerpts from *The Coming of the New Deal* by Arthur M. Schlesinger, Jr. Copyright © 1958 by Arthur M. Schlesinger Jr. Reprinted by permission of Houghton Mifflin Co.

> Perhaps no law passed during the Hundred Days expressed more passionately a central presidential concern. The concern arose only in part from Roosevelt's old absorption with land, forest and water. It arose equally from his continued search for a better design for national living. Utopia still presented itself to him in the cherished image of Hyde Park—tranquility in the midst or rich meadows and farmlands, deep forests and a splendid, flowing river. America, he felt, was overcommitted to urban living. In the twenties he had discussed the possibility of keeping people on the land by combining farming with part-time local industry. As Governor of New York, he had talked of redressing the population balance city and countryside—taking industry from crowded urban centers to airy villages, and giving scrawny kids from the slums opportunity for sun and growth in the country. The depression and the President provided new opportunity to move toward a balanced civilization.[2]

Arthur Morgan, the first Chairman of the TVA, the other two Directors, Reeves and the other early employees were among those who were captivated by the ideas of the President. The TVA Act, however, did not quite reflect these sweeping ideas. In fact the Act imposed some limitations and specified somewhat different priorities. The development of the river and power system and the rehabilitation of worn out lands absorbed most of the energies and resources of the TVA for most of its early years. Nevertheless the ideals of Roosevelt for the project guided the thinking and motivation of the leaders of TVA throughout his life time.

To help FDR tackle the complex problems facing him and the country he attracted to Washington a collection of brains, dedication and energy probably unequaled in the nation's history since its early days. As Schlesinger described the situation:

> Washington was deluged with an endless stream of bright young men. 'If ability could be measured in a tin bucket, William Kiplinger wrote in the Journal of the Commerce in 1934, I should say that the Roosevelt administration contained more gallons of ability than any of its recent predecessors. They brought with them an alertness, an excitement, an appetite for power, an instinct for crisis and a dedication to public service which became during the thirties the essence of Washington.' 'No group in government,' said Arthur Knock, 'has ever been more interesting, dull, brilliant, stupid, headstrong, pliable, competent, inefficient, more honorable in money matters, more ruthless in material methods . . .' The sounds of the New Dealers were rarely dreary or hollow. They altered the whole tempo and tone of Washington as a community.[3]

Floyd Reeves, forty-three years old at the time, fitted into this environment with elan. He not only got acquainted with FDR (and later Eleanor Roosevelt) through several conferences and other work with the President on TVA business but won his confidence as evidenced by the number of tasks which he undertook at the President's request in such fields as education, personnel administration, planning, programs for youth and returning veterans, and manpower. He also extended his range of colleagues, friends and acquaintances in labor leaders, planners, business leaders, agricultural economists, *et al.*[4]

On June 25, 1933, eight days after the first meeting of the TVA Board, Reeves, full of enthusiasm, wrote to his wife:

> I have never worked harder than during the past two weeks, yet I have never enjoyed my work so much. The intellectual stimulation I get is worth all the effort of the past twenty years which has made the present position possible. I live more in the two weeks of this work than in two months of any work I have had before. Furthermore I feel better physically than I have felt at any time since we moved to Chicago . . .[5]

On July 16, 1933, Reeves continued to express, to his wife, his pleasure and excitement in his contacts in Washington, including Frederic Delano and others.

Reeves loved the excitement of Washington and became a significant personage in the organizations with which he worked—including primarily, in the first two and a half years with the Tennessee Valley Authority. Washington and the New Deal were good for Reeves and Reeves was good for the New Deal as will be described subsequently.

Background information on the key historical factors which were part of the roots of the TVA; struggles and debates in the Congress regarding the best way—in the national interest—to deal with the long-term and short-term problems of developing the natural resources of the nation and specifically those of the Tennessee Valley; and some of the major actions taken by the TVA within the framework and specific provisions of the Act during the first twenty years are recorded in the basic publications which are listed in the notes on this Chapter.[6] But first the major provisions in the TVA Act.

The breadth of the Act is well expressed in the preamble:

> An Act—to improve the navigability and to provide for the flood control of the Tennessee River; to provide for reforestation and the proper use of marginal lands in the Tennessee Valley; to provide for the agricultural and

industrial development of said Valley, to provide for the national defense by the creation of a corporation for the operation of government properties at or near Muscle Shoals in the State of Alabama and for other purposes.

The Act, more specifically, provided for: (1) the creation of a Government Corporation headed by a three-man Board with headquarters in the Valley to conduct the business of the Authority and to report directly to the President; (2) fiscal and other managerial powers which made it possible to operate with the power of government but with the "flexibility of private enterprise", and (3) other provisions which created a framework in which the initiative, imagination and creativity of the Board and staff could be focused on the highly novel problem of maximum integrated development of the physical, social, economic and institutional resources of the potentially rich Tennessee Valley.

Joseph Swidler, General Counsel, commented on some key features of the TVA ACT:

> TVA is deeply rooted in the nation's history. Each phase of its program arose out of varying needs and problems, but it is a principal distinction of the TVA Act that it serves as a vehicle for uniting as a single resource development program these diverse but interrelated public interests. The key administrative feature of the TVA Act is the establishment of a framework adapted to the nature of the problems and responsibilities of the agency. The Act not only unites and integrates the various program activities but also, tailors the administrative arrangements to the special needs of the program. The goal of all federal administration is a balanced accommodation between executive responsibility and freedom on one hand and Congressional control of basic policies on the other. The record shows that the TVA Act is one of the most successful of the efforts of Congress to achieve such a balance.[7]

Several lawsuits, brought by the private power companies, which went the route of the lower courts, were finally resolved by the Supreme Court in favor of the TVA. The decisions validated the wisdom of the legislators and of the President.

Provisions of the Act of Particular Reference to the Work of Floyd Reeves as Director of Personnel

The breadth of the Act in program terms, and the unique provisions for the organization and administration of the programs, generally attracted and challenged the Board of Directors, and the staff, particularly of the early group of appointees. Apart from the pleasure of just getting a *job* (after varying periods of unemployment for many) the program challenge and opportunities set forth in the Act, which created an attractive setting in which to work, were instant challenges to qualified engineers, foresters, agriculturists, accountants, planners, public administrators and all the other professions, from all sections of the United States. The key provisions of the Act which made it possible to select personnel who could meet the challenge were Section 3 and 6

Section 3 reads:

> The Board shall without regard to the provisions of Civil Service Laws applicable to officers and employees of the United States, appoint such managers, assistant managers, officers, employees, attorneys, and agents, as are necessary for the transaction of its business, fix their compensation, define their duties, require bonds of them as the Board may designate, and provide a system of organization to fix responsibility and promote efficiency.

Section 6 reads:

> In the appointment of officials and the selection of employees for said Corporation, and the promotion of any such employees or officials, *no political test* or qualification shall be permitted *or given consideration but all such appointments* and promotions shall be given and made on the basis of merit and *efficiency* (italics added). Any member of said Board who is found by the President of the United States to be guilty of a violation of this section shall be removed from office by the President of the United States, and any appointee of said Board who is found by the Board to be guilty of a violation of this section shall be removed from office by said Board.

This novel language was felt to be necessary by Senators Norris and Hill, and other legislators in order to assure that the administration of the Act would not be compromised by federal employees who might have been recruited and promoted under rigid civil service rules and regulations on the one hand, or political or corporate influence on the other.

The founding legislators wrought better than they knew, for within the framework of freedom and responsibility provided in the Act, an exceptional human organization evolved. John Oliver, one-time General Manager of TVA, writing of the organization structure observed:

> This sketch of the evolution of TVA's organization structure provides little insight into the warmly human factors which were always in operation. From the beginning the Board and members of the staff addressed themselves to daring new experimentation in integrated resource development and in administrative concepts which made maximum demands on creativity and team work. The whole program of TVA in fact became for those involved in it a vital educational experiment. New combinations of highly specialized personnel were brought together to lay the ground work for an expanded regional economy which would use the developing capital plant and the newly integrated resources for the economic and social rehabilitation of the Tennessee Valley.[8]

Inability of the Civil Service System to do the TVA Job

The first problem for the TVA, if operating under the normal Civil Service System at that time would have been the problem of political appointments. This is not to say that the Civil Service System had not already progressed far beyond the spoils traditions of the Jacksonian era, but only to suggest that many of the principal officers of government agencies normally would have secured their appointments through political endorsements. Reeves and his associates had difficulties enough in staffing the TVA, but the situation would have been hopelessly confused if there had been a mixture of politically endorsed employees and those who were employed without reference to political preference. Herman Pritchett quotes President Hoover's concern regarding the personnel provisions of the Muscle Shoals bill of 1931, which he vetoed in these words:

> These directors are manifestly to have a political complexion and apparently the entire working force is likewise to have such a basis of selection, as the usual provision for the merit service required by law in most other federal activities is omitted.[9]

The framers of the TVA Act took President Hoover's fears to heart and made sure that a unique merit system was essential to achievement of the TVA objectives. The merit system started with the Directors—whose politics were not highlighted—if considered at all—nor was the "politics" (if he had any) of Floyd Reeves. The only criterion for selection of the three directors as stated in the Act, was that they attest to their "belief in the wisdom and feasibility of the Act." They would have been subject to dismissal if this provision had been ignored.

The stark fact was that large numbers of the unemployed or under-employed were Democrats, and the Democrats had been out of office for twelve long years. With the Civil Service incapable of meeting the recruitment demand, the pressures to give preference to Democrats in employment became hard to resist. Just how, and how successfully, various New Deal agencies dealt with this problem we need not examine here, but TVA with its specific legal prescription for appointments on the basis of "merit and efficiency," had a clear and unequivocal response to the Senator or Congressman seeking to bypass or water down the merit and efficiency principle. But this didn't keep them from trying. Some members of Congress simply couldn't believe that they had meant it when they wrote such a provision into law. Floyd Reeves had to take a good deal of the bluff and threats from quite a few irate Congressmen on this subject, but he knew what the TVA Act prescribed and that he had the full support of the Board in doing his job.

Then there was also the question about the efficacy of the Civil Service System's precise numerical rating of qualifications of professional personnel. A system of evaluating qualifications which permitted more judgment and flexibility, commonly practiced in private industry, was clearly called for in manning the TVA. Another overriding—but less objective consideration—was the fact that the Civil Service was not distinguished for attracting the most potentially competent personnel—especially professional and managerial personnel.

Another factor which would have inhibited the performance of TVA employees was the then unclear policy of Civil Service regarding in-service training programs for employees. TVA embraced the policy of providing in-service and other forms of training from the very beginning of its operations, as an integral and significant aspect of its comprehensive personnel program. It was never ambiguous about the use of prescribed pre-service and in-service programs, training for apprentices, clerks and office personnel and more varied programs for professional and managerial personnel.

The Creation of the TVA Personnel Program: Selection of the Staff

Much of the work load necessary to implement the personnel provisions of the TVA Act, especially in the early years, was carried by a few young persons, several of whom were selected and trained by

Reeves. Chief among these was Gordon R. Clapp, who was one of Reeves's graduate students at the University of Chicago, whom he appointed as his assistant on July 13, 1933—less than one month after the first meeting of the Board. Clapp's only work experience up to this point had been as Dean of Students at Lawrence College in Appleton, Wisconsin but he was a brilliant and dedicated young man. He was promoted successively, over twenty-two years with the TVA, to the positions of Assistant Director of Personnel, Director of Personnel (at the time of Reeves's departure from TVA), General Manager and Chairman of the Board. Others somewhat in order of appointment at essentially junior levels were: Paul David, a young economist, who had been selected by Chairman Morgan, and who was particularly helpful in the early work of dealing with the hundreds of applicants while the TVA offices were still in Washington; Arthur Jandrey, a lawyer and graduate student at the University of Chicago who performed high level policy and analytical work in close collaboration with Clapp and Reeves and who later served as Assistant and then Director of Personnel and Assistant General Manager; Ethel Larson, an able secretary and later administrative assistant, who was employed in July 1933 and continued her work with the Personnel Division for many years thereafter; J. Dudley Dawson, on leave from the chairmanship of the Mathematics Department at Antioch College, who had principal responsibility for the formulation and conduct of the early training programs; Carl Richey, possibly the only person with experience in governmental personnel administration, as Director of Employment and subsequently head of the Classification Division and also of the field offices; C. C. Killen, labor organizer who was appointed as "labor and wage investigator" and who became a key staff member on all matters related to organized labor; Maurice Seay, a colleague of Reeves at the University of Kentucky, appointed as Director of Training succeeding J. Dudley Dawson; and George F. Gant, who joined TVA as a young historian in the Social and Economic Division and who successfully served as Director of Training, Director of Personnel, and General Manager.

Staffing of the Personnel Division reflects Reeves's aptitude for selecting able young persons, essentially "amateurs" in public personnel work to whom he delegated broad responsibilities under only general supervision and who, over several years, typically grew in competence under such a work environment. Many of the early appointments made in the TVA—although none for political reasons, had an aura of personal favoritism. This point was brought out in the Joint

Congressional Investigation of TVA in 1938 during which certain Congressmen who had no special love for TVA raised questions about the competence and performance of the Personnel Division. Leonard D. White, a recognized leader in personnel and public administration and a former Commissioner of the U.S. Civil Service Commission, served as an expert consultant and witness to the Joint Committee. White, then a Professor of Political Science at the University of Chicago, summarized his response to the question "Is the staff of the Personnel Department adequately trained and competent for the proper performance of the work of the Department?"

> The staff of the Personnel Department compares favorably with the staff of other employment agencies; the responsible officials are well qualified for their respective duties; they are familiar with the best personnel procedures and have shown ability to adapt prevailing practices to the needs of the TVA; they have the confidence of organized labor and of other employees and supervisors; the *esprit de corps* of the Department is high. The satisfactory quality of their work is reflected in part in the high quality of personnel which has generally been supplied to the operating departments of the Authority.[10]

The Joint Committee made no recommendations on point of their investigation. White recommended, however, that the "Civil Service Law of 1883, as amended," be extended to the Tennessee Valley Authority, "excepting such classes of employment as the President, upon the recommendation of the Civil Service Commission after consultation with the TVA, may direct." After 6306 pages of testimony on the personnel and other management and program aspects of the TVA, the committee did not accept Leonard White's recommendation but rather rested the case with his overall appraisal of competence. But for many years thereafter there was continuous administrative and legislative pressure on TVA to conform to civil service rules and procedures. Some modifications were done selectively to adjust some personnel procedures (e.g., recognition of granting preference to veterans) while preserving the initial requirements of the TVA Act to develop an independent, non-political merit system of personnel administration. Furthermore, a number of the innovations of the TVA personnel system were adopted by the federal system.

The moral to the story may be that where there is a creative job to be done employ bright young persons who are not bogged down with detailed experience in long-standing approaches to personnel and other aspects of administration; and delegate responsibility to them and trust them and let them break new ground. This was basically Reeves's solution to this, as to many other problems, in the art of administration.

Significant Steps in the Evolution of the TVA Personnel Program

Establishment of the non-political merit personnel program had to be achieved concurrently with the employment of large numbers of employees under pressure of getting the regional development job underway and to relieve oppressive unemployment. This double-edged problem is reflected in Reeves's letters to his wife which describes the pressures under which he worked. Excerpts follow:

6/20/33 (four days after the first meeting of the Board)

> Our office is a mess at present. We have about 8000 applications for positions and nothing but temporary help. Our lines of personnel applicants seeking interviews consists of about 500 people a day . . . Have had two conferences with the Secretary of War and one with the Secretary of Agriculture.

6/22/33

> This morning I was besieged by the politicians. They are calling me all sorts of names now and threatening me with serious trouble when Roosevelt returns to Washington. I am standing pat on appointments and intend to continue to do so. I have employed Ethel Larson as Secretary. I had her telephone hooked up to mine in such a manner as to permit her to listen in on all of my conferences over the phone and take a transcript of what is said . . . I told her to do this because I want a witness. The politicians always come in pairs and unless I have Miss Larson present there would be one man's word against two . . .
>
> Yesterday I had a conference with the Secretary of Agriculture. Today the Secretary to the President and the Secretary to Mr. Farley* the Postmaster General and dispenser of patronage, came to my office and told me what they expected of me. I told them that they were making a mistake, and that I did not think they were truly representing Mr. Roosevelt.* I refused to let them persuade me to employ a politician as my major assistant . . .
>
> Senator Pat Harrison of Mississippi sent word to me this morning that

---

* Chairman Arthur Morgan who also took a great deal of "heat" from Mr. Farley.

he was going to stay in Washington until I placed some of his folks. I sent word back that I thought he could find a cooler place to spend the summer and that he would be here all summer unless he changed his mind.

6/25/33

We are still free from politics and I intend that we shall stay free . . .

Yesterday I received word from a committee of Congress that I was to have the skids put under me this week unless I changed my attitude, I shall sit tight and see what happens . . .

7/20/33

This week was a difficult one with the politicians. I have had an item at the office which I will send . . . The item stated that the man representing patronage was going to be on my tail yesterday. It happened just as stated. No member of the Board is here so I had to handle the situation alone. For the time being it is cared for but I expect more difficulty Monday. I was told by this man today, that he was going over my head to our Board, and if he did not get satisfaction, he would take the matter directly to the President, asking my immediate resignation. I told him to carry it as far up as he pleased and that would not change my present procedure except by direct order from our Board.

The Chairman and other members of the TVA Board never let Reeves down on this and his uncompromised adherence to the provisions of the TVA Act which barred political appointments.

8/11/33

As Reeves and his associates created procedures for selecting employees from the hundreds who were applying (for jobs) he mentioned the use of a questionnaire which was being sent to all references indicated by the applicants:

These questionnaire letters have caused many comments—all strongly negative or positive. For everyone who calls them trash, there are at least nine strongly favorable to the standard we set and the type of questions asked . . . The truck will leave for Knoxville with our 50,000 applications tomorrow.

8/22/33

I received word from Knoxville that there are 1000 personnel applicants appearing at the office each day. It is clogging up our machinery and we want to do something to stop it . . .

What was done to "stop it" was for Reeves to borrow Dr. L. J. O'Rourke, Director of Research for the U.S. Civil Service Commission who, in collaboration with the TVA personnel staff, devised a procedure for selection of construction workers which involved a written test to ascertain general levels of intelligence and ability to read written instructions; performance tests for certain jobs; interviews and reference checks. Gordon Clapp, who worked particularly closely with O'Rourke, describes the massive program—unheard of at that time for the selection of labor.

> In the fall of 1933 two examinations were held in 138 centers, covering all Tennessee and parts of Kentucky, Virginia, North Carolina, Alabama, Georgia, and Mississippi. The examination was of a general type, to test ability to follow written and oral instructions. Admission to the examination was by card issued to those whose applications met the requirement of residence within the Tennessee Valley. The application carried in the upper left-hand corner 'Form 10 TVA.' Of the tens of thousands of Form 10 applications freely distributed throughout the Valley, fifty thousand were filled out and returned, and almost thirty-nine thousand men ultimately took the examination.
>
> The thousands of men from farms and cities, from mountain caves and cotton-gin towns, who assembled, pencil in hand, on those two December days of 1933 were probably unaware that they were making history in a method for the recruitment and selection of a labor force. Their presence in the post-office rooms, schoolhouses, and churches which served as examination centers was a public demonstration of a new approach to construction work. They had already passed, unknowingly, through several sifting screens. They were men who had decided to assemble for this strange kind of examination instead of relying on the assurance of harassed political captains that a job would be obtained for the party faithfuls without going through special procedures. They had shown their confidence in the probity of the TVA by filling out Form 10 in spite of some scoffing at this fancy way of getting a job when, as the wise boys said, 'everyone knows a letter from the congressman will be enough.'[11]

Clapp went on to report that the use of "Form 10" laid the basis for public understanding of the non-political character of the TVA personnel policy.

During the Congressional hearings in 1938, after Reeves had returned to the University of Chicago, considerable attention was paid to TVA's operations of the merit provisions of the Act, with several specific instances examined in great detail. Clapp served as the principal witness to the work of the Personnel Department. The records of his testimony show 121 pages of grilling by unfriendly Congressmen, principally Representative Charles Wolverton of New Jersey but by others as well. He was questioned on all aspects of the program including training courses; training costs and quality of instructors; Negro employment and relations; grievance policies and specific cases of dismissal; political influence; policies and relations with unions; wage and salary rates and comparisons; costs of personnel and many other subjects. On all of these he kept his cool in spite of annoying and very personal questions about his own background and rapid progress in his career. Only two or three references were made to Reeves. One was to the period of time Clapp worked under the supervision of Reeves. The dialogue with one of the Congressmen went like this: "So you were tutored, so to speak, under him for 3–4 years before you were placed in charge." Clapp's response, "A very tough tutorage, I assure you."

Apropos of the same point, David Lilienthal in his foreword to Harry Case's article on *Gordon R. Clapp: The Role of Faith, Purpose and People in Administration* wrote:

> Long ago in the earliest days of TVA, Gordon Clapp attracted the attention of those of us who were responsible for erecting the enterprise, as a man to watch. Because of his relative youth and his even more youthful appearance, he was usually referred to as 'that red-headed boy in Floyd Reeves's office.' It was not long until that red-headed boy had established himself as a man of judgment in personnel matters. The rest of the story of his rise is history.[12]

One of the toughest opponents of TVA's personnel program was Senator McKellar, the Senior Senator from Tennessee, who was known for his well-developed concern for patronage to worthy supporters from the state he represented, which happened to be his "recognized" patronage territory. The TVA files show numerous early attempts, which persisted for several years, to cajole the Directors, Reeves and Clapp to appoint his constituents to positions in the Authority. But the provisions in the Act for a non-political merit system of personnel administration held firm. McKellar finally stated in the Senate that "I do not know of a man I have recommended who has been appointed by the TVA." A similar sentiment was expressed by Representative Maury Maverick—presumably about persons he had recommended for jobs with TVA. He said:

> Woe be to him who applies for a job with the endorsement of a Congressman or Senator. The Directors have little comprehension of the

political mind; and the personnel department, wholly inexperienced in dealing with the politics, writes unnecessarily sharp letters.[13]

The above Congressional appraisals of TVA's personnel policies and practices were corroborated by Leonard White, who in the Congressional hearings previously referred to, responded to the question: "Have appointments to the TVA been made on the basis of political recommendation, or has the rule of merit and efficiency been observed?"

> Despite the existence of many recommendations from Congressmen and Senators in the personnel file(s), there is no evidence that appointments have been made as a result of or in consequence of political influence; on the contrary there is convincing evidence that the rule of merit and efficiency has been carefully observed in making appointments in all branches of the work of the Authority.[14]

The files in the Harry Truman Library reveal that Clapp continued to search, several years after the first tests were made, for evidence of any political connections of employees and of any early appointments by the Directors which could possibly have been influenced by politicians or political considerations. Only four "suspicious" cases were located and none of these were verified.

Establishment of Personnel Procedures

Innovative employment procedures were also devised for the selection of professional and technical personnel. These involved the creation of open registers (which permitted applications to be processed at any time); evaluation into three broad groupings of not qualified, qualified, and exceptionally well qualified; interviews and reference checks; close collaboration with employing officials for selecting the best of the qualified persons or extending the search for additional applicants on a nation-wide basis if none of those presented by the personnel division were considered by the appointing official to be qualified; and other procedures to assure the selection of the most qualified persons. Initially, classification and pay plans were devised generally in conformity to U.S. Civil Service standards but TVA gradually modified some of these plans. Other aspects of personnel administration, e.g., performance ratings, rules on leave, policy on nepotism and many other policy and procedural matters were regularized and promulgated including a strong emphasis on involving operating officials in all aspects of personnel administration.

Training Program

Of special interest to Chairman Morgan, J. D. Dawson, the first Director of Training, and Reeves was the development of the training program which had its major initial application in Norris, Tennessee at the dam site and in the TVA built model town of Norris. The basic policies which undergirded the program were: (1) the general notions of the Chairman, who saw the TVA as a principal vehicle for adding an educational dimension for improving the life of the people of the Valley and (2) more precisely to utilize the period of construction of major dams (typically three years), to improve job performance and to equip participants in the program, most of whom were rural persons, to improve their agricultural and other skills and through such improved skills to raise their standards of living after completion of the construction. A unique feature of the TVA was to employ directly all construction workers by "force account" rather than under contracts with private builders. The offset of this policy was to have several thousand workers on each site who became the "clients" of the training programs. Chairman Morgan—who had extensive experience in engineering construction—was also acutely aware of the traditions of construction camps, which were typically unsuitable for families and single men. Construction workers rarely brought their families to such camps. The availability of good housing for families, combined with wood working and other shops, plus health and safety services and recreation facilities led to the creation of a large number and variety of educational activities—some directly related to improvement of job performance and others of a general educational and recreational character. The former included classes in blueprint reading, carpentry, mathematics, welding and other similar subjects which improved job performance and increased qualifications for promotion. The latter classification of activities offered a wider variety of educational and recreational and leisure-time activities including classes for the study of natural science, English, music and almost any subject which was of interest to employees and their families. An early memorandum sent by Reeves to John B. Blandford, Acting Coordinator, on May 18, 1934 (incidentally, exactly one year after the passage of the TVA Act) provides specific information on the details of the program as well as the philosophy which undergirded the program.

> The training program now being carried on and contemplated for the future serves two purposes: 1) it provides a constructive solution to certain specific problems growing out of the construction of Norris and Wheeler Dams; 2) it serves to demonstrate a technique of training which may be applied elsewhere and which may serve to solve problems more fundamental than those created incidental to the construction work of the Authority.
>
> In keeping with the recent trend to reduce working hours, the TVA has established a 33 hour-week, thereby releasing a substantial portion of the week as leisure time. Any construction project similarly managed would require a program to utilize or occupy this leisure time if for no other reason than to prevent the occurrence of serious problems pertaining to morale, discipline, health, and the like. The Authority met this problem by establishing a training program designed to utilize the leisure time of employees.[15]

The memorandum went on to describe the health and medical programs and the program of social studies which combined strictly practical considerations along with broader educational values.

A unique feature of the program, which had its origins at Norris and was later provided throughout the Valley under contractual arrangements with local library boards, was a mobile library service which served the construction campus and outlying areas as well. Books were made available for technical subjects and recreational subjects as well, under the same rationale as activities at the construction sites. Mary U(topia) Rothrock, a member of the training staff, created and developed this program and was recognized for her creativity by being elected as the first woman President of the American Library Association.

Reeves was very keen about the early program. He wrote several articles and made a number of speeches about the scope and employee response to the activities and continued his keen interest in adult and rural education when he returned to the University of Chicago.

Negro Employment and Relations

Despite Reeves's genuine interest in improving employment and training opportunities for Negroes in the Valley, not much progress was made until the crunch of getting the personnel program underway was over. Employment of Negroes was at the level of about 10% (which represented the ratio of Negroes to whites in the Valley) but practically all of them were in unskilled construction or service jobs. They were however given "equal pay for equal work." Reeves did set the stage for later developments with the employment of two professional Negroes on the training staff who were helpful in making some progress with support from other parts of the Personnel Division and general management. Some, but not spectacular progress was made in the area. Later on, the TVA Board authorized the elimination of all discriminatory symbols in the public access facilities and work areas, and a more aggressive recruitment procedure for the employment of professional and technically trained Negroes.

Although Reeves was a member of the Board of Trustees at Howard University and had very liberal views on racial matters, the crunch of work in getting the TVA underway, plus the scarcity of Negroes qualified for higher level positions, postponed a better solution to the employment of more highly qualified Negroes until much later.

Employee Relationship Policy

Another highly innovative feature in the evolution of TVA personnel policy was the creation of the "Employee Relationship Policy," (ERP) which was a joint major achievement of Reeves, Clapp, the full support of the Board, the General Manager, Legal Division, employee organizations, and supervisors at several levels. A chronology of communications in the evolution of the policy indicates that discussions began as early as October 1933 and continued until August 28, 1935 when the final draft of the policy was approved by the Board. The policy was thus nearly two years in the making. Reeves was particularly instrumental in securing the consulting services first of William A. Leiserson, a leading expert in labor relations with whom he had become acquainted while Leiserson was a member of the faculty at Antioch College, and later of Otto Beyer, Director of Labor Relations, Office of Coordinator of Transportation with whom Reeves had become acquainted. The introductory Statement sets forth the tone and general principles to guide employee-management relations:

> In the formulation of this policy the TVA recognizes that it is an agency of the sovereign government of the United States. As a consequence, the Employee Relationship Policy of the TVA must conform to national policy and the Federal Government must be in final control. In this respect, (however) TVA differs from a private employer. Subject to these conditions, TVA can establish governing principles upon which a progressive

> program of employee relations may be based. This statement represents an initial effort to formulate a labor policy for the TVA.
>
> The TVA will support as favorable labor standards and employment conditions as are consistent with the national welfare, having regard for the fact that the work of the TVA is being financed initially by the people of the United States.[16]

The Policy then declared that "employees of TVA shall have the right to organize and designate representatives of their own choosing. In the exercise of this right they shall be free from any and all restraining, interference, or coercion on the part of management and supervisory staff."[17]

Harry Case, the fifth TVA Director of Personnel, reflecting on this brief historical record, wrote the author as follows:

> The really innovative feature was the collective bargaining policy. The idea of having an employee relationship policy in writing, was also no doubt innovative, certainly in Federal agencies. But most of the ERP (Employee Relationship Policy) was relatively unimportant compared with the bargaining feature and this no doubt explains, at least in part, why it took so long to get it drafted, or why it was necessary to have such a policy.

With experience gained in large scale construction and operations and with the motivation of organized labor in the Valley, the significance of the collective bargaining policy became increasingly evident. Case, writing in 1955, commented:

> The areas in which labor now shares responsibility with TVA management cover much ground which is customarily thought of as 'management prerogative,' in addition to the ground which has traditionally come to be accepted as within the sphere of union responsibility. The latter includes the determination of wages, the settlement of jurisdictional questions, and the handling of grievances. The former, in which TVA is in more of a pioneering position, includes job training, job classification, and the joint cooperative program to promote efficiency, morale, health and safety.[18]

Reviews of TVA Personnel Administration

TVA personnel administration created a great deal of interest—and some criticism-among governmental personnel and public administration organizations and key leaders in these fields. Many administrative officials and scholars of personnel administration visited TVA and invited TVA personnel officials to address their meetings. Reeves also made many speeches on the personnel program, in and out of the Valley.

One of the most thorough professional examinations of the provisions of the TVA Act for personnel administration was made in 1934 by the "Commission of Inquiry on Public Service Personnel" created by the Social Science Research Council with funding from a private foundation. Hearings were held in various sections of the country, participated in by government officials, representatives of civic and reform groups, personnel administrators from public agencies and private industry, students of government and others acquainted with or involved in public affairs. The Commission was chaired by Lotus Coffman, President of the University of Minnesota, and included Louis Brownlow, Director of the Public Administration Clearing House, Ralph Budd, President of the Chicago Burlington and Quincy Railroad, Arthur Day, Vice President, Corning Glass Company and Charles E. Merriam of the University of Chicago. Luther Gulick, a leading student of personnel and public administration, headed the research staff. Their findings essentially verified the fact that the TVA (as partly a public utility) was properly exempted from the civil service as it had established its own career system.[19]

A later comprehensive review in 1938 by the Joint Committee of the Congress sustained the independent merit system of the TVA over the advice of Leonard D. White, an expert consultant to the Committee. Still later in 1940 Senator George Norris, testifying before the Senate Committee on Civil Service which was considering covering TVA in the federal civil service under a bill sponsored by Congressman Ramspeck, defended the TVA personnel system:

> The TVA is the only organization in the Government of the United States that has a system of civil service running from top to bottom.
>
> It has, in my judgment, a better civil service than is provided by our civil service law. And it is possible for this to be so because in the TVA we start at the top, with the heads of the organization.[20]

A still later review by the Senate Committee on Post Office and Civil Service concluded in 1953 that TVA, along with a few other smaller agencies, continue to be exempted from the U.S. Civil Service in these words: "Congress has seen fit to grant them additional flexibility in their operations and until the plans proposed in this report have proved equally flexible for the government as a whole, these agencies should continue to operate their programs free of the Civil Service Commission control.''[21]

A number of other efforts to modify TVA's basic personnel program were tried by Senator McKeller and others but not until later were these ''nibbling'' efforts successful and then only with reference to specific areas such as Veterans Preference.

Appraisal of Reeves' Contribution to Establishing the TVA Personnel Program

Many minds and much dedicated work on the part of many individuals went into the development and implementation of TVA's personnel policy and program. The most notable was certainly Gordon Clapp, the *primus inter pares* of the staff. Clair Killen contributed a great deal to enlighten and highly effective labor relations policy along with the leadership of the unions of the AFL as did Arthur Jandrey and others of the initial staff and later appointees. As TVA's first Director of Personnel, Reeves, however, carried the responsibility of employing the original staff and of recommending the initial policies and procedures to carry out the purposes of the Act. His influence was undoubtedly very great. Harry L. Case, who served for the longest period as the Director of Personnel (following Clapp, Jandrey and Gant) carried on the creative tradition and basic operating policies and procedures of the TVA Board. The record clearly shows that in the two and a half years between June 16, 1933 and January 1, 1936 Reeves's major contributions to the personnel program were:

- The early defense and implementation of the merit provisions of the Act. He was the chief spokesman with key officials of the New Deal Government, Congressmen and Senators, applicants and the general public—that the personnel program was to be based solidly on the principle of merit and efficiency.
- The establishment of effective working relationships with President Roosevelt and other key officials of the government with the support of Chairman Morgan, the other Directors and the staff.
- The creation and staffing of a personnel organization which, by June 1935, included sections for employment management, safety, camp management, labor relations, medical services and training.
- The development of an orderly and innovative procedure, with the help of the U.S. Civil Service Commission, for selecting over

twelve thousand clerical employees and construction workers who descended in droves on the TVA offices in Washington and Knoxville, Tennessee.

- The recruitment and selection of numerous key officials, from all parts of the United States for a few positions not being directly recruited by the Directors, and for reviewing and appraising other candidates proposed by the Directors and other officials before their appointment. Reeves's extensive experience with the organization and personnel of many of the leading colleges and universities in the United States made it easier to personally recruit several of the top officials of the TVA.
- Played an important role as Director of Personnel in creation of the "Employee Relationship Policy" which set new standards for employee relations in the federal service. The special relationships of Reeves and Clapp and their own estimates of the contributions each of them made to the TVA personnel program, is contained in an exchange of, heretofore unpublished letters between them, on Clapp's being given the "Stockberger Award" for distinguished service in the federal government. Reeves wrote:

> The judges made no mistake in their selection of the recipient of the Stockberger Award. Any accomplishment that may seem to some people to have been mine in the development of the personnel program in TVA were due largely to the work of others, and to yours more than any other person. Moreover, my work with TVA covered a period of only 2½ years. The personnel program at that time was only in the early stages of development. I do not minimize my own contribution to the success of the TVA in the field of personnel management, but it was of a different nature from yours and not of a kind for which awards are made or deserved. My most important contribution was in bringing you into the TVA and having you there ready to carry on and develop the personnel division when I left. This is the way I feel and nothing can change my mind.

Clapp responded:

> Thank you for your note about the Stockberger Award. There were at least a few people in the audience who realized as I did, that the Award should have been made to you. Whatever we have done in the TVA in developing a good personnel job would not be, had it not been for the foundation you laid for it and the high sights you set and I don't say that just to be throwing blarney around.

Clapp's appraisal of Reeves's contribution was also expressed by George Gant, successively Chief of Training, Director of Personnel and General Manager. Although not as close to Reeves as was Clapp, Gant came to TVA in 1935, and worked under Reeves's direction in the Social and Economic Division and later in the Personnel Division. Gant wrote:

> The major point here, I think is that Floyd showed great imagination and innovative skill in initiating or helping to initiate policies and programs not commonly known or practiced in those days but so well formulated as to be outstandingly successful and common practice in similar circumstances today. This quality of unhibited but responsible and effective policy diagnosis, planning and execution I think distinguished Floyd Reeves. Through those years I found him to be approachable, always friendly and warm, understanding and direct. He had integrity; he had an uncluttered mind and could cut through complications to the heart of the problem or situation.[22]

Although the personnel division was directed by persons of different temperaments and approaches—Reeves, Clapp, Jandrey, Gant and Case up to 1956—there was a clear continuity in the role which the Personnel Division played in TVA administration after Reeves resigned.

Reeves's Involvement in Planning for Social and Economic Development

Policy Framework

The far-sighted and long-held views of Roosevelt about the need for and benefits to be derived from broadly construed physical, social and economic planning were expressed in his message to Congress advocating the passage of the TVA Act:

> Many hard lessons have taught us the human waste that results from lack of planning. Here and there a few wise cities and counties have looked ahead and planned. But our nation has 'just grown.' It is time to extend planning to a wider field—in this instance comprehending in one great project many studies directly concerned with the basin of one of our

great rivers. This is in a true sense a return to the spirit and vision of the provider.

These views were put into legislative form in Sections 22 and 23 of the Act. In an Executive Order of June 8, 1933—less than one month after the passage of the TVA Act, President Roosevelt assigned to the TVA Board the research and planning functions spelled out in Sections 22 and 23 of the Act (Appendix D) which were left to his discretion. The language follows:

> In accordance with the provisions of Section 22 and Section 23 of the Tennessee Valley Authority Act of 1933 the President hereby authorizes and directs the Board of Directors of the Tennessee Valley Authority to make such surveys, general plans, studies, experiments and demonstrations as may be necessary and suitable to aid the proper use, conservation and development of the natural resources of the Tennessee River drainage basin and of such adjoining territory as may be related to or materially affected by the development and consequent to this Act, and to promote the general welfare of the citizens of said area; within the limits of appropriations made therefore by Congress.[23]

The first known indication that Reeves had been drawn into the general orbit of planning and employment relief is expressed in a letter to his wife written July 10, 1933, approximately a month after the President's Executive Order.

After indicating how involved he was in dealing with the employment problems and pressures of the TVA, he wrote:

> About four o'clock I received a telephone call from one of President Roosevelt's secretaries informing me that the President had appointed me to serve as a member of a committee to make recommendations for an organization to spend $25,000,000 of Public Works funds which the Act allocates for moving unemployed to suburban and other planned communities. We were asked to drop everything and meet at once in the Office of Col. Sawyer, the temporary director of the . . . Public Works Program . . . The Tennessee Valley Authority was represented by Mr. Morgan and me. The group elected Mr. Morgan chairman and we went to work with our plans . . . I worked with Mr. Morgan and one other member of the Committee, and together we prepared a planning organization to submit to the larger group. This plan was discussed from 7 until 12 o'clock and finally adopted without modification. Mr. Morgan is to present it to President Roosevelt at lunch tomorrow for his approval.

Although the record is not clear as to exactly what happened after these discussions they appear to have anticipated the creation of the Resettlement Administration. It is clear, however, that TVA, its Chairman and Reeves were drawn into the vortex of hastily developing plans to make jobs for the vast number of unemployed persons, and perhaps to large scale relocation to suburban and rural areas.

This was pretty heady stuff for Reeves and he responded with energy and ingenuity. At one point during the period he expressed to his wife the hope that he could get the personnel work of TVA under direction of someone else so that he could give all of his time to planning.

Direct TVA Involvement in Planning Activities

Reeves considered the extensive training program at Norris and other locations as parts of a planning process directed toward improvement of the economic, vocational and cultural opportunities of TVA employees and to provide demonstrations as to how the program could be applied elsewhere. At first these activities were essentially directly funded and staffed by the TVA under policy direction of Chairman Morgan and Reeves, but administered by Dudley Dawson. But the basis for a broader definition of possibilities in planning developed as a result of the deputation of Reeves to Harry Hopkins for the direction of a research program which was funded by the Civil Works Administration (CWA). The program involved 400 researchers who carried on an intensive program of compilation of basic economic, demographic, educational and other data throughout the seven states of the Valley area. Reeves described this program briefly in a speech to southern mountain workers in March 1934:

> This has been done in close cooperation with the faculties of colleges and universities and the heads of the various state departments of education, public health and public welfare. The TVA has been the coordinating agency in directing the utilization of this fund in a way that has been done to integrate the programs of state and local agencies in the program of study and development for the entire valley. This program was carried on not by suggesting what the various agencies might do that would meet the needs and requirements of any plan that the TVA might have in mind but rather by inviting existing agencies to suggest studies of importance to the state and local unit and for which public funds might legitimately be spent . . . The TVA obtained a vast amount of material that will be of value in the formulation of general plans and further studies and demon-

> strations; and the state and local agencies have obtained a vast amount of material that can be used to bring about changes and reforms in which they are logically interested and better prepared to consummate.[24]

In the conclusion of this speech, Reeves summed up the policy framework which became the basis for a number of important activities which were related, initially, to the construction of dams such as relocation of highways, schools, graves and churches; assistance to counties resulting from lose of tax revenues; effect of reservoirs on trade centers and transportation and marketing facilities and related problems. Reeves further observed that: "These problems must be faced and solved before the Authority or any other agency is prepared to formulate anything in the nature of a master plan, to say nothing of its execution."

Concurrently, the TVA Board evolved a policy of making its broader contribution to planning by formulating demonstrations in a variety of development areas.

The key word *demonstration* became essentially the limit of TVA's direct participation and funding (or partial funding) of which there were many examples in almost all fields of resource development activity in which TVA was engaged. Demonstrations were always developed in collaboration with valley governmental, educational or other organizations in agriculture, forestry, education and even in the organization for planning itself at the state and county levels.

Dr. Harcourt Morgan—the "other" Morgan on the TVA Board—who had the best sense of TVA's relationships with Valley educational and other institutions, articulated and advocated this basic policy as early as October 1933. Under this policy Reeves supervised the planning and operational activities, including health and safety activities.

TVA focused its regional planning activities, after Reeves's departure, in the Department of Regional Planning Studies. The Department included a central staff and three divisions as follows: General Planning to which was delegated responsibility for studies related to "valley-wide" development; a Property Layout and Design Division which was responsible for architectural planning and landscape and site planning; a Basic Data and Research Division which had a section for Land Classification; and a Social and Economic Research Division which was formerly under Reeves's direction. The Department continued to make social, economic and governmental studies for the guidance of policies for general management and the Board; prepared the data for TVA's allocation of power revenues to municipalities and cooperatives in lieu of taxes and did similar operational studies. But the idea of overall planning never really took hold in the TVA; nothing resembling a master plan for the Tennessee Valley was ever developed or seriously contemplated. In no sense did the Department of Regional Planning Studies over-ride the responsibilities delegated to other departments for planning their activities. In fact a cardinal idea in TVA was that planning is an essential part of all departments—coordinated by general management. The professional planners were, accordingly, frequently frustrated. And some master planners like Rexford Tugwell and some visitors from countries with five year plans were mystified by TVA's approach to planning. *It is probably correct to describe the TVA Act as the basic planning document to guide TVA operations.*

Reeves's Work as a Consultant to TVA

Reeves left full-time employment with TVA in January 1936. The Board of Directors announced his resignation on December 18, 1935 but indicated that "arrangements have been made with Dr. F. W. Reeves to serve as a consultant with the Authority." In the same announcement Gordon R. Clapp was named as Director of Personnel. The record of the formal contracts covering twenty years of time and scores of letters in which Reeves was kept abreast of important developments, or in which his opinions were sought, attest to his continuing interest in TVA and in his continued usefulness in helping guide policies and program developments.[25]

Between 1936 and 1953 TVA entered into eleven consulting contracts with Reeves for varying amounts of time from thirty days to open-ended contracts for unspecified time during any one contract period. A brief listing of the problems and program developments on which his judgment was sought included personnel policy, training programs, organizational changes, educational relations, post-war planning and some major personnel appointments.

After several reviews of the personnel policies and programs (and one particularly after about 17 years had elapsed) Reeves summarized his challenging observations in these words:

> Personnel administration in the TVA must justify its independence of the United States Civil Service Commission by its superiority over the personnel administration of those agencies of the Federal government that do not have such independence. Furthermore, personnel administra-

> tion in the TVA must take full advantage, within the limits of political wisdom, of laws designed to give the TVA some or all of the flexibility of private industry.

His comments on these general standards were followed by several specific suggestions regarding ways in which the Personnel Division could continue its contributions to general management; to "cooperate" with the Regional Studies Division in helping state and local agencies administer their programs which had initially been aided by TVA; and other facets of personnel administration not characteristic of conventional government personnel operations.

Two other illustrative program areas in which Reeves served as a consultant were in the area of government and inter-university research programs for regional development. One of the most interesting and complex program problems was to "render consulting and advisory services in connection with problems involving research in Southeastern universities in relation to the research programs of the Clinton Laboratories of the Manhattan district of the U.S. Army at Oak Ridge, Tennessee and in relation to the cooperative research activities of the Authority and Southeastern universities." Consultation on this complex set of problems came at the time when the super-secret "Oak Ridge Project" of the Army Engineers was in the process of being replaced by the U.S. Atomic Energy Commission soon after to be chaired by David E. Lilienthal. The problems involving the organization for atomic research as related to TVA policies and research programs made him an ideal consultant for this task. Reeves worked closely with John P. Ferris, Director of TVA's Commerce Department, to whom was delegated responsibility for representing TVA's invited interest in this new regional organization. Gordon Clapp, General Manager and David Lilienthal, Chairman of the Board were, of course, closely involved. The work required preparing and reviewing successive draft compacts which set up the organizational framework for what became the Oak Ridge Institute of Nuclear Studies (ORINS); attending meetings of various committees as an observer; advising Ferris on various issues; preparing and reviewing communications with Dr. Frank P. Graham, President of the University of North Carolina, who served as Chairman of a Committee of Presidents of Southeastern Universities, which collaborated with TVA in this new and novel organization of research efforts in a regional development context.

Another challenging consulting arrangement was to serve as Chairman of a panel of consultants established for the purpose of studying

TVA's Division of Regional Studies and to assist TVA's General Manager in the selection of a director for that Division. The panel included Edward Ackerman of the Bureau of the Budget, Gordon Blackwell, social scientist from the University of North Carolina, Arthur Maass of Harvard University, Charles McKinley, political scientist from Reed College, and Glen E. McLaughlin all of whom were knowledgeable about TVA but not involved in day-to-day operations of the Authority. The Committee was asked to address an agenda of problems provided by the General Manager.

Reeves's report to the General Manager on the results of the Committee's deliberations, (after referring to FDR's message to Congress advocating the creation of the TVA and section 22 of the Act) opened with the following quotation from Henry Steel Commanger's *The American Mind* which set the broad and challenging tone of the report.

> . . . The TVA was the first major attempt by government to use what John Dewey had proposed, plural and experimental methods in securing and maintaining an ever-increasing release of the powers of human nature in service of a freedom which is cooperative and a cooperation which is voluntary . . . It was the proving ground, as it were, of a dynamic democracy. Here were tested the broad construction of the Constitution, large-scale planning, the recasting of federalism along regional lines, new techniques of administration, and new standards of civil service, the alliance of science and politics, and the revitalization of democracy through a calculated program of economic and social reconstruction.[26]

Reeves's report continued:

> Your consultants are unanimous in the feeling that the "reality" of TVA today does not fully conform to those concepts of a regional planning agency; yet we feel that it should. TVA is not the "pace setter" in the field of regional resources development that we believe it was intended to be; yet the opportunity in terms of legislative authority and administrative structure are still more favorable here than elsewhere in the nation.
>
> It is in the making of broad plans for Valley development and in the setting of social objectives for these plans both essential to the broader role originally conceived for the Authority that the social scientists can make a very important contribution . . .

(These functions and others that should be performed by social scientists were then spelled out.)

The report furthermore urged the General Manager, the Board, and those other TVA officials charged with top administrative responsibilities to give more consideration to the problems of long-range planning. This recommendation was considered essential to the proper correlation and regional effectiveness of TVA's several operating programs. The establishment of an industrial development staff, concerned with integrated industrial location services, analysis of industrial development trends, and research on industrial possibilities arising from the region's resources was also recommended. This staff was also urged to give guidance to the operating divisions in making proposals as to what industries should be attracted to the region.

The report then proposed administrative machinery to give effect to the eleven bold and comprehensive recommendations including the appointment of an Assistant General Manager to work with and coordinate the activities of an Industrial Economist to do special studies in this area. Both of these recommended appointments were made. Gordon Clapp also made a report to Reeves sometime later on other actions taken by the Board on other recommendations of the panel.

Although the thinking of the panel was possibly a bit visionary (as were some of the earlier views of President Roosevelt and Chairman Morgan) it was convened at a time when the Board, under Clapp's Chairmanship, and that of the General Manager, apparently thought that the TVA needed a fresh look at and appraisal of what TVA was doing in the area of regional studies. One of Reeves's attributes was the capability of sometimes "sticking a needle" in organizations for which he had the highest respect and aspirations. He had the capacity to be constructively critical and deliberately provocative of forward thinking in the leadership of these organizations.

Although the author is informally aware of the fact that some small progress was made on the recommendations of the Committee, there was no further information in the Reeves collection of the Archives.

Informal Contacts

Besides the formal contractual relations, Reeves exchanged letters, had numerous informal conversations in Washington and Chicago with a dozen or more TVA officials, and secured the participation of TVA personnel in several activities in which he was actively engaged outside of TVA. Furthermore, he continued to lecture, write articles and teach his students about TVA policies and programs. The principal exchange of letters and visits were with Gordon Clapp.[27] Starting in 1936, when

Reeves returned to the University of Chicago, through 1952 and later, the files in the MSU Archives and Historical Collections record over fifty such exchanges. The tone of the letters was always professional and cordial with no indication of dependency. They started in the beginning with a "Dear Mr. Reeves" salutation to the informal "Dear Floyd" after a few years. Clapp made a point of keeping Reeves informed of major developments in the TVA on which Reeves had initiated or had been a principal participant and sought his reactions to and advice on many matters of policy. Conversely, Reeves sought Clapp's advice on matters of mutual interest and invited him to serve on several national committees and commissions such as the Advisory Committee on Education and other bodies.

Relationships with the TVA Board

An account of Floyd Reeves's career in the TVA would not be complete without some comments on his relationships with the three members of the TVA Board. As many students of the social sciences and persons interested in governmental operations knew, there were deep philosophical differences between the members of the Board—principally between Chairman Arthur E. Morgan and David E. Lilienthal, which were expressed in basic program policies and organizational and managerial actions. Frequently in the first three tumultuous years, Reeves by virtue of his pivotal position as Director of the Personnel and Social and Economic Divisions and by his early and close association with Chairman Morgan, was inevitably drawn into often emotionally charged differences between the members of the Board. The grave and almost catastrophic policy and managerial differences between the Board members were not finally resolved until Chairman Morgan was removed from his office by President Roosevelt on March 21, 1938, more than three years after Reeves had left the TVA. Inasmuch as the complex philosophical differences between the Board members—finally between David Lilienthal and H. A. Morgan "versus" Arthur Morgan—and the public policy and managerial issues which these differences precipated are well documented, the section of this account will be narrowly focused on the background factors and activities during the 2½ years Reeves was directly involved while Director of Personnel. These are documented in the Reeves collection of the Michigan State University Archives.[28]

Basic Philosophical Differences between the Directors

At the heart of the controversy were the fundamental differences between the philosophical orientation and the experience background of the three Directors. Arthur M. Schlesinger, Jr., in his monumental work on *The Coming of the New Deal* provides this interpretation:[29]

> Roosevelt had already made his choice for the Chairmanship of the three-man board to run the new Tennessee Valley Authority. Indeed, few American engineers had so much experience with flood control projects beginning with the famous Miami Conservancy District . . . to prevent a recurrence of the Dayton flood, and Morgan joined to his technical talents unusual personal qualities. He was a tall, lanky, gray impressive man of fifty-five, a Yankee moralist and mystic, honest and righteous, given to ethical meditations of a somewhat jejune but uplifting kind, a social thinker touched with utopianism . . . Since 1920 he had been President of Antioch College in Ohio. Part technician, part prophet, Morgan was possessed by an earnest passion to remake man and remake society . . . Morgan was thus well prepared to respond to Roosevelt's dream of the Valley. "The TVA," Morgan observed is "not primarily a dam-building job, a fertilizer job or power transmission job . . . we need something more than all of these." It was an experiment in social reconstruction: the improvement of the total well-being, in physical, social, and economic condition, is the total aim. (Page 321)

Schlesinger had this to say about the other two Directors:

> While Morgan was laying plans for the reordering of life in the Valley, Roosevelt (at the suggestion of Arthur Morgan) named his colleagues on the three-man board, Harcourt A. Morgan of Tennessee and David Lilienthal of Wisconsin. Harcourt Morgan was an agricultural scientists, sixty-six years old in 1933, who had been for fourteen years President of the University of Tennessee. He had promoted agricultural activities in the south since the nineties; and his work as Dean of the College of Agriculture at Tennessee and then President brought him into close relations with the extension service, which strongly urged his appointment. The people of the Valley trusted Harcourt Morgan, with his lean, weather-beaten face and his laconic ways. The third member of the Board was only thirty-four years old—over twenty years younger than Arthur Morgan, and nearly half the age of Harcourt Morgan . . . After graduating from DePauw University Lilienthal had moved on to the Harvard Law School, where his crisp personality and incisive intelligence attracted the attention of Felix Frankfurter. When Lilienthal left Cambridge, Frank-

> furter strongly recommended him to Donald Richberg, who was just then setting up a new (law) firm in Chicago. Lilienthal worked with Richberg in drafting the Railway Labor Act and soon became a successful lawyer in his own right, specializing in public utility regulation . . . Lilienthal gave up a profitable law practice and moved to Madison. His distinguished record on the (utility) Commission made him an obvious choice for the TVA. A quiet, solid man, with a round face, spectacles, receding sandy hair, a deceptive gentleness of manner, and a hard precision of mind, Lilienthal had a vocation of public service and a steely determination to protect the public interest. And he had, in addition, a vivid sense of the meaning of electricity for the national welfare. (Pages 328–329)

These differences in character, experience and philosophy, of course, had their effects expressed in three areas in which Reeves was importantly involved—in personnel appointments, program policy and planning and in organization and administration. The area of personnel appointments was not significantly involved, however, since all three Directors limited their personnel appointments to a few persons as personal assistants or top technical positions in their areas of special competence and responsibility. Reeves was responsible for recommending to the Board and approving all other major appointments. But there was an important difference between Chairman Morgan's and Lilienthal's general approach to personnel policy. A clue to the effect of this difference is provided in Chairman Morgan's book *The Making of the TVA*, in which he made no mention of labor relations with the Tennessee Valley Trades and Labor Council, although he was initially in charge of construction work where most of the labor was employed and where all of the labor relations problems arose and were ironed out. Reeves was clearly pro labor unions and was instrumental in getting the formulation of the progressive Employee Relationship Policy underway before he resigned as Director of Personnel.

The philosophical and pragmatic differences between the Directors with reference to policy issues, production in planning and relationships to local and state governments created more problems for Reeves. Arthur Morgan favored centralized and comprehensive planning, modified in part by his interest in cooperatives and handicrafts, while H. A. Morgan and Lilienthal (influenced particularly by H. A. Morgan's intimate knowledge of Valley educational and governmental institutions) favored involving these organizations as contractors, collaborators and demonstrators in the development of the region. Although Reeves was influenced by the expansive ideas, hopes and visions of Chairman Morgan and FDR in the early years, he readily concurred in the more pragmatic and realistic policy of collaborating with and strengthening local institutions through contracts for conducting demonstrations very soon after the TVA lawyers and regional planners began to see more clearly how sections 22 and 23 of the Act could be implemented. Furthermore, the organization was so involved in getting the whole program underway—especially the clearly statutory obligations for comprehensive development of the river system for flood control, navigation and power, that the differences of opinion, as to the best mode of operation for development of the region in program areas, other than those mentioned above did not really surface to any significant degree until Reeves had gone back to the University of Chicago.

The area of organization and management, focused most sharply on general management, was the one in which Reeves became more intimately involved. Even before taking up his duties in Knoxville, he had consulted with Charles Merriam of the University of Chicago about the organization of TVA and had prepared an organization chart which showed the Directors as a policy body and the administration of the policies being delegated to a General Manager. But in the fast moving pace of the early days and particularly since the Chairman had started to work before the other Directors were on the job, the Chairman had already begun to operate as Chairman and "General Manager" before any decision on how the Authority would be managed had been taken by the full Board. Lilienthal and H. A. Morgan found this unsatisfactory. The problem was temporarily resolved by each Director assuming primary responsibility for activities in his special areas of competence: Dr. A. E. Morgan for the construction, engineering and personnel program, Dr. H. A. Morgan for fertilizer production and agricultural development programs, and Lilienthal for the legal and power distribution policy and program. This plan left policy and operational matters, like the preparation of budgets, basically uncoordinated, confused and the source of controversy which became more personalized and acute as time passed. Reeves, as Director of Personnel under Chairman Morgan, had responsibility for organization as a function directly related to personnel administration. In this role he tried to resolve the organizational issue by recruiting a "Coordinator." But the Coordinator position was quickly taken over by the Chairman, Arthur Morgan. Some progress was made but it took until 1937 to firmly establish the position of General Manager. Some of the essential functions of the General Manager position were first performed by the

Coordinator who, by persistence, objective management and good judgment had earned the confidence of all three of the Directors and who later was named to the General Manager position in 1937.

But the resolution of this difficulty made tough times for Reeves, who in eleven letters to his wife starting as early as July 1933 expressed such views as:

> I am worried because things are not running smoothly within the Board itself . . . Unless our Board can begin functioning as a Board instead of three independent administrative officers we are lost . . . I do not believe that divided responsibility of that kind can possibly work without friction . . . Yesterday morning (since) it looked certain that there would be Board of the Authority by night, I arranged for the case to be laid before Roosevelt and he stayed in Washington one day longer and smoothed things out so that we can go on; things are still not well with the Board . . . Mr. M. (A. E. Morgan) wanted to propose my name as General Manager of the Authority and put it through even if he had to go to FDR to do so, but I refused to consider it. As the organization now functions, no one could succeed in such a position and I told him so.

But the work went on in spite of the controversy as Reeves reported to his wife:

> President Roosevelt has just ordered us to build another big dam, starting at once. It means that we will have to increase our forces greatly. The new dam will cost $22,000,000. Furthermore the pressure of the opponents of TVA—particularly the power companies was stepped up which didn't contribute to organizational tranquility.

The internal feud (which was largely contained within the upper reaches of the organization) continued and came to another peak when FDR renominated Lilienthal in 1936 for a second term of nine years over the objections of Chairman Morgan, who sought to persuade the President not to take the action. FDR, however, wrote a thoughtful letter in support of his action and requested the Chairman (Dr. A. E. Morgan) to understand and get on with the work. But the Chairman persisted in his objections and charges against the majority decision of the Board in speeches, in articles in *The New York Times* and in *The Saturday Evening Post* and the *Atlantic Monthly*. In various degrees these impugned the integrity of his colleagues. These actions precipitated a response from the other two Directors to the President defending their integrity.[30] The President again wrote a "Dear Arthur letter"[31] hoping that the Chairman would mend his ways but he persisted with another communication—this time to Congressman Maury Maverick on the same vitriolic theme. The President requested the Chairman to attend a third meeting at the White House for the purpose of attempting a reconciliation which the Chairman refused to attend.[32] This was the last straw. With support of a legal opinion of his Solicitor General as to the authority to do so, the President, with great reluctance, dismissed the Chairman for *contumacy*—an unprecedented action in the history of American public administration. On March 23, 1938 the President sent a special message to Congress in which he expressed the carefully considered opinion that Arthur Morgan "was temperamentally unfitted to exercise a divided authority."

Congressional Investigation

The controversy did not end however with the action of the President. The problem now, understandably, was taken up by the Congress, which created a Joint Committee to investigate the Tennessee Valley Authority. This Committee held hearings in Washington, D.C. and Knoxville, Tennessee from August to December 1938. The public hearings covered practically every conceivable aspect of the Authority's policies, expenditures, program decisions, all elements of the controversy in the Board, and the personnel policies, appointments and other actions some of which went back to Reeves's period of employment as Director of Personnel. Those were ably and convincingly defended by General Manager Gordon Clapp. The outcome of the investigation was objectively summarized by Marguerite Owen, the Washington Representative of TVA, as follows:

> . . . In January 1939, the Joint Committee issued a preliminary statement, in April a complete report. With a minority dissenting and recommending the dismemberment of TVA, it was a general affirmation of approval.[33]

Much more could be written about Reeves's role in the whole complex and emotion-charged affair. He came to TVA at the request of Arthur Morgan. For some of the early months, which required creative work in double quick cadence, he was doubtless thought of as the "Chairman's man." There was quite possibly some suspicion on the part of the other two Directors, who early on became painfully aware of the Chairman's method of work, which meant treatment of them as subordinates instead of equals. Reeves, an experienced student and practitioner of the administrative art, was inordinately busy fending off political pressures, in recruiting key officials, and in establishing orderly procedures to select hundreds of professional personnel, construction workers and clerks on the basis of merit as prescribed by the Act. Reeves was strongly motivated by the challenge for the integrated development of the resources of the Valley, as outlined in the Act, and initially was much impressed with the ideas of Arthur Morgan and President Roosevelt for improving the living standards of the people of the Valley. But he was also convinced that TVA could only achieve its high purposes under organizational arrangements of a full-time policy Board backed up by a General Manager to administer Board policies especially given the evolving animosity of the Chairman toward his colleagues on the Board and his chaotic, and sometimes reckless behavior. The idea of a Coordination Division was tried for a while and may have laid the basis for the creation of a strong full-fledged General Manager. But only after the Chairman's departure did the General Manager's office get a chance fully to demonstrate its efficacy. Reeves had a significant part to play in these developments but probably his chief contribution came in the selection and appointment of Gordon Clapp and other young associates who followed his leadership.

With reference to Reeves's relationship with Arthur Morgan and other members of the Board all of the records available to the author, including the Arthur Morgan collection at Antioch College, reveal no significant personal conflict between him and Floyd Reeves.

In Arthur Morgan's introspective, but still acrimonious reaction to his two colleagues, published in his *The Making of the TVA*,[34] he describes Reeves as "creative and competent in educational administration and in practical administration" and nowhere suggests a negative judgment of Reeves's contributions to TVA. Shortly before his death he expressed the wish that they would have had "an opportunity to visit." Reeves also maintained good relations with Lilienthal as a consultant to TVA and in other areas of mutual interest as he did with H. A. Morgan.

Chapter II

President's Committee on Administrative Management and Civil Service Improvement

Reeves had hardly shaken the Knoxville dust and soot off his feet and settled into his normal teaching and research activities at the University of Chicago when another call to service in the Roosevelt government was made to him in April 1936. This time it was to serve as a member of the research staff of the President's Committee on Administrative Management. It took only three years in Roosevelt's first term for him to become acutely aware of the enormous workload which fell upon the office of the Chief Executive, much increased by the varied economic and social problems of the depression and the redefinition of the role of the federal government fostered especially by his New Deal.

The roots of the problems were deep in the history of the Republic but were not highlighted until FDR became fully aware of the need for a reorganization of the Office of the President and the managerial instrumentalities available to the Chief Executive for operating the federal government in the 20th century. Accordingly, he created a Presidential committee on March 20, 1936 to examine the problem and to prepare recommendations for improving the capabilities of the federal government to respond to the old and new challenges for service to the public. The President leaned heavily on three experienced and trusted professionals to provide leadership in the production of a blueprint for reform and renovation—Louis Brownlow, as chairman, and Charles Merriam and Luther Gulick as members of the committee, all old friends and professional colleagues of Reeves. It was only one month after the creation of the committee when Reeves's was invited to Washington by the committee to discuss possible organization of the project and the personnel to do the job. Here are the highlights of Reeves's informative letter to his wife written on April 26, 1936 from the Hay Adams Hotel in Washington, D.C. the then informal headquarters for governmental consultants:

> Things have been moving so rapidly since I arrived in Washington that I scarcely know where I am, what I am going to do or what I ought to do. This survey of the Administrative Management of the federal government is clearly the most important study if properly done it will save ultimately billions of dollars to the nation and what is more important may actually determine the form our government will take in the future years. I had no conception of its real significance until I arrived. (A Reeves proclivity to see work in which he was asked to be associated in the largest terms of reference and to do his work accordingly.) . . . Immediately upon my arrival I was asked to serve as associate director of research—and to personally direct and prepare the report on personnel for all of the federal agencies . . . After considerable reluctance I accepted the associate directorship . . . I absolutely refused to accept the directorship of the personnel study. I did that first because I felt that under no conditions could I ask for further release from the University, and second because I felt, as I told the Committee, that there were at least ten men in America better qualified than I am for the job. Last night the Committee told me to produce the ten men so that they could select from them. I sat up most of the night thinking of the various individuals and could only find five. I presented their names this morning and all proved to be men who had been considered and rejected. Brownlow, Merriam and Gulick all say I . . . could do the job . . . and I was the first staff member that the President approved. I said I know I would not be acceptable to the speaker of the House of Representatives. They replied that he favored my appointment, primarily because I had turned down every request he had ever made of me. To prove this the speaker had dinner with us tonight and urged me to accept . . . I am in a tight place, because I honestly believe there must be several men in America better qualified for the job . . . As things now stand I am to . . . start the Personnel study with the understanding that I will try to find someone to take it over as soon as possible.

Although Reeves did, indeed, have a limited exposure to the organization and personnel policies and practices of the federal government, he did have a significant experience in both aspects of administration in the TVA. Furthermore, he had what was probably more important—the confidence of the President and colleagues, who were more knowledgeable of federal organization and personnel policies than he was. He also had the demonstrated unusual capacity to pick very able young persons and others as associates to do much of the work under his direction.

Financial remuneration for the work was not attractive. Reeves's attitude toward money and service to the government coupled with his continued insecurity about taking responsibility for the personnel sector of the work are revealed in the same letter to his wife as quoted above:

> We will not fare very well financially on this matter. It is expensive to live here and no one on the staff is to get more than $25 per day. The overhead committee works for nothing. The Committee could get an Executive Order from the President allowing me $50 a day and intended to do so but I stopped that because I do not want exceptions to be made in my behalf. Furthermore, I did not want anyone to think that the remuneration had anything to do with my reluctance to accept the job. I am honestly afraid I cannot do the personnel job. All the members of the Committee say they know I can and the President has said he knows no one else who can.

With these personal issues settled with Reeves, the Committee got down to the task of selecting members of the research staff, which was headed by Joseph P. Harris and included Reeves, Paul David and several of his then current or later friends and professional associates: Laverne Burchfield, who later was his research assistant in the rural education project at the University of Chicago and Editor of the *Public Administration Review*; Professor Charles McKinley of Reed College, who was a sometime consultant to the TVA; Arthur Holcombe, Professor of Government at Harvard University; William Y. Elliott, long-time Professor of Government at Harvard; G. Lyle Belsley of the Civil Service Assembly; and several others who became members of the twenty-eight member research staff.

Major Considerations in Launching the Reviews

There is no better summary of the major considerations taken into account by the Committee than their introduction to their final report to the President.[1] Excerpts from their introduction illuminate the breadth of the Committee's thinking and the scope of the research needed to prepare their recommendations:

> Scope of the Government of the U.S.: The government of the United States is the largest and most difficult task undertaken by the American people, and at the same time the most important and the noblest. Our Government does more for more men, women, and children than any other institution . . . It covers a wider range of aims and activities than any other enterprise; it sustains the frame of our national and our community life, our economic system, our individual rights and liberties . . .
>
> General vs. Private Interests: Our American Government rests on the truth that the general interest is superior to and has priority over any special or private interest, and that final decision in matters of common interest . . . should be made by free choice of the people of the Nation, expressed in such manner as they shall from time to time provide . . . Our goal is the constant raising of the level of the happiness and dignity of human life, the steady sharing of the gains of our Nation, whether material or spiritual, among those who make the Nation what it is.
>
> The American Executive: Our Presidency unites at least three important functions. From one point of view the President is a political leader—leader of a party, leader of the Congress, leader of a people. From another point of view he is head of the Nation in the ceremonial sense of the term, the symbol of our American national solidarity. From still another point of view the President is the Chief Executive and administrator within the Federal system and service. In many types of government these duties are divided or only in part combined, but in the United States they have always been united in one and the same person whose duty it is to perform all of these tasks . . .
>
> Focus of Committee Work: Your Committee . . . has been asked to investigate and report particularly upon the last function; namely, that of administrative management—the organization for the performance of the duties imposed upon the President in exercising the executive power vested in him by the Constitution of the United States . . .
>
> Foundations of Government Efficiency: The efficiency of government rests upon two factors: the consent of the governed and good management. In a democracy consent may be achieved readily, though not without some effort, as it is the cornerstone of the constitution . . .
>
> Administrative efficiency is not merely a matter of paper clips, time clocks, and standardized economies of motion. These are but minor gadgets. Real efficiency goes much deeper down. It must be built into the structure of a government just as it is built into a piece of machinery . . .[2]

Reeves participated generally, as a key member of the research staff, in the preparation of all major recommendations of the Committee. As he got into the work of the Committee in some depth, in areas other than education and personnel administration, however, he became somewhat ambivalent in the directions and emphases which his professional life should take. Furthermore, he found that he needed an expanded vocabulary—if not conceptual understandings, beyond those with which he was very familiar in the field of education. His ambivalence about his career choices and his unembarrassed and candid appraisal of his limitations to deal with concepts in government and public administration are expressed in another letter to his wife dated May 24, 1936.

> I realize as never before the importance of a broad background. Here I am at (age) 45 faced by the astonishing situation of having to decide whether my future will be in adult education, in political service, or in both . . . I never had a course in either political science or in the subdivision of political science we call public administration. I have read many specialized books in both fields but until yesterday I never read a text covering either field. Dr. Elliott of Harvard very tactfully suggested at our first staff meeting that it would be well for one of the junior members of our staff to make a list of terms with definitions for the use of members of the staff who have not had the advantage of extended formal study of public administration! I am the only such man. I seconded the proposal. It is being done.

Nevertheless, he learned quickly and contributed judgment and ideas to the broad spectrum of problems faced by the Committee and to the innovative recommendations which evolved. These recommendations were aimed at strengthening the capacity of the President to discharge his vast responsibility for the efficient organization and management of civilian branches of the government and also his responsibilities as Commander in Chief. The principal recommendations included: (1) the strengthening of the Office of the President with the appointment of six assistants (initially) who had the confidence of the President and who possessed a "passion for anonymity" to help the President coordinate the work of the Department through a better flow of information among key officials and through the Agencies which they administered; (2) the strengthening and development of the managerial agencies of the government—particularly the Bureau of the Budget; (3) the creation of an independent post-audit agency reporting directly to the Congress, without executive authority, to help strengthen internal auditing in the administrative unit of the government; (4) establishment of a national planning agency, without administrative authority, reporting directly to the President; (5) the reduction of the number of independent government organizations from over one hundred to twelve departments headed by cabinet secretaries, including reorganization of the independent regulatory agencies, government corporations and other agencies which had developed out of control of the President; and (6) the extension of the merit system to all non-policy determining positions and the strengthening of the organization and functions of the central personnel agency to help the President discharge his responsibilities for government personnel. Some of these recommendations were accepted by Congress and are still part of the operations of the Office of the President and administrative agencies of the U.S. government. Although it is not possible to separate out Reeves's contribution to the collective committee product, the fact that his services continued to be sought by the President on other public administration projects gave proof of his usefulness in these broader areas. Furthermore, he took principal responsibility for the personnel section of the report, which recommended major changes in the personnel management organization and procedures of the federal government.

Personnel Management Section of the Committee Report by Reeves and Paul T. David

As was typical of Reeves's major research undertakings he chose a younger scholar to carry much of the research load so that he could devote his energies to some policy matters and coordination with other aspects of the larger study. This arrangement was especially needed in this project because of his involvement in the New York Regents Study of Education; his duties in connection with the National Emergency Council; his continued work at the University of Chicago; and his admitted need for someone with more background in political science and public administration. He chose as his principal associate Paul T. David, who had worked with him with TVA as an administrative assistant in recruitment and selection of personnel in the earliest months of the TVA and who then transferred to the Social and Economic Division also headed by Reeves. David took his undergraduate work at the Georgia Institute of Technology and Antioch College. After graduation from the latter institution he received M.A. and Ph.D. degrees in Economics from Brown University and was a research fellow at the Brookings Institution before joining Reeves in the TVA.

He later collaborated with Reeves in the presidentially appointed Advisory Committee on Education and the American Youth Commission of the American Council on Education and still later spent four years with the Bureau of the Budget and ten more years as a senior staff member of the Brookings Institution. Since 1960 he has been a professor of government and foreign affairs at the University of Virginia.

For about nine months Reeves and David teamed up to give direction and personally to participate in an intensive examination of the federal personnel system while Reeves continued to participate in the general design and conduct of the whole committee's inquiry to relate the emerging findings regarding personnel practices into the broader findings with reference to the organization and staffing of the Executive Office, financial controls and accountability, departmental management and other sectors of the study. They cast a wide net of inquiry regarding federal personnel administration covering not only basic statistical information but also information as to the deficiencies of the present system, as well as suggestions for improvement based on the experience of those engaged in departmental personnel work. Questionnaires were sent to the Civil Service Commission, the Council of Personnel Administration, and departmental personnel officers. Some of them were accompanied by a Presidential letter requesting their cooperation. Several key officials having a depth of knowledge of and experience with federal personnel practices were interviewed.

Reeves arranged for drafts of the section on personnel to be sent to other members of the committee research staff, who provided important feedback on content and tone of the draft report—sometimes critical. With reference to the tone of the draft report one respondent wrote to the director of research:

> It is possible that my feeling of mild dissatisfaction with Mr. Reeves's discussion of principles is due to a stylistic preference for a less dogmatic form of presentation. While Mr. Reeves does make a good many qualifications of what seems, on first reading, to be a statement of 'absolutes,' it is the flavor of 'absolutism' that I get from reading that discussion. This may, however, be a mere matter of style . . . Please convey my congratulations to Mr. Reeves for his very interesting and stimulating report.

Reeves also got feedback from the director of the research staff on his formulation of principles, on the need for protection of the civil service against a raid by a politically minded President, on the deficiencies of the Civil Service Commission in recruitment of professional employees and other aspects of personnel administration. These points became subjects of discussion between Reeves and David and other members of the research staff.

As the work progressed and a draft report was available for final review, Reeves demonstrated his desire to get the widest reaction to his, David's and the Committee's thinking from additional persons knowledgeable about federal personnel policies and operations. Among these, most of whom were persons with whom Reeves had prior experience were: William H. McReynolds of the Treasury Department who became the Presidential Assistant for Personnel; Clarence Dykstra, City Manager of Cincinnati, Ohio, later President of the University of Wisconsin; Luther Steward, President, National Federation of Federal Employees; H. Eliot Kaplan, National Civil Service Reform League, and others having similar vantage points on the operations of civil service system policies and practices.

This involvement of persons known to have various perspectives on the problems doubtless more than made up for the deficiencies about federal personnel policies and practices which Reeves had frankly mentioned when initially urged to take on the task. This quality of mind and work method which emphasized getting the facts and judgments of knowledgeable persons about problems which Reeves undertook was his trademark and style of operation.[3]

Highlights and Judgments About the Federal Personnel Program

Excerpts from the Reeves-David findings which have the largest bearing on the major recommendations approved by the Committee and the President follows:[4]

> • The responsibilities of the Chief Executive in connection with the determination of personnel policies, although of the highest importance, have seldom in the history of the office received the attention they appear to merit. Presidential recommendations for personnel legislation have been relatively infrequent. The Civil Service rules have not been given thorough revision since 1903 and do not appear to meet the need for comprehensive and modern administrative code relating to personnel matters.*

---

*This deficiency was erased in FDR's message to the Congress on January 12, 1937 in which he endorsed the recommendations of the Committee on Personnel and other aspects of administrative management. Congress subsequently passed several laws which implemented some of the recommendations and the President also promulgated several executive orders to implement the recommendations.

• Good personnel may admittedly be very ineffective in the Federal Government if placed in an organization framework that is structurally unsound. Emphasis upon good personnel should not be allowed to minimize the emphasis that should be given to sound organization. Both problems are of major importance, and in fact interlock. It is difficult to attract good personnel to an organization that is faulty in structure, and it is likewise difficult to improve the structure of organization without the assistance of good personnel through whom to work.

Apart from the relationship of personnel policy and practice to organization (demonstrated to be effective in the TVA personnel program), Reeves and his associates had a comprehensive view of the various components of personnel administration which went beyond the initial appointment of personnel. More specifically, they were concerned with other interrelated major functions such as: (1) classification of positions to clarify responsibilities and duties and to permit salary coordination, (2) status changes as related to building a career service, (3) determination of appropriate salary levels and the administration of individual salary changes, (4) systematic training programs for supervisors and for the improvement of employee performance and their advancement, (5) conduct of employee management relations, (6) creation of working conditions to promote health, safety and efficiency, (7) administration of compensation policies for death, disabilities and injuries in the line of duty, and (8) retirement of superannuated and disabled employees. They saw these functions as being largely carried out by line officers responsible for results. They also saw line officers being aided by the work of departmental professional personnel officers who were knowledgeable of government-wide regulations—and for developing guidelines for departmental policies and for counseling the line officers in their application. Reeves, David and associates found the Civil Service Commission as doing its best work largely in: the administration of assembled examinations for large groups of standardized positions; the administration of personnel classifications; and the administration of the retirement system. The principal deficiencies of the Commission to create a more adequate modern central personnel service were analyzed as: having a lack of interest in creating such a system; being excessively concerned with initial examination and appointment procedures to the exclusion of other aspects of personnel administration; placing major emphasis on the negative and restrictive actions attendant upon the enforcement of the Civil Service laws and rules generally rather than on a positive and cooperative management approach. Furthermore, they saw a need for the creation of more adequate examination and classification procedures for higher and specialized positions and for improved recruitment, placement, training and morale building activities. Other deficiencies of the Civil Service Commission itself related to the organization, training program and "in breeding" of the staff.

Over time a number of these deficiencies have been corrected or eliminated—especially with the crunch of the expanded war-related and post-war programs. But as late as 1944 Reeves in re-reviewing the organization and program of the Civil Service Commission wrote a highly critical article under the title of *Civil Service as Usual* which is detailed later in this section.

Other aspects of federal personnel practices were examined including: relationship to the Bureau of the Budget, Federal Personnel Council, employee organizations, expenditures for personnel services, rule making and appelate functions, research, employee relations and related topics.

Principal Illustrative Recommendations

A brief summary of the most important recommendations were:

- The merit system should be extended upward, outward and downward to include all positions in the Executive Branch of the Government except those which are policy making in character.
- The extension of the merit system upward was to include all permanent positions except a very small number of executive and policy forming positions; outward to include permanent positions not under the Civil Service located in new or emergency agencies or those by-passed in older departments; and downward to include skilled workmen and laborers in the regular government service.*
- The extension of the merit system in the federal government requires the reorganization of the Civil Service Commission as the central personnel Agency.

The reorganization would involve the selection of a highly qualified non-political single executive officer to be known as the Civil Service Administrator. A part-time policy board was also recommended, con-

---

*On June 24, 1938 FDR issued Executive Order #7916 which extended the Civil Service to a group of positions involving approximately 24,000 persons.

sisting of seven persons drawn from private business, labor, education, agriculture, and public administration for overlapping terms and to be appointed by the President. The principal functions of the Board would be to nominate to the President persons for the position of Civil Service Administrator; advise the President on possible improvements in the laws or administration of matters affecting the personnel program; advise and assist the administrator in fostering the interest of institutions of learning, civic and professional organizations and labor and employee organizations in improving standards and more generally to act as a watch dog of the merit system and to represent the public interest in the improvement of the federal service.

- Other recommendations called for an increase in the number, quality and scope of responsibility of departmental personnel officers to better relate federal personnel and organizational policies and priorities to the special needs and functions of the several departments and to help in formulating more viable policies and practices with full recognition of merit principles.
- Also recommended was the revision of salary scales especially for the higher non-political positions to facilitate retaining the best qualified employees for a career in the service. Salaries of $20,000, $15,000 and $12,000 were recommended for heads of executive departments, under secretaries and assistant secretaries. (The ceiling for most top positions at the time was at $10,000.) This recommendation, plus other considerations, was doubtless influential in the creation of the present "super grades" for top executives ranging from approximately $61,296 to $69,000 with variations for the "Senior Executive Service" which are still considered by most personnel experts to be below comparable positions in the private sector.

This intensive review of all aspects of federal personnel policies, organization and operations and the quality of the thinking which supported the far reaching recommendations, led to the subsequent selection of Reeves to serve with a committee to deal with the special problems of attorneys and the higher executive levels in the federal service.

President's Committee on Civil Service Improvement

Approximately three years after Reeves served as a member of the President's Committee on Administrative Management, he was invited by Justice Stanley Reed to join a Presidentially appointed advisory group on civil service improvement with special attention to "Administrators." The invitation to serve in this new, and final, major effort of FDR to improve the Civil Service, was seconded in a letter to Reeves from Luther Gulick, Director of the Institute of Public Administration, who had been recommended by Justice Reed to be the Chairman of the Advisory Committee. The other members of the Committee included Reeves's old friends and professional associates: Louis Brownlow, then head of the Public Administration Clearing House; Clarence A. Dykstra, President of the University of Wisconsin; John Gaus, Professor of Political Science at the University of Wisconsin; Leonard White, Professor of Political Science at the University of Chicago; William E. Mosher, Dean of the Maxwell School of Citizenship and Public Affairs at Syracuse University; John F. Miller of the National Resources Committee; Walter Dietz, Western Electric Company; Delos Walter, R. H. Macy and Company; John H. Fahey, Chairman, Federal Home Loan Bank; Harry Marsh, Personnel Director, Department of Finance and Control, State of Connecticut; William H. McReynolds, who had been appointed Assistant to the President for Personnel; General Robert E. Wood, President of Sears Roebuck and several other public and private officials who were well acquainted with Reeves and his work.[5]

The mission of this Committee was focused primarily on the special problems of the professional, scientific and higher administrative classes of employees and attorneys in the Federal Service. The special problems of attorneys were, in a sense, overlooked in the review of personnel in the President's Committee on Administrative Management, although the emerging needs of the higher level technical and administrative personnel for special consideration had been acknowledged and corrective actions recommended by the Administrative Management Committee. They were not followed up by the Civil Service Commission and thus persisted as problems, along with those of attorneys. There were approximately 5,000 positions in these classes which were temporarily exempted from the Executive Order which had extended Civil Service to approximately 24,000 persons in other classes as recommended by the Committee on Administrative Management and were supported by Congressional legislation introduced by Congressman Ramspeck. The President postponed the application of the above Executive Order by issuing another Executive Order (No. 8044) to give additional consideration to methods of extending the Civil Service to the classes indicated above. Since many of the 5,000 employees were attorneys who were supported in their views by Supreme Court Justices, they resisted being lumped together with the other classes of employees.[6] One can only speculate as to the pressure which was put on the President to postpone action and give the attorneys another day "in court" to argue their case for separate treatment.

Nevertheless, the Advisory Committee on Civil Service Improvement after approximately two more years of deliberation recommended:

> That all of the (5,000) positions, with insignificant exceptions, committed to our study be brought within the classified civil service. We offer a series of minor recommendations designed to permit some added flexibility and efficacy in the existing civil service procedures. All members of the committee agree that the attorney positions, equally with all the others, should be brought within the classified civil service, but there is some difference of opinion as the processes which should be used for the initial selection of attorneys.[7]

Although Justice Murphy joined in the committee's recommendation, he wrote a separate letter to the President on the same day in which he expressed his partial dissent from the Committee's recommendation as follows:

> Your Committee on Civil Service Improvement is submitting to you a report which I believe to be helpful in many respects and in which I have concurred. It is also my belief, however, that this report does not constitute an adequate reply to the question raised by Executive Order No. 8044. I have therefore been impelled to prepare an independent memorandum . . . in which are embodied certain views formulated during several years' service as a public administrator.
>
> This action has been prompted principally by the conviction that if a system of personnel administration is basically sound, that system, with only minor modifications to meet unique conditions, will be appropriate and effective for all types of positions . . . It has therefore been my position that a proper execution of the Committee's task necessitates an inquiry into the character of the national civil service system as a whole.[8]

The Justice went on to detail specific objections to the proposals in the Committee report. With all due respect to the Justice, I suspect that the trouble was not entirely with the report but with the text of the Executive Order which constituted the framework for the Committee's deliberations. The President, in any event, on the basis of a memorandum signed by "STE" (doubtless Steven T. Early) approved the release of the Committee report on February 20, 1941.[9]

The Advisory Committee on Administrators, on which Reeves also served, focused its deliberations on approximately six hundred positions in the Civil Service with salaries ranging from $3,800 to $9,000 and above as of January 31, 1937. The titles of the positions under review included Bureau Chiefs, Directors and Assistant Directors, Heads of institutions and Administrative Assistants to high officials. A sharp distinction was made, however, between this group of administrative officials and those which, although having similar titles, combined policy making and political responsibilities.

Reeves was also involved in preparing recommendations which also applied to positions in engineering, natural science, social scientists, economists and architects which were set forth in two chapters titled *Toward an Improved Civil Service*. Many, if not most, of these recommendations were of the same order and character as those authored by Reeves and David and included in the report of the President's Committee on Administrative Management. Because these ideas are described in earlier sections of this chapter, the following notes are restricted to the issues and recommendations focused on the higher non-political levels of the Administrative Service. The principal recommendation of the committee was:

> That all positions whose duties are administrative in nature in grades CAF 11 and P4 or higher (the middle and top grades of the Civil Service), whether in the departmental or field service and whether in the competitive classified or exempt service be identified as an occupational group within the existing classification structure as the basis of authority now vested in the Civil Service Commission.[10]

This recommendation, although deceptively bland in expression, was in fact revolutionary because it recognized for the first time that administrative work in the federal service should be considered as having a character and importance of its own, and not as an upward extension of the clerical or professional series. The establishment of an administrative group was not, however, to be patterned after the British or other generalist administrative services as Reeves made clear in a letter to Gulick on September 26, 1939 in which he indicated his reactions to a draft report which had been sent to him for review. Apparently, Reeves was annoyed, or dissatisfied, with more than one item in the report since he wrote: "In view of the questions that are in my mind at present in connection with this report, I do not wish to have my name affixed to it. I favor another Committee meeting for further discussion." But on one point his views were clear and forcefully expressed in his letter to Gulick: "Do not establish an administrative service!" And further in a post-script he wrote: "Since drafting this letter, I have discussed this report with Brownlow. He tells me that he is very much opposed to setting up an administrative service of any kind. In view of his comments to me, it seems particularly important that we have another meeting of the Committee."[11]

Reeves's position on this critical point was sustained.

The final report of the Committee on this point makes clear in the following language exactly what the Committee had in mind on this central issue.

> We accept the view that the management of an institution, bureau or agency, which is based upon the application of a profession or science can best be performed by one who is familiar with such profession or science. In such cases, however, we observe that knowledge of the profession or science is not enough in itself; the director or supervisor must also possess the qualities which make for success in management, which are different from those which make for success in research or professional practice. In this recommendation we wish to safeguard the existing recognition of supervisory positions for which scientific or professional knowledge and experience are recognized as essential. In any case we do not recommend barriers or exclusion between these two divisions of a single occupational group. Men with professional or scientific training and administrative skill should clearly be eligible for appointment as administrators in nonprofessional or scientific agencies; and the converse should be equally possible, within the judgment and discretion of the proper appointing authorities.[12]

A further observation of the Committee which may well have been authored by Reeves denied the necessity of establishing an educational requirement as a prerequisite for appointment to an administrative position. "The only consideration is the possession of those qualities of character, intellect and personality which give promise of success in administrative work, and in the case of professional and scientific agencies the possession in addition to the degree of knowledge thought necessary."[13]

No formal predictive tests of administrative ability were thought to be available other than demonstrated competence in actual work.

Specially designed in-service training programs emphasizing planned assignments of operating duties, and short-term training details to other agencies were strongly advocated. The establishment of the position of General Manager for larger organizations was also strongly recommended. No open competitive examinations by the agency or by the Civil Service Commission were recommended, rather that selection "be made on the basis of a considered recommendation by the department personnel officer, strengthened by provision for a preliminary training period and by careful observation of personal aptitudes over a period of time." The Committee recognized the desirability, however, of making some "replacements at all grades from without the service in order to reinvigorate the high administration by new blood, fresh energy and developing ideas from private management."[14]

Post Script Evaluations by Clapp and Reeves of Federal Personnel Practices

A thoughtful critique of the total report, which doubtless reflected Reeves's views, was written by Gordon Clapp (his protege in the TVA) under the title of *The Role of Three It Puzzles Me*.[15] Clapp attacked the sections of the report dealing with the problem of assimilating lawyers into the Civil Service, which took the position that lawyers were different from other professional, technical and higher administrative personnel. Clapp made a strong case against the general assumption that lawyers were essentially different from other professional employees but made his strongest case against the "rule of three"—the requirement that appointments be made from the top three numerically rated persons on a personnel register. His views were considered as seminal among thoughtful persons in personnel administration.

TVA under Reeves and Clapp was instrumental in devising a more sensible and defensible approach to relating measures of merit to specific needs of operating officials in the TVA merit system—without a "rule of three."

Reeves's ten-year perspective on personnel administration in the federal service—starting in 1933 in the TVA followed by service on two presidentially-created committees on administrative management and civil service improvement and later in war manpower and other war agencies—was expressed in a reflective and highly critical and provocative article of civil service procedures under title of *Civil Service as Usual* published in 1944.[16]

In this article Reeves recapitulated the major findings and recommendations of his and David's studies previously referred to and the major findings of the Committee on Civil Service Improvement. On the positive side of the ledger he noted several constructive developments, the basis for which were fostered by the above Committee, as follows: the passage of the Hatch Act which provided for the exclusion of federal civil servants from active participation in political activities and the Ramspect Act which extended the classified service to virtually all positions—with the major exception of the TVA which had its own merit system; and the establishment of departmental personnel offices and the reconstruction of the Council of Personnel Administration.

The Civil Service Commission was also credited for a number of constructive measures particularly designed to improve personnel practices to help facilitate the war effort. Some of these, for which Reeves gave the Commission full credit included: administering a pool of qualified personnel for war service appointments, mostly temporary; developing an aggressive recruitment program, especially for scientific specialized, supervisory and administrative personnel; instituting open examination registers; decentralizing a number of personnel transactions; improving investigation of applicants; and creating a liaison staff of defense agencies. Most of these progressive measures were carried out cooperatively with departmental personnel officers.

On the negative side, Reeves pointed out the reversion to old policies and practices. One of these was the reversion to the "closed register" system (some of the registers being from three to five years old) in contrast to the "open-continuous" examination and register system adopted by TVA in 1933. The open register system, combined with more aggressive recruitment procedures, brought more able persons into the government and placed them in government agencies, the programs to which they could enthusiastically relate. Another was the reversion to the "rule of three," previously attacked by Clapp as described above, which, although having the appearance of providing an objective basis of selection of personnel actually introduced unnecessary and unsupportable rigidities.

Reeves also took out after the various subterfuges and evasions of rules and regulations which personnel directors and operating officials had to resort to—especially during the war effort—to get the job done. The Civil Service Commission was often a full partner in these subterfuges and in fact helped invent some of them. But the necessary and effective practices which were invented during the war had apparently no permanent effect on the Commission—since, among other factors, the Commission lost most of the imaginative and creative personnel whom they had recruited for the war effort and everything settled back to the old routines.

Chapter III

National Resources Planning Board (NRPB)[1]

The National Resources Planning Board and its predecessor agencies were born in the depth of a debilitating depression and flourished during the war emergency and post-war planning for a total of almost ten years and finally died at the hands of Congress for whom planning was anathema, if not downright "Communist."[2]

But it made important contributions to alleviating some of the worst problems of the depression, largely through support for an extensive public works program, and to highlighting and illuminating important interrelationships of natural and human resources. Its short organizational life has been evaluated by scholars as one of the major achievements of the New Deal Era.[3] Floyd Reeves was actively involved in the work of the NRPB as will be developed later in this chapter.

Beginnings

The basic framework and guiding philosophy of the NRPB is believed to have had its initial formulation in FDR's inaugural speech on March 4, 1933, when he said:

> Plenty is at our doorstep, but a generous use of it languishes in the very sight of the supply. Primarily this is because rulers of the exchange of mankind's goods have failed. The money-changers have fled their seats in the temple. The measure of that restoration lies in the extent to which we apply social values more noble than mere monetary profit. Restoration

> calls, however, not for changes in ethics alone. The nation asks for action and action now. Our greatest primary task is to put our people to work—it can be accomplished in part by direct recruiting by the government itself, but at the same time through the employment to stimulate and reorganize the use of our natural resources. It can be helped by national planning—but it can never be helped by merely talking about it. We must act and act quickly. In the event that the national emergency is still critical I shall ask Congress for broad executive powers to wage war against the emergency as if we are, in fact, invaded by a foreign foe.

Executive actions followed quickly thereafter.

On July 8, 1933 FDR appointed Harold Ickes, the Secretary of Interior, as Administrator of Public Works which was created on July 20 as the National Planning Board. During its first year the Board, in addition to a variety of specific actions to accelerate the public works program, provided planning assistance and financial aid to many new city, state and regional planning agencies. It initiated plans and programs in the fields of land, water and other resources, a key formulation of "Plan for Planning" for the Board and for the nation as a whole.

The principal leaders of this first year were, in addition to Secretary Ickes, Frederic A. Delano, (FDR's uncle) who had as impressive experiences in city and regional planning in Chicago, New York, and Washington and was also a recognized expert in land-use policies; Wesley C. Mitchell, a distinguished economist from Columbia University; Charles E. Merriam, a friend and co-worker in Chicago politics with Harold Ickes; and Charles W. Eliott II, who had worked with Delano for the National Capital Park and Planning Commission. Mitchell and Merriam had served as Chairman and Vice Chairman respectively for Herbert Hoover's Committee on *Recent Social Trends*, which put the planning effort in a non-partisan context. This tradition was faithfully followed by the NRPB.

As of July 1, 1934 the title of the agency was changed to The National Resources Board (NRB).[4] Ickes continued to serve as the nominal chairman, which assured some continuity with ideas articulated in the "Plan for Planning." The language of the Executive Order which created the NRB was then broadened to direct the new agency:

> to prepare and present to the President a program and a plan of procedure dealing with the physical, social, governmental and economic policies for the development and use of land, water and other national resources and

such other related subjects as may from time to time be referred to it by the President.

Reflecting some program and personality conflicts (which were not uncommon in the early year of the New Deal) the National Resources Board was renamed the National Resources Committee (NRC) by an Executive Order. Beardsley Ruml, a former professor at the University of Chicago in the Hutchins era, then the Treasurer and Vice President of Macy's Department Store, and Henry Dennison, a prominent businessman, were named to the NRC.

A final reorganization occurred in 1939 when the name was changed for the rest of its existence to the National Resources Planning Board (NRPB) as an independent agency in the Executive Office of the President. The NRPB had its own budget which had previously been subsumed in the budget of the Department of Interior under Ickes. The organizational changes did not affect Delano and Merriam, the principal architects of the program. Ickes, however, was to a degree "sidelined" in the reorganization. Merriam is reported by Arthur Schlesinger to have emerged as the dominant figure in the agency. The functions were more clearly defined to reflect functions already being performed as follows:

- To survey, collect data on and analyze problems pertaining to national resources, both natural and human, and to recommend to the President and the Congress long-time plans and proposals for the wise use and fullest development of such resources.
- To consult with federal, regional, state, local and private agencies in developing orderly programs of public works and to list for the President and the Congress all proposed public works in the order of their relative importance.
- To inform the President of the general trend of economic conditions and to recommend measures leading to their improvement or stabilization. (This innovation may have anticipated the functions now performed by the Council of Economic Advisors.)
- To act as a clearing house and means of coordination for planning activities linking together various levels and fields of planning.

Reeves's Participation in the Work of the NRPB

Before going into a further account of the work of the NRPB in 1941 to 1943, when Reeves was actively associated with it as a consultant, it is relevant to sketch out a few of the significant personal and professional linkages between Reeves, Merriam, and Delano and the work of the NRPB. The principal professional experience which was useful to the NRPB was Reeves's three years as Director of Personnel and of the Social and Economic Planning Division of TVA. The TVA program of comprehensive resource and regional development was directly relevant to the work of the NRPB. After leaving the TVA he served as Chairman of the President's Advisory Committee on Education which produced far reaching recommendations for the expansion of federal participation in education broadly related to the war effort. He had earlier been associated with Frederick Delano in the Advisory Committee on Education. While Reeves was serving as Director of Labor Supply for the War Production Board, Mr. Delano requested Sidney Hillman, Associate Director General of the War Production Board, to have him transferred to the NRPB. Reeves's relationship with Charles Merriam was longer in duration and more deeply personal and professional. They shared many interests including the work of the Public Administration Clearing House, affiliated with the University of Chicago.

Other University of Chicago faculty were also members of a larger group which were very active in New Deal organizations. This group included: William Fielding Ogburn, Marshall Dimock, Charles Colby, Herman Pritchett and several others.

Reeves was a full partner in these exciting enterprises and by background, disposition and values an ardent New Dealer in spirit.

NRPB Reports to Congress[5]

Excerpts from the introduction to the 1942 report highlight the policies and spirit of the NRPB in its ninth year of existence. The mission of the nation was epitomized in the President's statement, "We are going to win the war and we are going to win the peace that follows."

> American energies are now directed toward the development of a vast production program toward the mobilization as swiftly as possible of all the resources of the nation. We are engaged in what is termed total total war—a form of struggle in which all the resources of the States involved are hurled into the arena of conflict . . . *To Win the Peace*, we must prepare now—even while we are concentrating on winning the war . . . We are intent on winning the war, not only to safeguard our lives and our

> liberties, but also to make possible the 'pursuit of happiness' . . . the full fruition of our hopes and plans for progress and development. We must fight the dictators and all their forces, not only with greater force, but with ideas and faith . . . We are not going back to the 'status quo.' We are going forward with restored confidence in the basic foundations of faith, decency, and liberty which underlie our civilization.

The report went on to explain that the NRPB as the planning arm of the Executive Office of the President, along with other organizations established in 1939 such as the Bureau of the Budget and the Office of Emergency Management, were created to aid the President in administering the government. The NRPB functioned as the principal advisory agency to the President in a wide range of rural, urban, regional and national planning affairs. It reported directly to the President and functioned on the basis of an agenda approved by the President.

The rationale and wisdom of the planning effort was clearly stated in the 1942 report as follows:

> What happens to our national economy when in a defense and war period the national income goes up to $100 or more billions, has an important bearing on the maintenance of full use of our national powers after the immediate emergency is over. Collapse following the war would bring with it calamaties as hard to bear as those of conflict . . . that there is no magic, black or white, in the mere word 'planning' except as it helps to realize the national ideals and interests in sound and practical forms. Planning is an effort to make use of social intelligence in the shaping of basic policies, but plans have no life unless they meet with public approval and are shaped into policies by the responsible persons who are entrusted by the people with the power of decision.

The introduction to the 1942 report closed with a declaration of national policy—which expanded the provisions of the Bill of Rights.

> We look forward to securing, through planning and cooperative action, a greater freedom for the American people. Great changes have come in our century with the industrial revolution, the rapid settlement of the continent, the development of technology, the acceleration of transportation and communication, the growth of modern capitalism, and the rise of the national state with its economic programs. Too few corresponding adjustments have been made in our provisions for human freedom. In spite of all these changes, that great manifesto, the Bill of Rights, has stood unshaken 150 years. And now to the old freedoms we must add new freedoms and restate our objectives in modern terms.

Freedom of speech and expression, freedom to worship, freedom from want and freedom from fear: These are the universals of human life.

The report went on to provide specific activities for War and Post-war Planning. Under the War Planning category there were such sections as: Community Problems Arising Out of Federal Defense Activities, Conservation of Cultural Resources, Support Priorities and Allocation, Public Construction Trends and Economic Reporting. Post-war Planning included such sections as: Plans for Demobilization—public and private, Rural Public Works and Land Use, Full Employment, Urban Conservation and Development, Drainage Basin Development, Transportation, Energy, Plans for Financing and Fiscal Policy for State, City and Regional Participation and Service Activities such as Health, Nutrition and Medical Care, Recreation and Education. The sections typically included statements of the problems and specific recommendations for immediate or future action. Reeves was actually involved in post-war activities in education and readjustment of civilian and military personnel.

On Education

Reeves was principal author of two reports on education which were incorporated as parts of the NRPB reports to the President and the Congress. With Paul Hanna, of Stanford University, he wrote a report under the title of "Post-war Planning for Children and Youth" and with Dudley Hart, Paul Mort, *et al.*, on "Equal Access to Education." Both of these reports utilized much of the data and reiterated the principal recommendations of the Advisory Committee on Education, the American Youth Commission and other work in which Reeves had engaged. The topics and recommendations covered the needs for expansion of educational opportunity, employment, health, recreation, social services and several other areas. The significance of these reports was not in their content alone but in the context in which the needs of education were juxtaposed with the whole range of needs for improvement in resource development, private and public employment measures, health and social services, urban redevelopment, and all other needs which collectively would help to win the peace as well as to win the war. The NRPB reports made educational needs and problems integral aspects of the total planning process for war and peace which incorporated Reeves's convictions and outlook.[6]

Post-war Readjustment of Civilian and Military Personnel

The most important, sensitive, far-reaching, challenging and creative work which Reeves performed as a consultant to the National Resources Planning Board was his chairmanship of the Conference on Post-war Readjustment of Civilian and Military Personnel. The unusual term *Conference* was used for what would ordinarily have been called a Committee or Commission. The term was adopted, in part, because there was considerable uncertainty in the beginning of deliberations as to just what the group might produce in the way of politically, economically and logistically feasible suggestions or recommendations; to whom the group was responsible; and when and in what form a set of recommendations would be released. The one point was undoubtedly clear to the NRPB was that there were 20–30 million military personnel and civilians involved directly in the war effort who would—at some uncertain date—when the war was won—be returned to their pre-war jobs, locations and personal destinies.

The criteria for selection of members of the Conference group included highly placed personnel from the military services and from civilian government agencies who would have the technical capability and creative imagination to deal with the manpower problems which the conference was created to explore.

The President approved the appointment of the conferees. The selection of a chairman for such a group, made up of persons of highly divergent backgrounds, was undoubtedly a matter of considerable concern.[7] The selection of Floyd Reeves was not, however, a high risk selection since he had already performed highly important tasks for the President and was personally known to Mr. Delano and was a close colleague of Charles Merriam. Reeves had demonstrated his capacity to organize and direct research and policy making bodies of diverse backgrounds and to secure consensus of views and recommendations from their deliberations, usually under highly improbable deadlines. Thus at the first meeting of the group on July 17, 1942 Mr. Delano introduced Reeves as the permanent Chairman of the group. In addition to the appointed members of the Conference, a number of other officials from the military and civilian branches of the government and elsewhere provided technical information and policy suggestions to the Conference.

A review of the records of the meetings of the Conference and existing correspondence between Reeves, who was at the University of Chicago between meetings of the Conference, and the Secretary,

Leonard Outhwaite, reveals that the Secretary played a key role in preparing summaries of the meetings, keeping Reeves informed of relevant developments in Washington and in shuttling back and forth between the Conference and the NRPB officers and staff.

Proceedings of the First Six (of twenty-seven) Sessions of the Conference[8]

At the first meeting two important framework statements were made by Mr. Delano, the Acting Chairman and Charles Merriam. Mr. Delano said "It seemed unwise to the President at this time to appoint a formal committee on demobilization problems." This meeting and the ones to succeed it should be regarded rather as a continuing discussion of common problems by specially selected individuals representing various government agencies immediately concerned. There would be no publicity. It would be particularly unwise to raise false hopes because of premature discussion of demobilization plans. Merriam followed with his views of the task to the effect that the duty of the Conference was to evolve a "plan for a plan." He felt that the Conference might result in the presentation of a report on a set of recommendations but certainly publicity or publication would have to wait upon events. Possibly they should aim for a preliminary report to be delivered in October. Timeliness was of the essence. It was, of course, the importance of the subject they had under consideration that made it necessary to proceed deliberately and with caution, Reeves responded by agreeing with Merriam and said, further,

> that the Conference might produce a set of recommendations which, hopefully, would be signed by all members of the Conference. He invited free discussion and full participation, out of which the report would grow.

One of the military conferees was reported to have said that: in his opinion the question they had under consideration was so important that it was second only to the question of winning the war.

To avoid "official" rather than "personal" participation Reeves encouraged detachment of the conferees from their organizational connections and reported later in his letter of transmittal of the report that the Conference, though set up by the National Resources Planning Board, had worked as an independent body and had been entirely free in arriving at its recommendations. The various members of the Conference served as individuals and not as representatives of departments or other agencies of the federal government."

After these brief introductory remarks the Conference set out to identify a set of major issues of the task before them. Among the major points made were the following:

- There was not a sharp distinction to be made between demobilization and mobilization—the boundaries were not clear. Approximately three to five million persons were to be involved.
- The tremendous changes which were occurring as a result of mobilization for the war were affecting the fate of particular industries and even cities. It was impossible to separate the problems of the war from the problems of the post-war period. Recognition had to be given to the fact that different types of demobilization programs had to be considered for military personnel and civilians engaged in the war effort. Rehabilitation of certain adversely effected industries was also placed on the agenda for further discussion.
- General Hershey pointed out differences in the attitudes between World War I when "the world was made safe for democracy and peace was to follow as a matter of course" and what he perceived to be a much more complex situation in World War II. He suggested the necessity for a program of education to be considered which had proved to be effective in World War I. The effect of migration of workers from small towns and rural areas (3 million) to big cities and from industries focused on military hardware and software was put into the discussion hopper.
- The opinion was expressed that the large number of women who had been drawn into industry would seek to remain there and be gainfully employed in much larger numbers than in the pre-war period (a prophecy which turned out to be true).
- A labor economist reminded the Conference that the job of demobilization would be a bit easier than in World War I because of several assets to which he made reference: better organization of the labor market; the war training programs; more general knowledge of the working population; and the fact that the public was more disposed to accepting the idea that government would assume considerable responsibility for demobilization.
- In response to the question of responsibility of the federal government, Reeves asked if it did not seem clear that the federal government did, indeed, have responsibility toward young persons

who had been called into service or into war industries and whose education on this account had been interrupted. This principle became widely accepted by the Conference and later by the NRPB, the President, and later by the Congress which passed the necessary implementing legislation for the G. I. Bill of Rights.

- Estimates of the very large numbers of persons in military and civilian service involved in the war effort for whom educational and training programs would need to be devised was factored into the discussion. The idea that preparations for readjustment could start while these large numbers of persons were still in the service was agreed to.
- Reeves noted that: "while we had a limited number of people of whom higher skills and greater knowledge was required, we also had people of whom less skill was required. Consequently, if we tied our vocational education to what people were doing now in industry, our training programs would become very narrow. They might, as a result, be very ill adapted to the future needs of peacetime industry. On the other hand, rounded-out vocational programs might be in very great demand."
- Possible public works programs were discussed in a context of having a hedge against massive unemployment if private industry could not get restructured fast enough to provide employment. The concept of a "shelf of public works" was suggested as a desirable plan to consider.
- The rate and timing of demobilization of both military and civilian personnel to avoid massive dislocation, came in for extensive discussion. One formulation was phrased as follows: "An administration that had in advance pledged itself to immediate rapid demobilization would have either heedlessly gambled on the nation's economic future and the lives of its veterans or shamefully sold out to reactionary forces." An alternative wording of the point which was considered was: "That sound demobilization policy would permit and prepare for rapid demobilization but should not be so great as to precipitate an unemployment crisis; rather that the rate be as rapid as is consistent with the nation's military need and its economic condition."

By the time of the sixth meeting on September 24, 1942, approximately two months after the initial meeting, a consensus was reached that it would be highly desirable for the President to make a statement regarding post-war adjustments "tucked into some other important message." The idea was conveyed to the President but he did not concur in the timeliness of even a general mention of the subject.

By this time the conferees had become an effective working team. Reeves, as chairman, requested members of the group to undertake assignments for preparing data on policies and practices of government agencies, including some foreign governments, and industries with reference to plans for demobilization. He also asked the Secretary and others to prepare draft statements on certain policy points. He occasionally summarized what appeared to be items of concern and again items for further exploration. He also asked critical questions and invited suggestions and observations. The group was functioning as Chairman, Delano and Merriam had hoped that they would in discussion and the application of creative thinking.

More than seven* additional meetings were held to put the final touches to a report which would be acceptable to NRPB and the President and would fit in with the President's sense of timing for release of the report. The President approved the release of the report on June 30, 1943. The release of the report would give veterans, the executive agencies of the government, private industries and educational institutions ample time to test the recommendations and to take measures to implement them.

For the present only the highlights of the report which the Congress used in formulating the G. I. Bill of Rights, and the specific provisions for collegiate and non-collegiate programs follow.

Highlights of the Report[9]

In the introduction to the report by the NRPB, the Board indicated strong endorsement of the Conference report and urged immediate action upon the proposed measures. They noted that soldiers and others are already coming back, and others will follow. For these men the post-war period had already begun. They commented that:

> Simple equity and sound economic policy alike demand that there be an early and clear understanding of what may be counted upon by our armed forces returning to civilian life, what they can tie with confident expectation that they will stand when victory comes. Unpreparedness for peace can bring calamity as great as unpreparedness for war . . . We want not only to get men out of the armed services; we want also to get them

*Appendix E

> into the peace services where their skills and abilities can be fully recognized, utilized and rewarded. They must not be put in the position of rescuing the world from the grasp of aggression, only to return to a world in which they cannot find their place and their opportunity.

Specifically, the following recommendations were endorsed.

For Those Being Demobilized from the Armed Forces

- Three months' furlough at regular base pay not to exceed $100 a month, plus family allowances.
- Beyond that time, if necessary, unemployment insurance for 26 weeks for those who register with the U.S. Employment Service.
- Special aid and counsel regarding adjustment and rehabilitation.
- Special provision, including tuition and allowances, for those who wish to pick up the broken threads of their education or follow some special course of training.
- Veteran's credit for old age and survivors insurance on the basis of service in the armed forces.
- Opportunities for agricultural employment and settlement to be provided for a limited number of qualified service men. But in general, agriculture should not be looked upon as a dumping ground for the industrial unemployed, since the problem is broader than that of agriculture alone.

For War Workers in Industry and Government

- Establishment or readjustment centers through which counsel and assistance and retraining may be made available in readjustment to other jobs, and for strengthening the existing employment agencies for their heavier load.
- Pursuance of a moderate policy in the continuation or cancellation of war contracts—a policy calculated to avoid the dumping of workers on an overstocked market, so far as this is feasible.

National Responsibilities

- It is clear that demobilization should not be considered by and of itself, but a connection with the national policy of economic stability at a high level of employment and productivity. Expanding peace time industry is the only answer to demobilization of war time industry.

- The bulk of employment must be furnished by private industry . . . But government must do what it can to bring about optimum results . . . The government should prepare a shelf of public works to be used in case of need.
- With respect to the costs of the recommended program the Board quoted the Conference report as follows: "These provisions cannot and must not be interpreted as costs in addition to the costs of the war program. They represent in fact a part of the cost of the war."

More Specific Provisions for Education

Because of Reeves's special competence in college and university administration and also because of the importance given to the educational component in the total demobilization and readjustment program, some of the other major recommendations of the Conference are noted below. Appropriate educational programs were recommended for three types of war-connected participants: (1) for those who left schools or colleges during the war who wish to resume their education when hostilities cease; (2) for those in the armed services "voluntary education and training programs such as are now offered by the United States Armed Forces Institute . . . ," and (3) for those released from war industries and for certain classes of employees of the federal government. Policies for the administration of each of the three categories of education and training were also recommended.

For Military Service Personnel

- As a policy, all training and education programs for men in the armed services prior to their release from active military duty should be carried out under the direction of the services, and the men during this period should be subject to such regulations, disciplines and controls as may seem necessary to the officers of these services.
- But for those who have been demobilized, training and educational programs "should be subject to the direction of civilian authority and carried out by the regularly constituted educational institutions, and during this period the men themselves should be free from the discipline and control of the armed forces."

For Collegiate and Professional Programs

Three main tasks were identified to give effect to programs for demobilized personnel interested and eligible to participate in programs at collegiate and professional levels: overall planning and assistance by educational authorities in the drafting of suggested legislation; specific planning on the part of each college, university or professional school in order to determine its particular contribution to the program; and administration of the funds which may be appropriated to implement the program and supervision of standards and eligibility requirements. The report further recommended that:

- "Each institution of higher education participating in the program should determine how many and what kind of demobilized personnel it can accommodate, the program which it can best offer, and the internal adjustments necessary." (The then Michigan State College created a new "Basic College" to respond to this recommendation.)
- "The federal government should encourage national associations of educational institutions to develop a coordinated program for the education of demobilized personnel."
- "The federal government should also undertake to provide such supplementary funds for the support of education as may be needed to make possible the provision of a comprehensive program for demobilized service personnel."

To say the least this recommendation added a new dimension to federal participation in education in which *almost eight million GI's and numerous educational institutions participated.*[10]

Non Collegiate Educational Programs

Because responsibility for education at the high school level is focused in State Departments of Education, with which the United States Office of Education has close relation but no authority, the recommendations for this level of education were more diffused. Nevertheless, the Conference did recommend that:

- The Office of Education should inventory the facilities for specialized secondary and vocational education which may be available for post-war training.
- The Bureau of Labor Statistics and the United States Employment

Service should provide information regarding employment requirements and types of training programs of post-war industries.

- Industrial establishments which are to be restaffed for peace-time purposes should be encouraged to cooperate with educational institutions in developing apprentice and in-service training programs.

The vast scope of and implications for social and governmental change which are contained in the above highlights of the NRPB report, based on the recommendations of the Conference, chaired by Reeves, shows the breadth of public policy concerns with which Reeves was intimately involved. His skill in organizing persons of divergent backgrounds to focus steadily on complex problems and arrive at a high level of consensus on the issues and to develop practical recommendations for action was of the highest level of importance to the war and post-war period.

For several years after the Conference report was widely distributed and implementing legislation and funding were passed, Reeves taught a graduate course on "War and Post-war Planning for Education " at The University of Chicago and lectured and consulted widely at numerous other major universities and educational organizations with encouragement from colleagues of the NRPB and the President of the United States.

The thousands of beneficiares of the G. I. Bill (some of whom may be readers of this book) will appreciate the efforts of the Conference and Floyd Reeves to anticipate their needs for help in getting adjusted to post-war civilian life. Dr. Albert Lepawsky, Professor of Political Science at the University of California in Berkeley, appraised the NRPB generally and the work of the Committee and the contribution of Floyd Reeves in a letter to the author in these words: "The G. I. Bill emerged out of the planning of the NRPB and the Committee—much of the background work having been performed by Floyd Reeves."

Chapter IV

Labor Supply in War Manpower Activities: 1940–1941

Reeves's involvement with labor supply began with a letter from Owen D. Young to President Roosevelt on May 27, 1940. Excerpts from Young's letter dated May 27, 1940 to FDR follow:

> I called General Watson on Friday and told him that I would, of course, do whatever I could to aid in the outline of such a plan (for war manpower). Accordingly, I went to Washington on Friday evening and had a two hour talk with Secretary Hopkins at the White House on Saturday afternoon. It was a most satisfactory one because his mind works with that clarity and definition which aids greatly in dealing with such a sprawling situation as this necessarily is.
>
> As a result of my talk with him, I met (with) first Mr. Aubrey Williams and Major McSherry, the latter being familiar with the personnel requirements of the Army both in direct service and to some extent with the indirect needs of industry supplying the Army. On Sunday morning, with the acquiescence of Secretary Hopkins, I called together at the Mayflower, in addition to Mr. Williams and Major McSherry, Dr. John W. Studebaker, the Commissioner of Education, Mr. Isidor Lubin of the Bureau of Labor Statistics, Mr. James J. McEntee, Assistant Director of the Civilian Conservation Corps, and Dr. Floyd W. Reeves, Director of the American Youth Commission. Although Dr. Reeves is not directly in the Government service, I asked him to come because he is so familiar with the entire area of youth problems and activities and also because I felt that he might be free to act as a liaison officer without interference with his other duties. This group spent several hours in discussion of the problem.[1]

Mr. Young then went on to indicate two not inconsistent approaches to deal with the problem: (1) one would involve the training of youth to "supply the defense program only to the extent necessary to insure an adequate supply of labor whenever and wherever it might be needed" especially in the skill areas of greatest need such as welders, riveters, etc., or (2) to broaden the program to include the large numbers of "restless, unemployed youngsters who are either unmoved by national needs or receptive to subversive and disintegrating influences." Young, as Chairman, and Reeves as Director of the American Youth Commission had thoroughly documented all aspects of the youth population as was described in a previous chapter and had gained insights into the problems, needs and potential of youth and strongly supported this broader approach as did Secretary Hopkins and the President.

Young's (and Reeves's) natural proclivity to get the facts as a basis for action led Young to make assignments to Studebaker to report on facilities in the public school system which could be used for training young people in general or special skills; to Lubin and Altmeyer to report on apprentice schools and training services of private industry and to estimate what additional numbers could be trained in existing or expanded facilities; to McSherry to report on present and possible expansion of training facilities of the Army and Navy; and to Williams to report on the extent to which the facilities of the Youth Administration for vocational training could be expanded. These reports were to be in the hands of Reeves two days later for the preparation of an overall report to Secretary Hopkins covering the topics indicated above plus some estimates of the cost of an enlarged program of training.

As an indication of Young's confidence in Reeves's capacity to pull together data from several sources within severe time limits, and also his knowledge that Hopkins and the President would also have confidence in Reeves's unusual ability to deal with problems of this nature he continued in his letter to the President as follows:

> I have asked Dr. Reeves to report directly to Secretary Hopkins because it will be next to impossible for me to be present at the meeting on Wednesday afternoon for reasons which I explained to the Secretary. Indeed I do not know that there is any need for me to be at that meeting. The following week I could cancel engagements and be in Washington for two days if you or Secretary Hopkins felt it necessary.
>
> My task, as I understand it, is only to aid the Secretary in the

formulation of the plan. I think that you have in Washington men who can administer it satisfactorily once it is established. To the extent to which I might be helpful with the industrial groups, I should, of course, be glad to aid.

I have gone into this detail, Mr. President, partly to test whether this kind of an outline meets the approach which you had in mind.

Young sent a letter to Reeves, with a copy of the letter he had sent to the President, on the same day:

I send you, of course in complete confidence, a copy of my letter to the President, as it has to do with the meeting and report on Wednesday. Unless I hear to the contrary, I shall not be present at that meeting because of the absolute necessity of a Memorial Day engagement which nothing can interrupt except the direct request of the President himself.

The American Youth Commission was asked to allow Reeves to take leave from the Commission for a year to serve as Executive Assistant to Mr. Sidney Hillman for Labor Supply on a dollar a year basis plus a $25 per diem starting June 15, 1940.

Advisory Commission to the Council of National Defense

Without pretending to have made a definitive study of all facets of the thinking and the creation of organizational forms focused on the problems of war manpower a brief sketch of the organization and environment in which Reeves worked follows:[2]

The first of the organizations addressed to the war effort, including manpower, was the cumbersome, all inclusive organization to involve all the relevant components of preparing for war. The Commission was advisory to the Council of National Defense headed by the President and included the Secretaries of War, Navy, Interior, Agriculture, Commerce and Labor. The Secretary of the Council was William H. McReynolds. Included in the Commission were Divisions of Agriculture, Industrial Materials, Industrial Production, Price Stabilization, Consumer Protection, National Defense Purchases, Transportation and Labor. The Divisions were headed by persons who later occupied key positions in the continuing war effort including Chester Davis, Leon Henderson, William Knudsen, *et.al.* The Labor Division, headed by Sidney Hillman, President of the Amalgamated Clothing Workers, included sections for labor requirements, labor relations, housing, employment and labor supply and training. Owen D. Young served as advisor on training and Reeves as Executive Assistant for Labor Supply. The staff under Reeves's direction included W. W. Alexander of the Rosenwald Fund, Major F. J. McSherry of the War Department, Robert C. Weaver, U.S. Housing Authority, H. A. Sarre, Federal Works Agency and Thelma McKelvey of the National Youth Administration. Two other organizations were actively involved. The Coordinating Committee included Arthur J. Altmeyer of the Social Security Board, Wayne Coy, Federal Security Agency, Aubrey Williams, National Youth Administration, Isador Lubin, Bureau of Labor Statistics, and Arthur S. Fleming, representative of the Civil Service Commission. The Labor Policy Advisory Committee included representatives of the major labor unions. Supporting Bureaus included Research and Statistics headed by Stacy May, and State and Location Cooperation by Frank Bane. Reeves enjoyed his association with several of these officials and maintained contact with them on other projects in which he was engaged.

The Defense Advisory Commission was succeeded in January 1941 by the Office of Emergency Management in the Office of Production Management headed by W. S. Knudsen with Sidney Hillman as the Associate Director. The Labor Division under Reeves remained the same. As the preparations for war accelerated and further experience was gained, the War Production Board (WPB) was established in January 1942 and headed by Donald Nelson. The principal personnel of the WPB included Henry Stimson, Secretary of War, Frank Knox, Secretary of the Navy, William Knudsen, Leon Henderson, Henry Wallace, Harry Hopkins and Sidney Hillman.[3]

Reeves's Work in the Labor Division[4]

The Labor Division was responsible for advising several federal agencies with reference to their policies regarding the coordination of their activities relating to labor supply and training. The principal agencies involved were the U.S. Employment Service, U.S. Office of Education, Apprenticeship Unit of the Department of Labor, National Youth Administration, Civil Service Commission and the Works Projects Administration. All of the agencies were highly cooperative with Reeves and his staff except the U.S. Office of Education under John Studebaker. The deficiencies of the office were detailed in a "very confidential" memo to Sidney Hillman reporting the non-cooperation of the U.S. Office of Education, and his great "sense" of urgency to get on with the job. Reeves again wrote to Hillman on January 13, 1941 with recommendations on organizational alternatives for getting on with the job:

> My recommendations are therefore: (a) that there be worked out an administrative relationship with the agencies carrying on defense training rather than an advisory one; or (b) that the office for coordination of labor supply and training be provided with an adequate field staff to properly accomplish the objectives of the program.

Hillman chose the second alternative (b) which was satisfactory to Reeves.

Reeves, for himself and key associates, made almost weekly reports (thirty-six by actual count) in which Hillman was advised in detail on salient aspects of the war manpower situation including such topics as: status of registration at employment offices; effect of third shift in government establishments; modification of Civil Service specifications for jobs; placement of Negroes in vocational education programs; training and employment of girls and women in war production jobs; clearance of labor between regions; status of labor relations including disputes and work shortages; exemption to age limitations, occupational analyses and job testing; and the status of training-within-industry (TWI) programs. Numerous conferences with labor committees, officials of employment offices, personnel and training officers of war production plants, defense committee of the American Medical Association and other groups were held. A sample of Reeves's informal style in conducting meetings is illustrated by a conference of women on the "problems of women's work in defense industries." He stated the purpose of the conference:

> I am frank to say that the major purpose I had was to get a little education on this point. It seemed that the members of this group were the proper people to give me a little education. I want to know what are the problems that are likely to face us with reference to women's work in defense industries in the months and years ahead. What are the problems? What are the various agencies prepared to do about it and what, if anything should we do? Now that, in a nut shell, is the purpose of this meeting.

Public education programs in which Reeves participated included a national radio forum on "Jobs for Defense" conducted by Eric Sevareid in a major speech before the Annual Institute of Government at the University of Southern California. This speech provided an opportunity to give a comprehensive account of the policy framework, motivation and specific activities of the Labor Division during his year of service. Accordingly, the speech was more than a speech in the usual sense of the word but an accounting of his perceptions of the task, his motivation and his performance. Highlights of the speech follow:

On Policy Framework: The Job to be Done

The (now) mobilization of manpower for defense is more difficult and more complicated today than ever before. War, formerly mainly a matter of soldiers, has become primarily a matter of machines . . . What is under test today is the struggle of the democratic nations against the totalitarian nations, is not only the relative abilities and morale of their armies and naval forces, but the relative abilities of economic systems to produce the all-necessary material—airplanes that can fly fastest and farthest, . . . tanks that can outspeed and out fight the rival army's tanks . . . The free workshops of democracy must outdo the slave workshops of the totalitarian nations in manufacturing the implements of war . . .

Major Factors in the Job

First there is the factor of time. The democracies were peaceably minded; hence they started late. While the productive capacity of Great Britain was barely getting started, and our own had not begun, Hitler . . . overran Czechoslovakia, Poland, Luxemborg, Belgium, The Netherlands, Denmark, Norway and France. Since our own defense effort began, just a year ago, Germany and Italy have added Romania and the Balkan states . . . The industrial capacities of these conquered nations have been added to the original capacities of the aggressors; so that now the belated democracies must overtake and surpass the war production of virtually all of continental Europe. . . .

Secondly, there is the factor of organization . . . Our own production has been diffused . . . we had to bring about an integration of productive forces such as, under a dictatorship, is achieved by compulsion and command.

The third aspect of the problem is the sheer size of the task. Our defense program at present calls for an expenditure of more than 40 billion dollars.

And the fourth aspect is the unusual requirement of labor skill . . . Modern ordinance, tanks, airplanes, warships, must be made with thousandths-of-an-inch precision . . . Hundreds of skilled trades are involved—many of them scarce, for the defense production emphasizes an output unfamiliar to our normal economy.

Some Specifics of the Job

Shortage of Skilled Workers (illustrative)

Our national system of public employment offices, in the two-month period ending June 1, 1941 received fifteen times as many employer requisitions for die designers as they had die designers registered. They received 16 times as many requests for tool designers . . . For shipyard loftsmen the ratio of employer requisitions to listings was 35 to 1; for boat builders, 40 to 1; detailed assemblers in aircraft 50 to 1 . . . These figures cannot be interpreted as meaning that those needed skilled men do not exist; but they are certainly not on the great register of more than 5,000,000 available workers which the 1,500 offices of the federal-state employment system have compiled. . . .

Specific Remedial Measures

Three needs were apparent on *prima-facie* indications and we proceeded to provide against them without waiting for statistical proof. The need of upgrading or supplementing the skills of presently employed skilled workers and adapting them to the precise needs of defense; the need of reviving or refreshing the rusty skills of those workers, in misplaced employment; and the need of a widespread increase in the vocational training system for the purpose of giving inexperienced people, old and young, whether unemployed or in relief employment, the basic training upon which semi-skills, and in time higher skills could be built . . . training within industry itself was later added.

The solution to the problems lay in the coordination of the vast potentially useful services of the federal security agency, WPA, NYA, Civil Service Commission, U.S. Office of Education, Federal Committee on apprenticeships, the labor unions, selected industries and other organizations to engage in various types and kinds of training activities.

Difficulties

But the job wasn't easy as Reeves pointed out. We are all, as government workers, familiar—too familiar—with the vested-interest psychology of individual agencies which often makes their relationship to other agencies one of competition rather than cooperation . . . (But) such negative individualism of this type that did exist among public agencies has materially diminished . . . As a result, we are training workers for the direct needs of national defense on the largest scale in the history of the United States.

Some Statistical Evidence of Work Accomplished

- Pre-employment courses given in vocational schools—55,000 trainees per year on the average.
- Supplementary courses, typically out-of-hours courses for employed or experienced workers designed to upgrade them to higher skills—98,000 trainees on the average for the past year for a total of 524,000.
- Courses for out-of-school youth (largely rural)—both general and specialized for an average annual number of trainees of 132,000 for a total of 471,300.
- Engineering courses, given by universities and their extension systems for 3,700 enrolled in-school and 58,300 enrolled in out-of-school or part-time courses.
- Out-of-school work program of the NYA, which involved "more than 300,000 young persons between the ages of 17 or 25 in workshop projects, learning through actual work experience elementary skills related to defense occupations."
- Training-within-industry, 22 TWI centers developed under the guidance of Channing Dooley and Walter Dietz who joined the labor division from the Socony Vacuum and Western Electric Corporations respectively.

Other problems discussed and to a degree resolved were: replacement provisions for key workers injured or otherwise unable to continue their work and "uncontrolled migration of workers" who respond to rumors about the availability of jobs in certain areas only to find that they are not available or that housing is not available or for other reasons jobs were not available.

Reeves closed his speech with a resounding call to patriotic participation in solving manpower problems:

> In democracy, all our lives are rooted. We breathe its air, its strength is our strength, the attempted revolution which would replace it is a threat to our very foundations. To some, Europe's war has seemed remote; it is remote no longer. It was not without a full grasp of the facts that our President proclaimed an unlimited national emergency; and that emergency to every lover of democracy, is an opportunity. It is our opportunity to see that no fighter for democracy goes into battle under armed, under protected, under equipped. . . .

Reeves was recognized for his competence in organizing and coordinating efforts to deal with manpower problems by a Presidential appointment made on August 27, 1940 in the form of a memorandum to the Secretaries of War and Navy as follows:

> I am designating the following persons to work with the Joint Army and Navy Selective Service Committee in planning the procurement of manpower for our National Defense under the Compulsory Military Training Bill pending before Congress:
> Frederick Osborn
> W. H. Draper, Jr.
> Floyd W. Reeves
> Joseph P. Harris.

No details are available to the author on work done under this assignment.

Recognition of the specific work done with the Labor Division under Sidney Hillman was expressed in Hillman's letter to Reeves dated June 24, 1941.

> I regret profoundly that the pressure of your work with the American Youth Commission and the National Resources Planning Board prevents you from remaining in charge of the Labor Supply and Training Section of the Labor Division. It is with the deepest reluctance that I accept this decision on your part. Your contribution, during the first year of the defense program, in formulating and directing the recruitment, training, and placement of defense workers has not only been extraordinarily efficient and successful but also has laid a firm groundwork for meeting this great problem in the future.
>
> In view of your unique experience in, and knowledge of this field, I am taking this opportunity to urge, even to insist, that you continue in a consultant capacity on my staff and be available to participate in developing policies which relate to the defense labor supply program. I am also gratified that you will be able to serve as liaison between the Labor Division and the defense and post-defense planning of the National Resources Planning Board.
>
> Please be assured that my entire staff joins with me in grateful recognition and appreciation of your brilliant accomplishment during the first year in the defense program . . .

Reeves agreed to serve as a consultant to Hillman.

A tribute to Reeves from his colleague, Thelma McKelvey on their work relationship was doubtless especially rewarding to Reeves:

> I am writing this note to you because I feel it is better than the spoken word to tell you how much this year has meant to me in a richness of

experience and the deepest sense of vision and understanding. I doubt if I ever again will have such a satisfactory working relationship. Your leadership has been stimulating and there has been no faltering in the course which you laid out to follow. I know that your heart has been with the American Youth Commission and that you have given this year at great personal sacrifice. However, I am sure no other person could have done the job and have left it as well equipped to meet the coming months of stress and uncertainty.

Please accept my deepest appreciation for your confidence in me, and may I offer my continuing service whenever you feel I can be of assistance to you.

Similar tributes were made by Reeves's colleagues in the American Youth Commission who had to get along without his services while on leave to work with Sidney Hillman. Dorothy Canfield Fisher wrote a letter to George Zook, Executive Director of the Commission, who had sent her, as a member of the Commission, a copy of the exchange of correspondence between Reeves and Hillman. She wrote:

Thanks for your letter of the 11th with the extremely interesting correspondence between Dr. Reeves and Mr. Sidney Hillman. I think the tribute to Dr. Reeves' extraordinary ability in the letter from Mr. Hillman is remarkable. And, as all we on the American Youth Commission know, entirely deserved and well earned. To have seen Dr. Reeves at work is one of the most heartening experiences I have had.

Reeves continued to be involved in manpower problems after returning to the American Youth Commission—in speaking engagements and conferences. One such involvement was a request of Paul McNutt, Administrator of the Federal Security Agency, who wrote Reeves as follows on September 30, 1940:

The Army is at this time withdrawing many of the ablest reserve officers who have served in the Civilian Conservation Corps. This raises the question of the future personnel of the Corps, their recruiting and training.

The President has requested me to appoint a special committee to go into this whole matter of the training of leadership for the Civilian Conservation Corps. I would be glad if you could serve on this committee.

The following are being asked to serve on the committee:

Dean James M. Landis, Harvard Law School
Professor Harold Lasswell, Yale Law School
Mr. Virgil Simmons, Department of Conservation of Indiana
Mr. Wayne Coy, Assistant Federal Security Administrator

> Dr. W. W. Alexander, Federal Security Agency—Chairman
>
> It is the plan to make this a small working committee to actually recommend a program of training which could be put into effect. The first meeting of the committee will be on Saturday and Sunday, October 12 and 13, 1940.
>
> It is anticipated that the report of the committee will be made soon after November 1, and it is desirable that the matter should be kept confidential until that time.
>
> I hope that it will be possible for you to undertake this service.

Reeves agreed to serve on the committee.

Reeves was also offered a position in 1948 as "technical expert" to the Adjutant General's Office of the War Department to review the extent to which the "Industrial College of the Armed Forces" was accomplishing its training mission. He was also strongly recommended to General Hines, Administrator of the Veterans Administration by his colleague, Leonard Outhwaite, of the Bureau of the Budget, who had earlier worked with Reeves on the National Resources Planning Board's study of "Postwar Adjustment of Civilian and Military Personnel," for a study of the Veterans Administration policies and practices in response to the passage of the G. I. Bill of Rights. Much later, in May 1966 when Reeves was 76 years old, he was asked by Lynn M. Bartlett, former Superintendent of the Michigan Department of Education and then Assistant Secretary of Defense (for Manpower) to "privately and informally review a report for us and give us your professional advice." Reeves apparently dictated a tape which elicited the following comment from Bartlett:

> It is clear, lucid, constructive and I'm sure will be of great help to us in dealing with the problem . . . Everyone in the office was greatly impressed with your clear analysis and manner of approaching such a problem. I am of the opinion that you have all the spirit and enthusiasm to aid your government just as you did many years ago when you were a dollar a year man.

Chapter V

National Institute of Public Affairs (NIPA)[1]

The last professional activity engaged in by Reeves was to serve on the Board of Trustees of the National Institute of Public Affairs from 1962–1968. He was appointed for a three-year term in 1962 and reappointed to a second three-year term. He remained active until 1968 when he suffered a heart attack and resigned. He was particularly instrumental in helping NIPA get its first large grant of $1,250,000 from the Ford Foundation and in helping formulate the program for research and training in urban and metropolitan affairs as a member of the special program committee. Service on the Board of Trustees provided Reeves with an exciting opportunity to renew his professional friendships and to become actively involved in innovative programs designed to improve governmental performance—especially directed to the high level personnel of the public service.

The NIPA was incorporated in 1934 as a non-profit, organization to foster and coordinate educational programs designed to improve the performance of the federal government. Later this mission was expanded to include state and local government and the encouragement of understanding and collaboration between government and private industry. The Institute came into being as part of a wave of efforts arising largely out of initiative of President Roosevelt and his New Deal advisors and organizations such as the President's Committees on Administrative Management and on Civil Service Improvement and other organizations and efforts to modernize governmental operations and to attract and retain competent young persons in governmental service. Concurrently, private foundations were becoming interested in investing some of their resources in programs to improve the greatly expanded governmental programs. The first NIPA program was focused on internships designed to bring well qualified college graduates into the public service in cooperation with the United States Civil Service Commission. By 1948 some four hundred especially promising young persons were involved in the program which was considered successful enough to be made a regular program of the Civil Service Commission without assistance from the NIPA.

The Institute was inactive between 1948 and 1961 but it was reactivated in 1962, under a reorganized Board of Trustees, and with a well funded, and highly innovative program, which was responsive to a wide variety of needs and opportunities which are described in the following.

NIPA was under the direction of a distinguished Board of Trustees, the members of which included several well-known political scientists and leaders in education, civic affairs and business.[2]

Principal Programs of NIPA

Career Education Awards

By far the most extensive program was the Career Education Awards initiated in 1962. The Ford Foundation made two grants of $1,250,000 each for the years 1962–65 and 1965–68. These awards permitted carefully selected mid-career civil servants, chiefly at the federal level but later expanded to include state and local levels, to participate in specially designed nine-month educational non-degree programs at one of the following universities: Cornell, Harvard, Chicago, Indiana, Princeton, Southern California, Stanford, Virginia and Washington. The universities were given grants to pay for special instructional costs and tuition for the participants. The federal government continued to pay the salaries, moving expenses and $1,000 for miscellaneous expenses for each trainee. Each awardee chose the university whose program best fitted his or her needs and career objectives. By way of example, the program at the Woodrow Wilson School of Public Affairs at Princeton University, under the direction of three professors, included: a choice of study in five different fields such as American Foreign Policy, Systems Analysis, Economic and Public Policies, Urban Affairs and International Affairs; special seminars, workshops and policy conferences; and the preparation of an essay—"a think piece" on a critical problem or a preliminary research design. Carl Stover, Executive Director of NIPA, succinctly described the aim of the program in these words, "The aim is not the refinement of a specialty but the development of a broader understanding and the ability to relate knowledge effectively to policy action." A more expanded list of objectives and rationale for the program was expressed by Stover as follows:

> A continuous problem in every government agency is to keep a steady supply of capable persons coming along to fill vacancies and new positions at upper levels. To redeem fully responsibilities for the execution of large and difficult programs and for making or advising on major policies requires more than technical competence and routine experience in agency operations . . . Programs were designed to help each trainee: to enlarge his capacity to listen and read critically; to speak and write effectively; to analyze and argue soundly; to deepen his appreciation of the principles to which this Nation is dedicated and of their meaning in our time; to refine his understanding of what knowledge can contribute to action and become more skilled in its use; to become more fully informed about the nature of the modern world, how it came to be, and where it is tending; to gain insight into the institutions and processes of government and learn better how to protect and strengthen their integrity; and perhaps most important; to achieve a higher vision of the mission that is his to fulfill and a better sense of the capacities that are his to employ in fulfilling it.

Industry-Government Seminars

During the years 1964–65 selected high-level government officials, e.g., the U.S. Comptroller-General, a member of the Federal Reserve Board, and comparable executives of private industry met once a month at the Woodrow Wilson School at Princeton University to discuss "public policy issues related to the economy and the role of the corporation." At the request of several business leaders similar seminars were sponsored by NIPA in 1966 and 1967. Reeves long-hand comment on the Board of Trustees agenda item for this program indicated his enthusiasm for the program, "A sample of the many demands which NIPA accepts from throughout the United States for services which we provide . . . It does not seem probable that we shall ever lack non-governmental support for our programs."

A more extensive Industry-Government Executive Interchange Program was formulated for implementation on a pilot basis for four or five exchanges to start in 1968. This program was adopted by the White House in 1969.

Programs on Problems of Metropolitan Areas

A special committee of the Board of Trustees, on which Reeves served, planned and supervised an extensive program, starting in 1967, of conferences on problems in metropolitan areas throughout the country—among them Atlanta, Boston, Cleveland, Dallas, Houston, Fort Worth, Detroit, Nashville, New York, Seattle and Tacoma under the title "The Metropolitan Area: Its Prospects and Problems." Career officials concerned with metropolitan problems, discussed such topics as comprehensive planning for the metropolitan area, urban governmental structure and technology and the future metropolis. The conferences were limited to twenty persons ranging in ages from 35–50 years and lasted for twelve days. Travel, rooms and meals were paid for the participants.

A special experimental mid-career program for government officials in the metropolitan Detroit region was influential in developing the larger program described above. This experimental program was developed in 1966 by faculty of Wayne State University, University of Michigan, Michigan State University and the University of Detroit for full-time and part-time fellows to study at Wayne State University, Credit was earned toward the Master's Degree. The core courses emphasized economics and political science augmented by non-credit seminars and conferences with decision makers in the field.

Systematic Analysis Educational Program

In 1965, with a grant of $10,000 from the Sloan Foundation, the Civil Service Commission and the Bureau of the Budget with NIPA assistance, sponsored a special training program in "systematic analysis." The program was designed to train selected mid-career officials in using new techniques of economic analysis creatively in the solution of complex problems. Trainees attended nine-month programs at the Carnegie Institute of Technology, and the Universities of Chicago, Maryland, Harvard, Princeton, Stanford and Wisconsin.

Language in Public Affairs

A $15,000 grant from the Carnegie Corporation was used as a first effort to deal with government ''gobble-de-gook'' or more politely to ''study the relationship between institutional writing, its writers and its readers'' for the purpose of developing ''suggestions for improvement of the teaching of English and of its use in public affairs.''

Other research, training and service programs fostered during the period while Reeves was on the Board of Trustees included: seminars for industry and government officials, funded by the Sloan Foundation, ''on the use of advanced technology and in such problem areas as environmental pollution, urban renewal and the control of crime and delinquency;'' a seminar series financed by a grant from the Carnegie Corporation on ''such matters as federal tax policies, enforcement of anti-trust laws and the balance of payments problem;'' and a research project, funded by a grant from the Ford Foundation, to evaluate four studies on ''how the advanced technological systems capabilities of private industries might be used in non-defense industries.''

In summary Carl Stover characterized the function and varied programs of the Institute in these words: ''By virtue of its neutrality, flexibility, breadth and involvement with diverse sectors of the total society, it is able to perform a variety of services that help to counteract the separation and rigidity endemic to an era of increasing specialization and massive institutions and thereby encourage individuals exercising public responsibility from public or private stations to grow more adequate to their tasks.'' This kind of policy framework excited and thrilled Reeves to participate and his contributions were not unappreciated.

Richard E. McArdle, the first Executive Director, wrote Reeves in 1964 as follows: ''Before I leave NIPA at the end of this month I want you to know that I shall always be grateful for your help and encouragement. I've taken comfort just in knowing that you are there if I need you. Knowing this I usually managed to work my way out of whatever difficulty I was in at the time. I'm glad you've been on the Board . . .''

In July 1968 in response to the resignation of Reeves from the Board, for health reasons, Carl Stover, then President of the Institute, wrote: ''I hope you know that it has been a great pleasure for me to work with you, that you have my great admiration and respect, and that I deeply appreciate the assistance you have given me and this organization. I will miss seeing you at our meetings. I hope, however, that we will have other occasions for visits in East Lansing or here.''

And finally the Board expressed in December 1968* their appreciation for Reeves's services as follows:

> Be it resolved that the Board of Trustees of the National Institute of Public Affairs commend Dr. Floyd W. Reeves, upon his retirement from the Board, for his exemplary service to the Institute, in assisting in its reorganization in 1962 and fostering its purposes and programs since that time, and also for his lifelong dedication to the improvement of those in public service.

Reeves found it impossible to travel and attend meetings in 1968 when he was 78 years old but he kept track of what was going on in NIPA. The whole experience was a fitting climax to a long and useful life in the public service.

*In 1970 the Institute was merged with the National Academy of Public Administration.

Chapter VI

Reeves and The Art of Administration

Floyd Reeves wrote, usually in collaboration with colleagues, a considerable number of published reports and articles, many speeches and lectures on administration. They have typically been addressed, however, to specific projects in which he was involved. It is not possible, therefore to present a comprehensive statement from his own pen, on the theory of administration. In fact, it bothered him, in his later years, that he had not got around to spelling out what he thought might be a *definitive* theory of administration, though the idea intrigued him. Perhaps he felt that as a professor of administration in a university somewhat distinguished in that field, he was presumably obligated to write at least one comprehensive book on the subject, but he didn't. He did write at one time:

> A science of administration consists of a body of related facts. A fact is knowledge obtained by either (1) personal experience, (2) experiences of others, (3) research that one does himself or that others have done and, (4) trial and error, Speculation or a guess or introspection of a voice of an oracle or the voice of God do not serve as a basis for a *science* of administration. These may represent knowledge to the individual concerned, but they do not constitute knowledge which will serve as a basis for scientific conclusions.

And elsewhere he wrote, under the title of ''Principles of Democratic Administration'':

> Public administration, broadly defined, means the whole range of processes by which a community or a state obtains the execution of its collective will regarding functions which it has decided to perform through public agencies for the common welfare. One of the largest and most important of these functions is public education. By democratic administration I mean the optimum arrangement whereby all persons affected are adequately represented in the policy making, whereby proper degrees of deference are given to the wishes of different classes of patrons and beneficiaries of the service, and whereby appropriate reliance is placed upon the special skills of different grades of professional and technical employees. Underlying the whole are two basic principles:
>
> (1) Universal respect for individual human worth and dignity, regardless of rank or class or race or creed; (2) ever increasing emphasis upon ways and means of cooperation for the common good, with equal and concurrent stress upon the development of individual rights and personal potentials.

These principles are very broad indeed, but more akin to philosophy than science. The fact is Reeves was not an academician of the customary type and there is no point in trying to characterize him as one. If we want to identify comprehensive principles of administration, applicable to a wide range of organizations, from Reeves, we have to get them principally from others—from persons who worked with him at close range to solve complex policy and administrative problems through sustained discussion of alternatives which led them to agree on actions which were most feasible and in the public interest. With notable exceptions, he deliberately avoided the kind of responsibility which put him in the role of president, chief executive, or administrator of educational or governmental organizations, despite a number of opportunities to do so. His principal contributions to administration, approximating the level of genius, were in the *work methods* which he demonstrated in the role of a consultant, advisor, director of research, committee or commission chairman.

A careful review of the evaluative comments of his associates, plus some of his articulation of *operational principles*, which are quoted in several chapters of this volume, may be thought of as constituting the *building blocks* of a definitive theory of administration, but they are not put together in a single formulation, as some seminal thinkers have done on *some* complex aspects of administration. We find these in publications, for example, in Elton Mayo on *The Human Problems of Industrial Civization*; Luther Gulick and L. F. Urwick in *The Papers on the Science of Administration:* Mary Parker Follett on *Dynamic*

Administration; Chester I Barnard on The *Funcations of the Executive* and other books and essays on the organization and administration of business enterprises; Henri Fayol on *General and Industrial Administration*; Maynard Keynes's seminal writings on Economic Theory: Herbert A Simon on *Administrative Behaviour*; and Peter Drucker on *The Practice of Management*.

These writers were essentially contemporaries of Reeves and their work preceded publications on System Science.

Although some of the above distinguished thinkers and writers on certain aspects of administration, which together might constitute a definitive theory of administration, in the opinion of the author, do not achieve this elusive goal. The fact is, the many subtle variables involved in administration including motivation, judgment, cultural traditions, leadership, values, and ethics make this goal almost impossible. The lack of attention to or ignorance of principles or guidelines will, however, inevitably lead to indifferent or even disastrous results in administration. It is thus, not surprising that Reeves did not accomplish his goal!

Accordingly we have to look to some factors, less comprehensive, in Reeves's career. The principal basis of Reeves's well deserved reputation in the field of administration does not derive from his limited experience as an administrator *per se*, but in essentially his staff work expressed as a consultant, advisor, or director of research. He and his associates did help a large number of administrators of highly important educational and governmental organizations to better organize and administer the programs under their direction. Most notably was FDR's authorization of changes in the organization and operation of the personnel system of the Federal Government; his expanded federal aid to education; in the executive policies and programs for returning veterans; and in constructive programs for youth. He was also helpful to Robert M. Hutchins and John A. Hannah and the faculties of the University of Chicago and Michigan State University, in improving the organization and administration of these two universities. His work with the officers of the North Central Association to establish more flexible and pragmatic or defensible ground-rules of accrediting colleges and universities was an area in which he was highly influential. He also contributed ideas and policies to better achieve programs of the American Council on Education to reduce discriminatory policies and practices of colleges and universities and in providing programs for youth, including the Civilian Conservation Corps. Governor Thomas E. Dewey was significantly influenced by research which

Reeves directed for the creation of the University of the State of New York. Other educational and governmental administrations were beneficiaries of Reeves's ideas and recommendations.

The key attributes and skill which Reeves brought to his work are briefly summarized in the following:

Capacity to Listen

One of the special talents of Reeves, possibly the most important to single out, one which he never articulated as a principle, but which was a key ingredient of his work method, was to *listen* to the people with whom he worked as a consultant, advisor, or committee chairman; to dialogue with them; to understand the goals they attempted or were obliged to achieve; to help them establish their priorities, and then to organize them for the purpose of coming to an individual or group decision. In generalizing about the "secret" of Floyd Reeves's unquestionable success in handling varied assignments at the policy level of public administration, it would be hard to improve upon the reflections of John A. Hannah, himself an administrator as President of Michigan State University, when he wrote in his book *A Memoir*;

> Floyd Reeves's greatest strength was his ability to take a group of people who didn't agree on much of anything, start asking questions and keep asking them, and listen to their answers. He kept the questions and answers going, so that over a period of a few hours, days or weeks, they would change their thinking and become full participants in dealing with the problem at hand.

There may be a bit of exaggeration or artistry in the way Hannah puts this, but it successfully conveys an impression of a recognizable characteristic of the way Reeves worked.

Another description of the same key attribute was provided in a letter to Carl Pacacha, candidate for the Ph.D. degree at Michigan State University in Education by Paul T. David, who worked as Reeves's assistant on the President's (FDR) Advisory Committee on Education and several other projects.

> He had an extraordinary skill in dealing with other major participants in a policy situation. He could achieve great empathy with people with whom he is fundamentally in disagreement with on substantive policy. Frequently they were not aware of the disagreement until it comes to the

> final crunch where people have to be counted. He had great skill in extracting information from other people that will reveal their views, motivations and probable position in oncoming policy situations. As a committee chairman he did not inject many of his own ideas while the comittee was actually meeting, let the discussion run free and produce summarizing comments that gave direction on many occasions. . . .

Capacity to Work with Others, Values and Timing

A second key attribute of Reeves's work method was described by Luther Gulick as his capacity to work with others and his sense of timing and values. Luther Gulick, one of the major authors and practitioners of public administration further evaluated Reeves's style and work method in a letter to the author, as follows:

> All of his theories were developed from practice and hard knocks and his field of concentration and management were dictated by the drives of world history, especially the New Deal, the invention of the TVA, World War II and the challenges arising from the major surveys and committees on which or for which he was called to serve. He always worked effectively with other people and was a master of compromise as to timing, but never gave up his fundamental commitments. While there are educators who surpassed his social graces, there were none who could surpass Reeves's diligence and dedication to the values of Abe Lincoln.

Other Attributes

Other attributes of Reeves's demonstrated capacity to achieve results fortified the principles which he espoused. Although they cannot be classified as principles of administration *per se*, they were significant components in his practice of the art of administration. A partial summary of these would be:

- Strong belief in the importance and purpose of the activities in which he engaged.
- Broad understanding, sympathy and sustained concern for disadvantaged persons for whatever reasons for their disadvantages.
- Contribution of creative (sometimes bold) ideas and suggestions to all projects with which he was significantly associated.
- Capacity to choose and delegate responsibility to young persons of promise and capacity to grow with work experience.

- Indefatigable energy, speaking and persuasive writing ability to get action on recommendations of committees and commissions. Reports on the projects were not put on the shelf to gather dust.

Conclusion

To anyone interested in the art of administration at the higher levels, where questions of definition both of purpose and method of execution are presented, where differing views have to be reconciled, and decisions reached on often pressing time schedules, these generalizations about how Floyd Reeves was seen to be doing a job are deserving of careful study and throw a good deal of light on the art of administration. The reader will have noticed many illustrations of Reeves's application of the art in the preceding pages.

If the objective is clear-cut and the technology of carrying out the objective is highly developed—as for example bridging a broad river—the Reeves type of mind is not what is needed. The main questions have already been asked and answered, and the problem is to get on with it. If the objective is more general—say the staffing of a new kind of governmental agency, or putting millions of youths returning from war to constructive and rewarding employment, and hardly any of the questions have been answered, let alone asked, then the Reeves type of mind is definitely what is needed.

Floyd Reeves came along fortunately, at one of those times in American history when new questions had to be asked and new answers given. Here, administration looks much less like a science and much more like an art—essentially the art of human relations.

* * *

Harry L Case and the author collaborated in the preparation of the final chapter. His ideas, draft script, and general counsel are gratefully acknowledged

* * *

Additional responses of colleagues, not previously listed, are quotes in Appendix F.

Appendices

Appendix A

The Introduction to *Recent Social Trends* which indicates the scope of the survey and some of the major findings which are particularly relevant to Reeves's interest and work in education and public administration, are developed in the chapters in Parts I and II and commented on in the following:

Scope of the Survey

> The first third of the twentieth century has been filled with epoch-making events and crowded with problems of great variety and complexity. The World War, the inflation and deflation of agriculture and business, our emergence as a creditor nation, the spectacular increase in efficiency and productivity and the tragic spread of unemployment and business distress, the experiment of prohibition, birth control, race riots, stoppage of immigration, women's suffrage, the struggles of the Progressive and the Farmer Labor parties, governmental corruption, crime and racketeering, the sprawl of great cities, the decadence of rural government, the birth of the League of Nations, the expansion of education, the rise and weakening of organized labor, the growth of spectacular fortunes, the advance of medical science, the emphasis on sports and recreation, the renewed interest in child welfare—these are a few of the many happenings which have marked one of the most eventful periods of our history.

Interrelations of the Committee Findings in Recent Trends

The committee then went on to express the important interrelationships of these trends which it is reasonable to assume influenced

Roosevelt's "Fireside Chats" to help the American public, including educators, see these relationships. There is little doubt that Reeves saw these interrelationships which were reflected in the areas in which he worked—for example in the comprehensive (19 volume) studies of the American Youth Commission, which he directed.

> It may indeed be said that the primary value of this report is to be found in the effort to interrelate the disjointed factors and elements in the social life of America, in the attempt to view the situation as a whole rather than as a cluster of parts. The various inquiries which have been conducted by the Committee are subordinated to the main purpose of getting a central view of the American problem as revealed by social trends . . . social change is to be found not merely in the analysis of the separate trends, many of which have been examined before, but in their interrelationship—in the effort to look at America as a whole, as a national union the parts of which too often are isolated, not only in scientific studies but in everyday affairs.

Labor Organization, Rural Life and Adult Education

Reeves's interest in labor organization, rural life and rural institutions, and in the emphasis which he gave to the implications which increased leisure had for education—including adult education—was expressed by the Committee:

> The economic structure (previously described) of course affects the other institutions of society, setting the stage for many of the activities of mankind and modifying the potentialities of life in innumerable directions, its influence is particularly powerful on that great group we call labor, on our consumption habits and on the conditions of rural life. It also affects various other groups and such institutions as the family, the church and the school, and has much to do with the way in which we spend our leisure time. And all of these social institutions and habits affect the economic organization as well. All, indeed, are interrelated, and often the economic changes come first and occur more rapidly than the correlated changes in other parts of the social structure.

Unemployment and Work Programs

After extensive examination of the strengths of the American economic system, the Committee pointed out the weakness of the system as indicated by problems of unemployment. Reeves saw the unemployment of out-of-school youth and the later prospect of massive unemployment following demobilization of manpower after the war as clearly as did the Committee. His strong advocacy of combining education in the programs of the Civilian Conservation Corps (CCC) and the National Youth Administration (NYA) and in the work programs as integral aspects of comprehensive school curricula are evidence of his understanding of the relationship of economic trends and problems to education and the governmental programs to alleviate the problems.

Discrimination

A blot on American culture which was most disturbing to Reeves and on which he spent enormous amounts of his energy to change was (and still is) the discriminatory practices in education and employment for Negroes. Reeves expressed his concern in the design of the research program of the American Youth Commission, and in the work of committees on discrimination of the American Council on Education. Although he was doubtless influenced by early experiences with the Indians of South Dakota and by the vast literature on the subject, the broad views of the Committee became part of his knowledge and motivation to affect corrective practices in education. The Committee expressed its views in the following:

> Social discrimination, injustice and inequality of opportunity often block the path of adaptation both in the case of the foreign born and of native color groups. In the past the relations of Negroes and whites have been marred by evidence of friction and injustice, but more recently there has been a growing spirit of accommodation. As Negroes have moved northward and westward from southern towns and cotton fields, new questions have arisen over their entrance into industry and politics, questions which may become more widespread in the future.

Other References to Trends in Education

Other trends which were documented in the committee report which influenced Reeves's thinking were related to his advocacy of curricular changes in schools to make them more responsive to social, political and economic changes. His early support of counseling programs to help young people sort out vocational and other alternatives in a complex world was noteworthy as was his teaching, research and vigorous support of adult education. His strong and innovative support, expressed in surveys and accreditation of colleges and universities, of more flexible standards to allow greater amounts of experimentation in institutions of higher education to adapt their educational policies and practices to changing conditions, were all part of his pattern of priorities for affecting changes in education.

Government in Rural Areas

The old saying that you can get a boy out of the country but difficult to get the country out of the boy applied in an unusual degree to Floyd Reeves. His persistent concern with the importance of rural people and rural institutions, particularly rural schools, was reflected in the research which backed up the recommendations of the Advisory Committee on Education, in the studies of the American Youth Commission, and in his stimulation and direction of research and teaching programs at the University of Chicago. Multiplicity and overlapping of counties, school districts and rural services which increased the costs and diminished the quality of educational services, prompted Reeves to write his dissertation on this problem. He was cognizant of the effect of roads, telephones and other structural changes and of population migration, marketing and other social and economic changes on the lives of rural people. Merriam, who authored the chapter on government, expressed the multiplicity of trends affecting rural government in the following:

> In rural government the changes in population, wealth and mobility, together with the new emphasis on the functions of public health, education, welfare and highways, led in the latter part of this period to serious maladjustment and to the beginnings of very important reorganization. These conditions led to a variety of measures for relief, including the consolidation of existing districts, or their joint action, the transfer of functions to other agencies, as to the county or state or in some cases the carving out of entirely new units of government.

Relation of Government to Education and Other Social Trends

Reeves's interests in education were very broad. He was equally interested in organization, administration, finance, curriculum, teacher training, counseling, research and all other aspects of the complex subject. Furthermore, he saw education in the context of social trends and dynamics and of the central role of government, at all levels, in providing guidance to and allocation of resources for its support. He was unafraid—in fact he embraced and advocated, greatly increased federal government expenditures for education, particularly addressed to measures to equalize educational opportunities.

Appendix B

Inglis Lecture

The choice of Reeves to give the prestigious *Inglis Lecture*[6] at Harvard University in 1942 provided him with an opportunity to put together his extensive experience and thinking about secondary education (and other educational programs as well) in a comprehensive manner. The substance of his remarks are reflected in the following:

> Shortly after the fall of France, it was an American journalist I believe, who remarked that Germany had prepared for this war, France had prepared for the last war and England had prepared for no war at all. If one looks at American secondary schools, he finds that a great many of them are preparing them realistically for today's and a third group unfortunately which in effect does not appear to be preparing them for any real world at all . . .
>
> (The) realization of how important the role of youth will be in the (post-war) period has led to a very widespread demand for changes in our secondary schools. That demand is increasingly made not by *educators alone* but by large sections of the public and above all by youth itself.

Prophetically, Reeves remarked:

> Our youth are growing up in a world at war. They and we, if we are honest with ourselves, may fairly predict that the whole world will pass through many crises of explosive violence, and in some instances revolution, before it reaches a period of stabilization, or of relatively enduring peace. If the future citizens of America are to play a part in the determi-

nation of the policy and the protection of institutions of the nation, they must understand the dynamics of a world at war and understand too the forces that will be let loose in the post-war era of reconstruction.

More specifically Reeves pointed out:

> The nessity is necessary to study and to teach the elements of economic history and economic geography, as well as the strategic social tensions that lay at the base of and which still fortify, the acquisition of world power by National Socialism . . . where today are the minerals, the oil, tin, iron, coal, rubber in the Eastern and Western hemispheres? What is the distribution of staple food stuffs among nations? . . . What nations control these materials of life and these munitions of conflict, and how can their rational distribution be made to serve the purpose of the world at peace to producing abundantly, rather than a world of enforced scarcity and conflict? Again, what racial antagonisms, what psychological tensions have promoted the present war, and which of them, unless removed, will continue to promote divisions within and between nations?

On a philosophical level of less scope his conception of the importance of reading follows:

> In an age in which we all recognize that words are sometimes the tools of special interests, just as sometimes votes are, and also that words may be weapons as destructive to free institutions as an invading army, a generation equipped with mature reading skills will be better able to distinguish between verbalisms from truth, to detect a propaganda bias, and to read more for enlightenment and less to kill time or indulge individual prejudices . . . Unfortunately the positive handling of reading materials in many classrooms seems ingeniously designed to retard incompetent readers and to make bad ones out of good ones. Excessive policing of assignments, the recitational habit of minute analyses of meaning, create the idea that to read a book is to dissent and torture it sentence by sentence, and that all reading is a sort of minor branch of logistics.

His experience in manpower training and industry coupled with his knowledge and study of educational curricula prompted him to generalize as follows:

> Vocationally speaking, we live in a world of mass production which calls upon the schools mainly for general education . . . with specialized training provided largely on the job after employment is obtained . . .

> Basic training, rather than specific craft and trade education is what most applicants in the labor market need. They need education which fits youth for learning a job quickly and which, if the job vanishes through technological changes, enables them to move easily to another without serious delay or maladjustment. The useful habits and basic traits roughly associated with the word 'character' plus flexibility of mind and hand, with a wide range of interests, are today the most important keys to success in a working life.

His experience with labor unions and his active collaboration with labor leaders, doubtless influenced him in making this prediction:

> A majority of urban and rural youth will one day be at work in the mines, mills, stores and offices of the nation. Of these, large numbers will probably associate themselves with labor unions. From the standpoint of public policy and the welfare of the nation, their action and influence in such organizations may well be more vital at certain times than any ballot they cast in a stictly political election.

Reeves also expressed positive views about the importance of health education, school lunch programs, vocational and social guidance, leisure and citizenship training through the use of "community laboratories" where first-hand knowledge of community problems could be experienced.

Appendix C

Contents of a Letter from Paul A. Miller (Referred to in Chapter VII Part I)

When President Hannah established in approximately 1959 the Commission on the Future of the University, I was, as I recall, the only administrator on that body of 16. Dr. Reeves was my faithful consultant in preparing to serve on the Commission, directing me to readings that would expand the understanding of a rural sociologist with reference to the role of the university in the society of that day. As the Commission's work unfolded, Dr. Reeves continued to help me to grow into a much wider awareness of the university as a phenomenon. It was in such moments as those that he was able to discern that I was somewhat ambivalent about the proper style of academic governance; in short, whether to come down hard as a line administrator or to develop a more collegial mode. Dr. Reeves was among several people who influenced me toward the collegial mode.

Dr. Reeves had a very substantial part to play in what for me was the most difficult issue of my tenure as Provost, namely the reorganization of the College of Arts and Sciences into three colleges. I had not ever been very bothered by academic organization, feeling that good people with reasonable goals would get the job done regardless of what the organization table said. Reeves had much to say about university organization, and in many sessions helped persuade me that more attention should be paid it. And in such a connection, I recall one day his arguing, and I've never forgotten it in the years since, that one should remind the faculty that for every new course to be added that there should be a willingness to drop one. It was a discipline that he taught to others as well, and it was to stand me in good stead in the years to come.

Dr. Reeves possessed an incredible reservoir of knowledge about education, not that he would ever indicate as much, but one could always sense that his mind was sifting through countless books and monographs which he had read, as well as his teaching and consulting experiences, and almost like some latter day computer, would finally come out in a distilled reaction, almost always dominated by sparkling eyes under his bushy eyebrows . . . Dr. Reeves somehow felt that the American university as we had constructed it kept falling short of its full potential. Its slowness to change in response to societal realities was something that he seemed to have taken on as a personal challenge. That he saw in MSU a university which could become the sensitive, responsive, integrating mechanism was surely a stimulation that endeared the institution to Reeves.

His ability to relate at once to faculty and administrators, his loyalty to Dr. Hannah and other leaders of the institution, his ability to distill an incredible professional expertise and point it to the improvement of MSU, constitutes a task that seems almost impossible to be accomplished, especially when one considers that his role in the University was based on no formal authority whatsoever. That he accomplished so much in the role of consultant, friend, colleague and instigator resulted from the respect which so many people had for a great competence matched with great integrity. Along with President Hannah and others, Dr. Reeves represented that curious situation at MSU where the administration was always picking on 'youngsters' to take on big jobs when they were very young and scarcely up to it. That penchant for choosing quite youthful leaders, and helping them to grow was a trademark of MSU, and it was a process to which Dr. Reeves gave much of his mind and activity.

Appendix D

Sections of the TVA Act (Referred to in Chapter I Part II)

Section 22 of the TVA Act

To aid further the proper use, conservation, and development of the natural resources of the Tennessee River drainage basin and of such adjoining territory as may be related to or materially affected by the development consequent to this Act, and to provide for the general welfare of the citizens of said areas, the President is hereby authorized, by such means or methods as he may deem proper within the limits of appropriations made therefore by Congress, to make such surveys of and general plans for said Tennessee basin and adjoining territory as may be useful to the Congress and to the several States in guiding and controlling the extent, sequence, and nature of development that may be equitably and economically advanced through the expenditure of public funds, or through the guidance or control of public authority, all for the general purpose of fostering an orderly and proper physical, economic, and social development of said areas; and the President is further authorized in making said surveys and plans to cooperate with the States affected thereby, or subdivisions or agencies of such States, or with cooperative or other organizations, and to make such studies, experiments, or demonstrations as may be necessary and suitable to that end.[24]

Section 23 of the TVA Act

The President shall, from time to time, as the work provided for in the preceding section progresses, recommend to Congress such legislation as he deems proper to carry out the general purposes stated in said section, and for the especial purpose of bringing about in said Tennessee drainage basin and adjoining territory in conformity with said general purposes (1) the maximum amount of flood control; (2) the maximum development of said Tennessee River for navigation purposes; (3) the maximum generation of electric power consistent with flood control and navigation; (4) the proper use of marginal lands; (5) the proper method of reforestation of all lands in said drainage basis suitable for reforestation; and (6) the economic and social well-being of the people living in said river basis.[25]

Appendix E

Seventh and Subsequent Meetings of the Conference on Post-War Readjustment of Civilian and Military Personnel (Referred to in Chapter III Part I)

A basic question was raised by one of the conferees as "to whom the Conference was responsible and if the Conference should formulate a program, where would it go?" Reeves, probably with some understandings reached with Delano and Merriam, replied without hesitation "*that the report would go to the NRPB and through the Board to the President*." (Italics added) Two meetings later, Reeves indicated that members of the NRPB had discussed the work of the Conference with the President who responded only that it was too early to make a formal public statement.

By the twelfth meeting, detailed consideration was given to demobilization pay, unemployment compensation and elements of an appropriate educational program. The records of the meetings contained this statement: the general feeling was expressed that men who had been in the services for any period of time would be reluctant to return to any conventional type of school program. There was felt to be a need for continuation of high schools providing education on an adult level. The readiness of a large group of colleges and universities to support a system of recognizing and recommending for academic credit, training and education which had been taken during military service—subject to tests of accomplishments, the intellectual maturity of individuals and relationship of attainments to various specialized fields, was also recognized as being germaine in developing policies.

In summary, there was consensus that there was need for various educational programs to which nearly all demobilized personnel would be eligible which would be: broad in scope but limited in duration; provide for tuition and a modest subssistence; would include vocational training, general and specialized academic training; and provide for more advanced and specialized programs, on a competitive basis, for those who, while in service, had entered upon a protracted and serious course of study.

At later meetings intensive discussion was given to disclocations in agriculture caused by the war effort—a million two hundred thousand young farmers taken off the farms to enter military service and the problems of their reentry. To bring various matters to a head for the preparation and review of draft policy recommendations Chairman Reeves called for various members of the conference to prepare reports on: Objectives of Post-war Readjustment; Selective Service Mobilization and Demobilization; the Navy's proposed plan for post-war readjustment; potential demobilization activities of the Federal Security Agency; private initiative and post-war adjustment; post-war studies of the Bureau of Labor Statistics; post-war plans of the Agriculture Department; role of education in post-war occupational adjustment; and suggestions for policy consideration which Reeves assigned to himself.

All of the above background materials and specific recommendations were reflected in an outline of an interim report and in reviews of successive drafts of a final report. The Conference was ready to report, but clearance had not been had with the President for its release. On June 30, 1943 Leonard Outwaite wrote to Reeves in Chicago that he just had a talk with Dr. Merriam who had seen the President that afternoon and reported that the President seemed disinclined to approve the publication of a report at this time. Outwaite further indicated that Dr. Merriam had pointed out to the President several aspects of the situation that required his early decision regarding the release of the conference report. Included in the list was the fact that newspapers were beginning to carry stories on the subject; that the states were wondering what the plans of the federal government might be; that the report of the Osborn Committee, made up exclusively of military personnel, was more or less dependent upon the Conference report and it would be advisable if this more general report appeared first. Dr. Merriam also reported that he had, without revealing the source of the suggestions, discussed the main provisions for veterans with a number of men who were in the services or who had been in the services. He was also able to report that these men had been very pleased by the recommendations.

He then showed the President the galley of the introduction which summarized the provisions for veterans and some of the other provisions. At this point the President seemed very favorably impressed. It was Dr. Merriam's impression that the report might be published some time within the month, but no final decision was taken. The President asked, however, that page proofs be made ready as soon as possible. A copy of the galley was left with the President.

Dr. Merriam said in closing that: if the President desired further information or discussion on the report Reeves could come on from Chicago for this purpose.

In his letter of transmittal to Chairman Delano, Reeves pointed out that the responsibility of the Conference to deal with the post-war readjustment problems of both military and civilian personnel required the Conference to face many problems that would not have arisen had its responsibility been limited to dealing with only one of these two groups. He went on further to report that the decision to include both was a wise one and that "the problems of military and civilian readjustment are in fact simply different aspects of the task—namely, that of providing measures whereby returning soldiers and civilian war workers may find their place in a reconstructed civilian economy in which all have an opportunity and an incentive for constructive work."

The official transmittal of the NRPB report to the President was also dated June 30, 1943 which suggests that the President make up his mind almost instantly after the session which Merriam reported above. The President did make up his mind and released the report.

Appendix F

Other Attributes of Reeves Which Were Related to His Operating Principles

On his personality, style, and influence on personnel administration Marshall E. Dimock, a distinguished professor of political science and public administration and author of numerous books on administration, appraised Reeves's influence on personnel administration in a letter to the author as follows:

> Reeves's contribution to public administration was formidable. Reeves was an originator of ideas. He once told me that his earthy approach to things came from the fact that he came out of a worker's environment. At an early age he rubbed elbows with working people in a variety of settings. As a consequence he was not attracted to complicated concepts and vocabularies, but told it as it was. Beneath his rather reserved mien there was a great deal of fire. His advice was always realistic and farsighted. I can understand why he and Owen D. Young were attracted to each other because temperamentally they were much alike. With reference to his influences on personnel administration, I would put him in the same circle as Elton Mayo. What little progress has been made in humanizing personnel administration in this country the past fifty years is due more to Reeves than to anyone else.

AS an advisor to a key official in the United States Government, John Macy, former Administrator of the U.S. Civil Service Commission, university president, and Chairman of the Public Broadcasting Service wrote to the author as follows:

> My association with Floyd was more than of a student to leader in this field. Most of my association was during the early days of my service

when I read about his views of the development of the public service, and his analysis of the merit system and its procedures. Along with Luther Gulick, Louis Brownlow, Herb Emmerich and a few other giants of that period he represented the intellectual thrust for the development of public administration as a profession.

During my tenure at the Civil Service Commission both as an Executive Director and as Chairman, I called upon Floyd for advice on a number of occasions. He was always forthcoming with thoughtful and candid views. In many instances they departed from the direction that I had charted, but I found his course sufficiently wise to adjust my course as a result.

On his personal qualities and relations with people. Avery Leiserson, emeritus professor of Political Science at Vanderbilt University, wrote to the author as follows:

His work and his impact were greater than the man. I do not mean that he was a "little man"—he was extraordinarily likable and wonderful company. The way he worked and dealt with people is of course, not unconnected with personality. But it was his impact on people and what he contributed to the enterprise he was connected with, not his personality, that made Reeves one of the most important figures in American public administration for thirty years.

On his intellectual qualities and his influence on decision makers, Donald Stone, Adjunct Professor of Public Management at Carnegie-Mellon University and a former official at the U.S. Office of Budget and Management, said of Reeves.

I remember him as a person who had a quiet persevering manner, got to the heart of the issues, developed good solutions and perseveringly tried to educate others who needed to be informed and who ultimately made the decisions. One never had a sense that he was running for office or wished to receive credit. He certainly had a grasp of the requisites of good management and of processes in which policy, program and administrative improvements would be achieved.

Notes

Part I

Origins and Influences

1. Most of the background material on the early education and work experience of Reeves was provided by the Reeves collection in the Michigan State University Archives and Historical Collections (MSUAHC).

2. A document in the Reeves Collection (MSUAHC) based on Opal David's conversations with Reeves.

3. Nicholas, Barbara Ann, Ph.D. Dissertation on "Floyd Reeves on Curriculum," Michigan State University, 1971.

4. *Recent Social Trends in the United States*, McGraw Hill Book Company, London and New York, 1933. See also Appendix A.

Chapter I
University of Chicago

1. Most of the material for this chapter was made available by the Michigan State University Archives and Historical Collections—Reeves Collection (MSUAHC) and the University of Chicago Library and Special Collections (UC).

2. UC—Charles Hubbard files.

3. UC—Ralph Tyler files.

4. MSUAHC—memo from Harvey C. Daines, Comptroller of the University of Chicago, to Reeves dated 4/27/48.
5. Five to ten MSUAHC files.
11. Letter to the author from D. B. Varner dated February 15, 1982.
12. MSUAHC files.
13. MSUAHC files.
14. University of Chicago Press, 1945.
15. University of Chicago Press.
16. MSUAHC files.
17. Letter from Ralph Tyler dated 1/8/82.
18. Hutchins, Robert M., "Shall We Train for Public Administration? Impossible," from Dwight Waldo, Ideas and Issues in Public Administration, McGraw Hill, 1953.
19. University of Chicago Press, 1955.

Chapter II
Surveys of Colleges

1. Eells, Walter Crosby, *Surveys of Higher Education*, Carnegie Foundation for the Advancement of Teaching, New York, N.Y., 1937. The author relied heavily for the background of this chapter of Eells survey, which in its 538 pages covered almost every conceivable aspect of the subject.
2. *Ibid*, page IV.
3. *Ibid*, page V.
4. *Ibid*, page 196.
5. *Ibid*, page 197.
6. *Ibid*, page 137.
7. Letter to the author dated November 18, 1982.
8. Letter to the author dated April 6, 1985.
9. Reeves, Floyd and Russell, John Dale, *The Liberal Arts College*, University of Chicago Press, Chicago, Illinois.

The colleges involved included eight of the "Wesleyans" and some well known institutions such as DePauw University, Lawrence College (now University), Wilamette University and Northwestern University.

10. Reeves, Floyd W., *et.al.*, *Organization and Administration*, Vol. 11, University of Chicago Survey, University of Chicago Press, Chicago, Illinois, 1933.
11. Judd Files, University of Chicago Library and Special Collections.
12. Reeves, F. W., Fansler, T. and Houle, C. O., *Adult Education*, The Regents Inquiry, McGraw-Hill Book Co., New York, N.Y., 1938.
13. *Ibid*, page IX.
14. *Ibid*, page XII.
15. *Ibid*, page 125.
16. *Ibid*, page 137.

17. *Ibid*, page 145.
18. *Ibid*, page 164.
19. In addition to numerous files of materials on the work of the Commission in the Reeves files in the MSU Archives and Historical Collections, two books were also informative and useful.

(a) Josephine Young Case, Everett Needham Case, *Owen D. Young—and the American Enterprise*, Boston, David R. Godine, 1982.

This volume documents and interprets a number of the major activities of Mr. Young including the following activities in which he was engaged with Floyd W. Reeves: Franklin Delano Roosevelt's Committee on Education, American Youth Commission, National Resources Planning Board, National Defense Advisory Committee, and the Regents Inquiry into the Character and Cost of Public Education in the State of New York. The latter activity provided an opening wedge into the complex educational problems of the State which were addressed by the Commission. Young, like Reeves, worked closely with FDR and was once urged by Walter Lippman, Newton D. Baker and others to seek the Presidency of the United States which he respectfully declined to consider. He numbered Bernard Baruch, Marie Currie, Adlai Stevenson, Frederick Delano and many other political, civic and educational leaders among his close friends. The fact that he called on Floyd Reeves to serve as Director of Studies of the Commission after working with him in at least five other major committees and commissions indicates the degree of trust and confidence which he had in Reeves as a research scholar and collaborator in policy formation and implementation. They were highly compatible in their professional relationships, values and common interests in expanding educational opportunities. In their working relationships Young provided the leadership and personal prestige and Reeves provided facts and technical know-how. They, buttressed by several highly competent members of the Commission and the equally competent research staff assembled by Reeves, were able to achieve an educational and public policy consensus to solve the serious problems of post-secondary education in New York State.

(b) Oliver Carmichael, Jr., *New York Establishes a State University: A Case Study in Policy Formation*, Vanderbilt (Tenn.) Press, 1955.

This volume provided a complete documentation of the educational, political, and social problems faced by the Commission; highlights of the deliberations of the Commission; the leadership of Owen D. Young, the Chairman of the Commission, and of his relationship to Floyd W. Reeves, the Director of Studies and other members of the research staff. His prestige with the Governor and legislators of the state, nonpartisan approach, sympathetic understanding of the needs of youth and other sectors of the population, and his use of data and thinking of the research staff, were central in achieving constructive results in a highly emotion-charged educational problem.

20. "Message of the Governor Proposing a Commission to Study the Needs of our System of Higher Education," Legislative Document No. 26, 1946, State of New York.

21. Carmichael, *Ibid*, pages 58–59.

22. Henderson, Algo D., "Skyhooks" (an autobiography written for his grandchildren) Reverchon Press, Dallas, Texas, 1981, briefly describes his work on the Commission with Reeves, pages 179–188.

23. Case and Case *Ibid.*, page 770.

24. Carmichael, *Ibid.*, pages 113–115.

25. Final Report of the Commission (Legislative Document No. 30) Albany, State of New York.

26. The full set of publications of the Commission follows:

Preliminary Report of the Temporary Commission on the Need for a State University (Legislative Document), 1947, No. 33.

Report of the Temporary Commission on the Need for a State University (Legislative Document), 1948, No. 30.

Matching Needs and Facilities in Higher Education (Legislative Document), 1948, No. 31, by Floyd W. Reeves, Algo D. Henderson and Philip A. Cowen.

Education for the Health Services (Legislative Document), 1948, No. 32, by George St. J. Perrott, John T. O'Rourke, Lucile Petry and E. Richard Weinerman.

Inequality of Opportunity in Higher Education: A Study of Minority Group and Related Barriers to College Admission (Legislative Document), 1948, No. 33, by David S. Berkowitz, with Supplementary Studies by Franklin Frazier and Robert D. Leigh.

Costs and Financing of Higher Education (Legislative Document), 1948, No. 34, by Paul Studenski, Assisted by Edith T. Baikie.

27. Letter to the author, September 1982.

28. The author is indebted to Louis G. Geiger for his *Voluntary Accreditation*—a history of the North Central Association fro 1945–70 published by George Banta Company, Menasha, Wisconsin, Geiger focused primarily on the period from 1945–70 but referred to earlier developments described by Calvin O. Davis who chronicled the history from 1895–45. Geiger, a professor of history at Colorado College, saw the evolution of this important accrediting body through the eyes of a social historian and thus related educational developments in the larger context of social forces which impinged on education.

29. North Central Association Quarterly, published by the NCA, Boulder, Co., June 1930 issue, page 44.

30. The "Commission on Institutions of Higher Education" was one of three permanent Commissions (plus several committees) of the Association. The Commission consisted of forty-eight members, elected by the members,

organized in two groups—one for colleges and one for secondary schools. "The duties of this Commission as indicated in the Constitution are as follows: "to prepare a statement of standards to be met by institutions of higher education seeking the approval of the Association, which standards shall be submitted to the Executive Committee of the Association for approval or rejection; shall receive and consider statements made by institutions within his territory seeking approval by the Association; shall provide such inspection as it deems necessary; shall prepare lists of institutions which conform to the standards prescribed; and shall submit lists to the Executive Committee for final approval and publication. This Commission may, with the approval of the Executive Committee, grant an institution of higher education to waive certain standards that the institution may carry on an educational experiment that the Commission has approved" (*North Central Association Quarterly*, June 20, 1928, page 5).

The reason for describing this policy machinery is to indicate that any research or studies undertaken on behalf of the Commission had a fairly formidable review and implementation process to be engaged in under the general policy of being "advisory" to member institutions.

31. *North Central Association Quarterly*, March 1928.

32. "*The Evaluation of Higher Institutions*: A Series of Monographs Based on the Investigation Conducted for the Committee on Revision of Standards," Commission on Higher Institutions of the North Central Association of Colleges and Secondary Schools, Chicago, University of Chicago Press, 1936.

Chapter III
Advisory Committee on Education

1. Most of the background for this chapter was gleaned from voluminous materials in the Reeves' collection of the Michigan State University Archives and Historical Collection and from the Advisory Committee on Education files of the FDR Presidential library and archives in Hyde Park, New York.

2. Members and backgrounds of the Committee members:

Committee

The membership of the unpaid Committee reflected the scope of the problem of education and some of the principal organizations and individuals who had demonstrated an interest in critical policy issues and prospects for the creation of a more viable national educational system. Abbreviated bio-data on each of them follows:

William Rowland Allen, personnel director of the L. S. Ayres Company in Indianapolis, Indiana and active in civic activities and in personnel and labor relations.

Edmund de S. Brunner, Professor of Rural Education, Teachers College, Columbia University and active in sociological research on rural, religious and community problems.

Oscar L. Chapman, attorney and secretary of the Department of Interior with interest in child welfare.

Elizabeth Christman, secretary-treasurer of the National Women's Trade Union League, and active in such organizations as the International Industrial Relations Association, League of Women Voters, National Conference of Social Work and related organizations.

Gordon R. Clapp, Director of Personnel of the Tennessee Valley Authority and former associate of Reeves at the TVA and a student of his at the University of Chicago.

Ernest G. Draper, manufacturer and member of the Board of Governors of the Federal Reserve System. He served as Assistant Secretary of the U.S. Department of Commerce and on various commissions and committees on unemployment, wages and labor legislation.

Alice L. Edwards, home economist and former professor and dean of home economics at the Universities of Illinois and Minnesota and executive secretary of the Home Economics Association for twelve years prior to her appointment to the Committee.

Mordecai Ezekial, economist and economic advisor to the Secretary of Agriculture, active in economic and statistical work with the Federal Farm Board, American Farm Economics Association and similar organizations.

George L. Googe,* southern representative of the American Federation of Labor.

Frank P. Graham,* President of the University of North Carolina and well known liberal and progressive educator.

Luther H. Gulick,* Director of the Institute of Public Administration, New York City, Professor of Municipal Science and Administration, Columbia University and member President's Committee on Administrative Management and the (New York) Regent's Inquiry into the Character and Cost of Public Education. In both of these latter organizations he had been associated with Reeves.

George Johnson, Director, Department of Education, National Catholic Welfare Conference, an ordained priest and otherwise active in Catholic educational activities. He had served with Reeves on the American Youth Commission of the American Council on Education, the White House Conference on Child Health and Protection and other activities.

Charles Hubbard Judd,* Psychologist and Head of the Department of Education at the University of Chicago and associated with Reeves on numerous surveys on educational institutions, Regents Inquiry into the Cost and Character of Education in New York and other educational organizations and activities.

Thomas Kennedy, Secretary-Treasurer, United Mine Workers of America.

Katharine F. Lenroot, social worker and Chief of the Children's Bureau of the U.S. Department of Labor and active in child welfare and social work organizations.

*Arthur B. Moehlman,** Professor of Administration and Supervision, School of Education, University of Michigan and widely experienced in school surveys and educational research organizations and activities.

Henry C. Taylor, agricultural economist and Director of the Farm Foundation. Active in agricultural research, farm tenancy, National Grange and other farm and rural development activities.

T. J. Thomas, Assistant to the President of the Chicago, Burlington and Quincy Railroad Company and other industrial and commercial enterprises especially related to coal and other minerals.

John H. Zink, President, Heat and Power Corporation and otherwise active in engineering and construction enterprises.

*George F. Zook,** President of the American Council on Education (ACE) and formerly President of the University of Akron and U.S. Commissioner of Education. He worked closely with Reeves on the work of the ACE, the North Central Association of Colleges and Secondary Schools and in many other activities.

3. *The Advisory Committee on Education*, U.S. Government Printing Office, Washington, D.C., 1938.
4. FDR Library, Advisory Committee on Education file.
5. FDR Library, Advisory Committee on Education file.
6. FDR Library, Advisory Committee on Education file.
7. FDR Library, Advisory Committee on Education file.
8. FDR Library, Advisory Committee on Education file.
9. Reeves' principles for guidance of the committee:

Principle 1. The welfare of society demands that opportunity be offered every individual for the well-rounded development of his capabilities along socially desirable lines.

Principle 2. There is no clear line of demarcation between general education and vocational education.

Principle 3. The major obligation of the public school in the field of vocational education preparation is to train broadly for general occupational opportunity, rather than narrowly for specialized jobs.

Principle 4. Vocational counsel, vocational training, and initial follow-up in employment, are inseparable parts of any well conceived plan of education.

Principle 5. Training for occupational employment in any local center should be based upon the total local and national picture of vocational opportunity.

Principle 6. Preparation for a specific occupation, to be effective, should be given as closely as possible to the actual entry on employment.

Principle 7. It is socially and economically undesirable for immature youth to be gainfully employed in full-time occupations.

Principle 8. Training for public service occupations should be provided at public expense.

---

*Additional members appointed when the scope of the Committee's assignment was broadened.

Principle 9. Three types of vocational training on the adult level are an obligation of government: (a) retraining for those who have suffered loss of employment opportunities through technological change and through loss of skill during unemployment; training for those whom society failed to give adequate training in their youth; (c) training for those who will be enabled thereby to render more efficient service in their present or related lines of work.

Principle 10. The population will always contain a limited percentage of permanently unemployable adults.

Principle 11. The Federal Government has three responsibilities in the field of education: (a) stimulation of State and local effort; (b) equalization of educational opportunity between states; (c) research and reporting of information.

Principle 12. It is a Federal and State responsibility to provide well-trained teachers for all educational programs proposed and developed.

Principle 13. The Federal Government cannot escape the responsibility for following its financial assistance with enough control to insure that the assistance is in fact used to increase equality of opportunity rather than to decrease it, but should limit its control to general policies and the maintenance of financial accountability.[8]

10. FDR Library, Advisory Committee on Education file.

Chapter IV
Needs of Youth

1. Letter Joseph Lash to the author dated November 1, 1982.
2. *Advisory Committee on Education*, U.S. Government Printing Office, Washington, D.C., 1938.
3. The recommendations of the Advisory Committee are quoted or paraphrased from a summary of the committee in its final report, pages 207–211.
4. Background material for the AYC was provided by the Reeves Collection, MSUAHC.
5. Letter to Reeves from George F. Zook, dated May 24, 1939, MSUAHC.
6. Letter from Luther Gulick to Reeves dated May 23, 1939, MSUAHC.
7. "Youth and the Future," published by the American Council on Education, Washington, D.C., Reeves Collection, MSUAHC.
8. Reeves Collection, MSUAHC.
9. *Members of the Executive Committee.*

Arthur J. Altmeyer, Assistant Secretary, Department of Labor;

John W. Studebaker, U.S. Commissioner of Education;

M. L. Wilson, Assistant Secretary of Agriculture;

Lee Pressman, General Counsel of the Resettlement Administration.

National Advisory Committee

Charles W. Taussig, President of the American Molasses Corporation (Chairman);

W. W. Charters, Professor of Education at Ohio State University;
Henry Dennison, President of Dennison Manufacturing Company;
William Green, President of the American Federation of Labor;
Sidney Hillman, National Defense Advisory Commission;
Owen D. Young, Chairman of the Board of the General Electric Corporation;
George F. Zook, President of the American Council on Education;
Charles Hubbard Judd, Head, Department of Education, University of Chicago;
Dexter Keezer, President of Reed College (and later head of the Consumer Division of the Office of Price Administration for which Reeves served as a Consultant) and several others.

10. Letter Aubrey Williams to Reeves, MSUAHC.

11. Background material and quotations from American Student Union Collection in MSU's Special Collections Archives.

12. Material from *Student Advocate* (American Student Union), Vol. 1–3, Greenwood Reprint Corporation, New York, 1968, MSU Special Collections Archives.

13. Lash, Joseph, *Love Eleanor: Eleanor and Her Friends*, Doubleday, Garden City, N.Y., 1982.

It is quite clear that Mrs. Roosevelt was not naive about some of the allegations or the facts about the limited number of Communists involved in youth organizations but she never stopped dialoguing with them in their meetings or at the White House, or never lost faith in the good sense or motivations of youth. She gained their friendship and respect.

See also Roosevelt, Eleanor, *This I Remember*, Chapter XII, Greenwood Press, Westport, Conn., 1949.

14. Reeves Collection, MSUAHC.

15. Reeves Collection, MSUAHC.

16. Children's Bureau, U.S. Department of Labor, "Conference on Children in a Democracy"—paper and discussions at the initial session, April 26, 1939, U.S. Government Printing Office, pages 3–4.

17. *Children in a Democracy*—General Report by the White House Conference on Children in a Democracy," January 19, 1940, Superintendent of Documents, Washington, D.C.

18. Children's Bureau, U.S. Department of Labor, "Recommendations of the White House Conference on Children in a Democracy," January 18–20, 1940.

19. Reeves Collection, MSUAHC.

Chapter V
Reduction of Discrimination and Expansion of Educational Opportunities

1. The text of this chapter has been based primarily on the Reeves Collection MSUAHC.

2. The text of a letter written to Reeves on September 26, 1946:

I was instructed by the Board of Directors, meeting on September 20, 1946, to inform you that the Board received your resignation and thereupon adopted the following resolution:

WHEREAS, Professor Floyd Reeves has accepted an office in the North Central Association of Colleges and Secondary Schools and therefore finds it necessary to resign from directorships in colleges accredited by that Association;

AND WHEREAS, Mr. Reeves was one of the incorporators of Roosevelt College;

AND WHEREAS, at one point the entire future of Roosevelt College turned upon his endorsement;

AND WHEREAS, Mr. Reeves gave generously of his time and valued advice during the first year of the institution's development;

NOW THEREFORE, BE IT RESOLVED, that the Board of Directors of Roosevelt College express to Mr. Reeves their deep gratitude for his contributions to the establishment of the College and their regret in accepting his resignation . . .

Chapter VI
International Activities

1. Unless otherwise cited, material for this chapter was provided by the Reeves Collection in the MSUAHC.

2. Hannah, John A., *et.al.*, *A Study of the University of the Philippines*, University of the Philippines, 1958.

3. Case, H. L. and Bunnel, Robert, *The University of the Philippines External Assistance and Development*, Institute for International Studies in Education, College of Education, Michigan State University, East Lansing, Michigan, 1970.

4. Reeves Collection MSUAHC.

5. Raper, Arthur, et.al., *Rural Development in Action*, Cornell University Press, Ithaca, NY, 1970.

6. *Ibid.*, Raper, "Foreword."

Chapter VII
Michigan State University

1. Madison Kuhn's, Michigan State, The First Hundred Years (1855–1955) published in 1955 by the Michigan State University Press, Lansing, Michigan provides an excellent account of the growth and evolution of Michigan College into Michigan State University.

2. John A. Hannah's, *A Memoir* published in 1980 by the Michigan State

University Press provides a personal record of Hannah's background and his forty-six active and productive years in building the University. The book is written as a series of responses to questions formulated by his long-time assistants James Denison and William Combs.

3. *Ibid*, page 49.

4. *Ibid*, page 49. Reeves's involvement in the policies and administrative arrangements with colleges, universities and other educational institutions which were set forth in the legislation familiarly known as the "G. I. Bill" is described in Chapter 4, Part II.

5. This and all subsequent references to minutes of meetings of the Administrative Group, the State Board of Education, or other quoted materials regarding Michigan State University developments are from the Reeves collection in the MSUAHC.

6. The members of the Administrative Group were the Deans of the Colleges, the Comptroller, Registrar and for the war period the top military officer for campus military training programs. They met weekly as did the "Breakfast Group" made up of the top administrative officials and the President. The State Board of Agriculture met monthly.

7. Kuhn, *op.cit.*, pages 419–420. See also Kuhn's references to the Basic College and Reeves' participation in its creation on page 424.

See also Hamilton, Thomas and Blackman, Edward, *The Basic College and Michigan* State, MSU Press, Lansing, Michigan, 1955, for a description of the history of the College, contents of the courses and other aspects of the evolution of the College; also Noll, Victor, *Preparation of Teachers at Michigan State* University, College of Education at MSU, 1968 for information on the impact of college on teacher preparation. The author is also indebted to an unpublished but highly informative manuscript on the College written by Floyd V. Monaghann in May 1955 available in the Reeves Collection in the MSUAHC.

9. Hannah, *op.cit.*, pages 49–51.

10. The provision in the contract with Reeves, approved by the Board at its meeting on April 21, 1944, that he be available for consultation on major matters of interest to MSC while he was on the campus of the University of Chicago or at Claremont College in California was utilized for the following, among other calls on his services.

(a) Participation by Reeves in securing (on a confidential basis) the attitude of the University of Chicago officials, in response to President Hannah's communication to the "Chairman of the Committee of Faculty Representatives of the Intercollegiate Conference" with reference to MSC replacing the University of Chicago as a member of the Big Ten Athletic Conference when the University of Chicago dropped out of the Conference. Reeves made the requested inquiries regarding his question and responded to President Hannah's request within a month (on March 21, 1946). His response included a confidential analysis of MSC's prospects vis-a-vis other universities who were interested in taking the place of the

University of Chicago. He expressed the opinion that the key University of Chicago official "will be inclined to favor Michigan State College." All of the correspondence mentioned above is in the Reeves Collection of the MSUAHC.

(b) Attendance by Reeves representing the University of Chicago at a regional conference convened by MSC on "Education in a World of Crisis."

(c) Response to a letter dated April 14, 1953 from President Hannah regarding a question raised by Lee Thurston (Superintendent of the Michigan State Department of Education) of the "desirability of transferring responsibility for students in training to be secondary teachers from the schools of their major field to the School of Education . . ." My immediate interest in a sound evaluation of the wisdom of such a project. I am posing this question to you not as a prospective member of the School of Education but as a prospective advisor to the President. Rather than have you answer this in writing, I would like to have you arrange to come to East Lansing for a few days some time soon and at a time when I can be there for a meeting of the administrative group, including Lee Thurston, to open up this subject for discussion . . ."

11. Background material for this section was drawn from materials in the Reeves Collection in the MSUAHC, especially Lowell Treaster's unpublished manuscript on the reorganization of the Extension Service.

12. Reeves Collection, MSUAHC.

13. Reeves Collection, MSUAHC.

14. Reeves Collection, MSUAHC.

15. Reeves Collection, MSUAHC.

Chapter VIII
Reflections and Appraisals

1. Published in the *American Teacher*, *Educational Digest*, *Educational Record*, *School Review*, *School and Society*, *Parents Magazine*, *Rural America*, *School Executives Magazine*, *Adult Education Bulletin*, *High School Journal*, *Occupations*, *Elementary School Journal*, *National Parent Teachers*, *Survey Mid Monthly* and several books, chapters in books, reports and other writings previously referred to.

2. *American Teacher*, December 1941.

3. *Inglis Lecture*, Harvard University Press, 1942. (See also Appendix B.)

4. *Journal of the American Association of University Women*, June 1942.

5. *Educational Record*, May 1942.

6. Letter from D. Algo Henderson, former President of Antioch College and Associate Director of the Temporary Committee on the Need for a State University in New York.

7. Letter from Dr. Norman Burns, successor to Reeves as Executive Secretary of the North Central Association's Commission of Institutions of Higher Education and Professor of Education at the University of Chicago.

8. Letter from Dr. Milton Eisenhower, President Emeritus of Johns Hopkins University and former President of the University of Kansas.

9. Letter from Dr. Francis Chase, former colleague of Reeves at the University of Chicago and former Chairman of the Department of Education at the University of Chicago.

10. Letter from Dr. T. W. Schultz, Professor of Economics, University of Chicago, Nobel Laureate.

11. Letter from Dr. Paul R. Hanna, who was an associate of Reeves on the UNESCO Mission to the Philippines and Senior Fellow of the "Hoover Institution on War, Revolution and Peace."

12. Letter from Dr. Herman B. Wells, Chancellor of Indiana University and long-time colleague of Reeves.

13. Letter from David S. Berkowitz, former professor at Brandeis and Harvard Universities and member of the staff of the "Temporary Commission to Study the Need for a University of the State of New York."

14. Letter from Stanley Izerda, former Dean of the Honors College at Michigan State University.

15. Letter from Dr. John X. Jamrich, President (Emeritus) of Northern Michigan University and former Associate Dean of Michigan State University.

Part II

Chapter I
Tennessee Valley Authority

1. Schlesinger, Arthur M., Jr., *The Coming of the New Deal*, Boston, Houghton-Mifflin Co., 1959, page 3.

For other accounts of the social, economic and political background of the TVA see:

Lilienthal, David E., *Democracy on the March*, Pocket Books, New York, 1944 and his *Journals*, Vol. I on the TVA, Harper and Rowe, New York, 1964.

Owen, Marguerite, *The Tennessee Valley Authority*, New York Praeger Publishers, 1973. Marguerite Owen was Washington Representative of the TVA for more than twenty years.

Munzer, Martha, *Valley of Vision: The TVA Years*, New York, Alfred A. Knopf, 1969. This book was written under the auspices of the Conservation Foundation.

Morgan, Arthur E., *The Making of the TVA*, Buffalo, Prometheus Books, 1974. Arthur Morgan's own account of his experiences in the TVA and his conflicts with his fellow Board members.

Clapp, Gordon R., *The TVA: An Approach to the Development of a Region*, Walgreen Lectures, University of Chicago, Chicago, University of Chicago Press, Chicago, 1955.

Finer, Herman, *The TVA Lessons of International Application*, Montreal, International Labour Office, 1944.

Keun, Odette, *A Foreigner Looks at TVA*, New York, Longmans Green & Co., 1937.

Callahan, North, *Bridge Over Troubled Waters: A History of the Tennessee Valley Authority*, A. S. Barnes, New York, 1980.

2. Schlesinger, *op.cit.*, page 319.

3. Schlesinger, *op.cit.*, page 16.

4. These references and many others in this chapter are gleaned from correspondence in the Reeves Collection of Michigan State University Archives and Historical Collections (MSUAHC).

5. This reference to a letter from Reeves to his wife is one of several quoted below. He also wrote:

I am having so many interesting experiences these days that I wish I had time to record them in a diary. Since I do not have time to do this you might keep my letters if you care to do so and someday I may write something of my experiences using the letters as a basis for my facts.

6. Most of the material in this section is quoted or paraphrased from Chapter 2 on "Legal Foundations" by Joseph C. Swidler published in *TVA: The First Twenty Years*; a staff report edited by Roscoe C. Martin, University of Alabama and Tennessee Presses, 1956. The staff report was prepared for a course in public administration taught by TVA officials at Florida State University.

7. Swidler, *op.cit.*, page 34. See also Appendix B for Sections 22 and 23 of this Act.

8. Martin, *op.cit.*, page 42.

9. Pritchett, Herman C., *The Tennessee Valley Authority: A Study in Public Administration* (Chapter 9), Chapel Hill, The University of North Carolina Press. Pritchett provided additional background information on the need of the TVA for greater flexibility in creating a personnel system to meet the special needs of the organization.

For a later report on how the personnel policy and program matured, see Case, Harry L., *Personnel Policy in a Public Agency: The TVA Experience*, New York, Harper and Brothers, 1955.

10. Report of Leonard D. White to the Honorable Vic Donahey, Chairman, *Joint Committee on the Investigation of the Tennessee Valley Authority*, September 27, 1938, Reeves Collection (MSUAHC).

11. Clapp, Gordon R., The TVA: *An Approach to the Development of a Region*, Walgreen Lectures, University of Chicago, University of Chicago Press, pages 32–34.

12. Case, Harry L., *Public Administration Review*, Vol. XXII, No. 2, 1964.
13. Pritchett, *op.cit.*, page 283.
14. White, *op.cit.*
15. TVA Archival Files on the Training Program.
16. TVA Archival Files on the Personnel Department.
17. TVA Archival Files on the Personnel Department.
18. Case, Harry L., *Personnel Policy in a Public Agency: The TVA Experience,* Harper and Brothers, New York, 1955, pages 44–45.
19. Commission of Inquiry on Public Service Personnel, *Better Government Personnel*, Whittlesey House, New York, 1935, page 68.
20. Case, *Ibid*, page 106.
21. Case, *Ibid*, page 107.
22. The letter from George F. Gant was dated December 17, 1980. Gant was subsequently Associate Director, Board for Southern Regional Education; Director, South and South East Asia Program of the Ford Foundation; and Professor of Public Administration at the University of Wisconsin. (He has died recently.)
23. FDR Archives on TVA.
24. TVA Archives—Personnel Department. Reeves also made a number of other speeches on planning.
25. TVA Archives—Personnel Department.
26. Commanger, Henry Stelle, *The American Mind*, Yale University Press, New Haven, Connecticut, 1950.
27. Reeves Collection, MSUAHC.

Other exchanges of letters over a span of 20 years included: George Gant and John Oliver (General Managers; A. J. Wagner and David E. Lilienthal (Board Chairmen); Marguerite Owen (Assistant General Manager in Washington and Representative); Harry L. Case (Director of Personnel); John F. Ferris (Director of the Commerce Division) and others.

28. Investigation of the Tennessee Valley Authority Hearings before the Joint Committee on the Investigation of the Tennessee Valley Authority, 75th Congress, U.S. Government Printing Office. See also David E. Lilienthal's *Journal: The TVA Years*; and A. E. Morgan's *The Making of the TVA* and McGraw, Thomas K., *Morgan and Lilienthal: The Feud Within the TVA*, Loyola University Press, 1970.
29. Schlesinger, *op.cit.*, page 329.
30. FDR Archives on TVA.
31. FDR Archives on TVA.
32. FDR Archives on TVA.
33. Owen, *op.cit.*, pages 77–78.
34. Morgan, Arthur, *The Making of the TVA*, Prometheus Books, Buffalo, N.Y., 1974.

Chapter II
Committee on Administrative Management

1. *The President's Committee on Administrative Management: Report of the Committee with Studies of Administrative Management in the Federal Government*, U.S. Government Printing Office, Washington, 1937.

2. *The other sections of the report of the Committee were*:
- Resume of the Report of the President's Committee
  - Financial Control and Accountability
  - The General Accounting Office
  - The Problem of the Independent Regulatory Commissions
  - Departmental Management
  - Executive Management and the Federal Service
  - Government Corporations and Independent Supervisory Agencies
  - The Exercise of Rule Making Power
  - The Preparation of Proposed Legislative Measures by Administrative Departments

3. Several operational papers, draft reports and correspondence regarding the work of the whole Committee and especially with reference to the section on personnel management are filed in the *FDR Library and Archives*. They provided the basis for several citations and for my summary of how the President's Committee went about its job.

4. President's Committee on Administrative Management, *op.cit.*, pages 59–138.

5. The other advisory committees, with equally distinguished members, were concerned with Lawyers, the General and Specialized Engineering Fields, Architects, Natural Scientists, Social Scientists and Economists and Retirement.

6. The attorneys on the committee in addition to Justice Murphy included Justice Felix Frankfurter, Justice Frank Murphy and Attorney General Robert H. Wood.

7. Letter from Justice Stanley Reed to the President dated February 18, 1941 and signed by all members of the Committee, FDR Archives.

8. Letter from Justice Murphy to President Roosevelt dated February 18, 1941, FDR Archives.

9. FDR Archives, the memo was signed "FDR."

10. Report of the *President's Committee on Civil Service Improvement*, House Document No. 118, 77th Congress, 1st Session issued February 1941, page 57.

11. Letter Reeves to Luther Gulick dated September 26, 1939 with penciled note: "Copy of this letter sent President Dykstra, October 5, 1939, Reeves Collection, MSUAHC.

12. Committee report, *op.cit.*, page 58.

13. *Ibid*, page 60.

14. *Ibid*, page 62.
15. Clapp, Gordon, *The Rule of Three It Puzzles Me, Public Administration Review*, Vol. 1, No. 3, Spring 1941.
16. Reeves, Floyd W., *Civil Service as Usual, Public Administration Review*, Vol. IV, No. 4, Autumn 1944.

Chapter III
National Resources Planning Board

1. Background information was provided by materials in the Reeves Collection, MSUAHC.
2. Robert E. Sherwood in his *Roosevelt and Hopkins: An Intimate History* (Harper and Brothers, New York, 1948), reports that FDR and he were working on a speech in 1943:

. . . for the purpose of trying to save the National Resources Planning Board from death at the hands of Congress; the NRPB was very dear to Roosevelt's heart, but to the conservative majority on Capitol Hill, the very word 'plan' was considered a communist invention and any planning board must be a part of a plot to disrupt the capitalist system of free enterprise. Roosevelt made the point in his speech that he had planned the North Africa campaign more than a year ago and he had planned the Sicilian campaign more than six months ago and was not too soon to start planning for post-war reconstruction; he presented for the first time the proposal for a G. I. Bill of Rights—the plan for which he had been drawn by the NRPB''—page 741.

3. The principal source of information for appraisal of the NRPB is Albert Lepawsky's comprehensive and analytical article entitled: ''Style and Substance in Contemporary Planning: The American New Deal's National Resources Planning Board as a Model'' published in Plan Canada, 18/3, Sept.-Dec. 1978. Lepawsky's overall appraisal:

''Planning under the New Deal became, for the first time in United States history, government-wide and nation-wide in extent, transgovernmental and socio-economic in impact, and top level in political influence. It radiated outward from the White House itself where the New Deal's prestigious but vulnerable National Resources Planning Board (NRPB) maintained a foothold throughout the 'Planning Decade.' In its quality, moreover, New Deal planning was, at least in its own day, generally compelling, if not always convincing. More often than not, it was basic in content, suitable in kind, foresighted in vision.

However, this is not to image uniformity accorded New Deal planning in either professional or popular circles, neither at that time nor today. For despite their definitive character or exemplary status in general, the specific New Deal plans were sometimes defective and often disappointing. They were at times, irrelevant and tangential, impractical and utopian, short-sighted and expedient, difficult and discussive . . . It was abolished in 1943 at the climax of the Second World War following a warm Congressional debate which reflected a controversial rather than an ineffectual record . . . Nevertheless, there are distinguished exceptions and there is movement to the contrary. Harvard economist Wassily Leontief, who won the 1973 Nobel Prize for designing the macro-economic input-output tables which NRPB itself experimented with, asks bluntly in 1974: 'Isn't it high time to revive Franklin D. Roosevelt's National Resources Planning Board?' "

4. At a meeting on June 3, 1934 with Frederic Delano, Wesley C. Mitchell, Charles E. Merriam and Charles W. Eliot II, when they were discussing how the planning mission could best be defined, Arthur M. Schlesinger, Jr., in his *Coming of the New Deal* reported what happened as follows:

"The President groped for a phrase like 'land and water planning.' Eliot suggested natural resources, and Mitchell commented that human beings were perhaps America's most important resource. Merriam then suggested 'National Resources.' the President repeated the phrase several times, liked it sound and remarked, 'That's right, friend Eliot, get that down, that's settled.' " (page 350).

5. National Resources Planning Board Report, 1943, U.S. Government Printing Office, Washington, D.C.

6. *Ibid*, from Part III, Section 9, pages 113ff and Section IX, pages 68–74. The Reeves/Hartley Report was also reprinted in full in the *High School Journal*, Vol. 26, No. 4, May 1943.

7. Members of the Conference:

Dr. Francis J. Brown, Education Adviser, Joint Army-Navy Committee on Welfare and Recreation;

Dr. Edward C. Eliot, Chief, Professional and Technical Employment and Training Division, War Manpower Commission;

Dr. William Haber, Director, Bureau of Program Requirements, War Manpower Commission;

Brigadier General Frank T. Hines, Administrator, Veterans Administration;

Major General Lewis B. Hershey, Director, Bureau of Selective Service, War Manpower Commission;

Dr. A. F. Hinrichs, Acting Commissioner of Labor Statistics, Department of Labor;

Lieutenant Commander Ralph A. Sentman, U.S.N. (Ret.), Officer in Charge of Educational Services Section, Training Division, Bureau of Naval Personnel, Navy Department;

Colonel Francis T. Spaulding, Chief, Education Branch, Special Service Division, War Department;

Mr. Howard R. Tolley, Chief, Bureau of Agricultural Economics, Department of Agriculture;

Dr. Thomas J. Woofter, Jr., Director of Research, Federal Security Agency;

Mr. Leonard Outhwaite, National Resources Planning Board, Secretary.

8. From Reeves Collection, MSUAHC.

9. "Demobilization and Readjustment," Report of the Conference on Post-War Readjustment of Civilian and Military Personnel, Superintendent of Documents, Washington, D.C., June 1943. See also Appendix C.

10. Committee Report, 84th Congress, 2nd Session, *Federal Aid to Students for Higher Education*—A report prepared in the Legislative Reference Service of the Library of Congress by Charles A. Quattlebaum, Specialist in Education. U.S. Government Printing Office, 1956, pages 71–72.

"About 2,200,000 veterans attended colleges and universities with federal assistance under the bill. The rest of the 7,800,000 educational beneficiaries attended schools below college level, receiving on-the-job training or institutional or farm training. No other national program ever gave so many people skills in so many pursuits as did the G. I. Bill. The results from allowing those pursuing higher education to have freedom of choice of educational goals, with the aid of competent counseling is significant. About 774,000 veterans chose training to become scientists. A much smaller number, about 460,000 chose training in the humanities. Only about 100,000 chose social studies and preparation for social work. In 1952 a select committee of the House of Representatives, after an extensive investigation of the G. I. Bill programs, issued a report containing the following statements in reference to the federal assistance given veterans for educational pursuits:

> 'Almost every American knows a young service man who entered training, found his life's work, settled down, and is now doing well . . . The good that has been accomplished and which will show itself more clearly in each succeeding year and in succeeding generations is incalculable.' "

The G. I. Bill (Public Law 346) was passed by the 78th Congress.

Also McGrath, Earl James, *Selected Issues in College Administration,* Teachers College Press, Columbia University, 1967, page 82, quoting Peter F. Drucker had this to say about the G. I. Bill of Rights:

"The first item in my agenda for a college president is, therefore, to think through the alternatives. I suggested that I know one. It may not be the right one but at least it is one we have had. One that is not a policy innovation but one that is fairly well understood and has worked very well. Incidentally, it worked very well for the state universities too; a great many places that were cow colleges in the thirties and are now 'great universities' (or at least large universities) were built by the G. I. Bill of Rights."

Chapter IV
Labor Supply

1. Letter from Owen D. Young to Franklin D. Roosevelt dated May 27, 1940 and a letter from Young to Floyd W. Reeves of the same date. FDR Library.

2. Background information on the organization of the war effort is from the FDR Library.

3. Hillman was not pleased with this reorganization as evidenced by a note in the FDR Library (War Manpower Commission) which reads as follows: "The President sent (a) telegram to Mr. Hillman while in the Doctor's Hospital saying he has signed an executive order setting up the War Manpower Commission under McNutt and that of necessity takes training and labor supply functions away from the Labor Division of the WPB. Said he is changing the labor division presently into a Labor Production Division, with the objective of having it funnel labor information and needs primarily to Nelson (Donald, head of WPB) without going through other divisions of WPB. President said that he feels strongly that Mr. Hillman properly did not want that kind of work with WPB, but it is very important that the government and especially to him personally, that he have Mr. Hillman as labor advisor and he is therefore appointing Mr. Hillman as 'Special Assistant to the President in labor matters.' This will mean that Mr. Hillman's relationship to the President in the government will be very similar to that of Harry Hopkins."

Two years later—in November 1944—when Hillman resigned from the government, a note in the FDR Library follows: "The President wrote. One thing I want to make perfectly clear to Sidney is my appreciation. It was a great campaign and nobody knows better than I do how much you contributed to its success. I was glad to learn that the CIO in Chicago authorized the continuation of the PAC. I can think of nothing more important in the years to come than the continuing political education and political energy of the people, who do the jobs of this land, in determining that the American nation shall do the great job it can do for all of us. I send you no condolences for the licks you took in the campaign. You and I and Fala have seen what happened to the people who gave them."

Note: Reeves was not an organization democrat but it is obvious that he was close to Hillman professionally and shared at least some of his value system.

4. Unless otherwise indicated all of the background material and quotations are from the Reeves Collection in the MSU Archives and Historical Collections.

Chapter V
National Institute of Public Affairs

1. All of the material for quoted and unquoted comments on NIPA were from the Reeves gift of his papers to the Michigan State University Archives and Historical Collections.

2. CHARLES B. STAUFFACHER, Chairman
Executive Vice President
for Finance and Administration
Continental Can Company

MISS ANNA LORD STRAUSS, Vice Chairman
New York, New York

Earlier trustees had included Herbert Emmerich of the University of Virginia, Robert D. Calkins, President of the Brookings Institution, Archibald McLeish, former Librarian of Congress, Louis Brownlow, one of the chief architects of New Deal administrative reforms, and several others of comparable distinction in public affairs.

Its two executives after 1962 have been Richard E. McArdle and Carl F. Stover both of whom had exceptionally strong backgrounds to initiate and administer a wide variety of programs.

Index